Media and the War in Ukraine

Simon Cottle
Series Editor

Vol. 29

Media and the War in Ukraine

Edited by
Mette Mortensen and Mervi Pantti

PETER LANG

New York · Berlin · Bruxelles · Chennai · Lausanne · Oxford

Library of Congress Cataloging-in-Publication Data

Names: Mortensen, Mette, editor. | Pantti, Mervi, editor.
Title: Media and the war in Ukraine / edited by Mette Mortensen and Mervi Pantti.
Description: First edition. | New York : Peter Lang, 2023. | Series: Global crises and the media, 1947–2587 ; vol. 29 | Includes bibliographical references and index. |
Identifiers: LCCN 2023033300 (print) | LCCN 2023033301 (ebook) |
ISBN 9781433199301 (paperback) | ISBN 9781433199295 (hardback) |
ISBN 9781433199318 (ebook) | ISBN 9781433199318 (epub)
Subjects: LCSH: Ukraine–History–Russian Invasion, 2022—Mass media and the war. | Ukraine–History–Russian Invasion, 2022—Press coverage. | Mass media–Political aspects–Ukraine. | Disinformation–Ukraine. | Information warfare–Ukraine. | Mass media–Political aspects–Russia (Federation) | Disinformation–Russia (Federation) | Information warfare–Russia (Federation) | Mass media–Political aspects–History–21st century. | Social media–Political aspects–History–21st century.
Classification: LCC DK508.852 .M433 2023 (print) | LCC DK508.852 (ebook) |
DDC 947.7086–dc23/eng/20230831
LC record available at https://lccn.loc.gov/2023033300
LC ebook record available at https://lccn.loc.gov/2023033301
DOI 10.3726/b21210

Bibliographic information published by the Deutsche Nationalbibliothek.
The German National Library lists this publication in the German
National Bibliography; detailed bibliographic data is available
on the Internet at http://dnb.d-nb.de.

Cover design by Peter Lang Group AG

ISSN 1974-2587 (print)
ISBN 9781433199301 (paperback)
ISBN 9781433199295 (hardback)
ISBN 9781433199318 (ebook)
ISBN 9781433199325 (epub)
DOI 10.3726/b21210

© 2023 Peter Lang Group AG, Lausanne
Published by Peter Lang Publishing Inc., New York, USA
info@peterlang.com - www.peterlang.com

All rights reserved.
All parts of this publication are protected by copyright.
Any utilization outside the strict limits of the copyright law, without the permission of the publisher, is forbidden and liable to prosecution.
This applies in particular to reproductions, translations, microfilming, and storage and processing in electronic retrieval systems.

This publication has been peer reviewed.

SERIES EDITOR'S FOREWORD
Simon Cottle

Russia's invasion of Ukraine in February 2022 followed on the heels of the COP26 conference at the end of 2021, the latest UN Climate Change Conference of the Parties warning of catastrophic consequences if the world does not wake up to the reality of climate change, a reality that is now having devastating impact on ecosystems and millions of lives around the planet. As the United Secretary General António Guterres warned, 'humanity is on thin ice' and 'the climate time-bomb is ticking'. The morally egregious and bloody Russian invasion of Ukraine rapidly displaced the politics and pledges of COP 26 from daily news agendas as the world moved vicariously, courtesy of a plethora of global news outlets and a multitude of social media networks, to bear witness to this atrocious war.

The Russian war in Ukraine, as with COVID-19, deepening climate change and the ecological emergency, amongst other global crises, soon demonstrated the complex entanglement and interplay between different global crises as well as their destructive consequences in Europe and beyond. This became evident in heightened energy insecurity and renewed reliance on fossil fuels; a cost-of-living crisis, economic instability and recession; failing supply chains, food shortages and increased world hunger; forced migrancy, refugee precarity and conflict-spawned humanitarian emergencies; as well as, for those with ecological eyes to see, an increased outpouring of military carbon and the wilful destruction of ecology and environments as well as cities and urban infrastructure. The political and military ramifications of collective security enacted and enlarged through the war in Ukraine, as well as the explicit threats of nuclear war, also speak to a world of increased interconnectedness, interdependency – and rising existential precarity. Evidently global crises today, including war, are complexly entangled with other global crises, both compounding and exacerbating them.

Today's 'world civilizational community of fate', to borrow a prophetic term from Ulrich Beck, author of *World Risk Society*, is confronting a host of systemic existential threats and accelerating crises that now unfold and cascade in complex interactions. Many of them are registering in the world's ecosystems and biosphere. How today's global crises become communicatively constituted in different media proves critical to their subsequent trajectory and reverberation around the world. Communicatively speaking, global crises are epistemological and discursive in nature and generally contested, as well as predominantly economic and ecological in origin and consequence. How this is so has formed the focus of many of the 30-plus volumes to date of the *Global Crises and Media Series*. In today's world-in-crisis this moving terrain will demand to be thoroughly as well as theoretically explored in the year's ahead.

Mervi Pantti and Mette Mortensen's *Media and the War in Ukraine* provides an invaluable collection of scholarly studies examining Russia's latest invasion of Ukraine and follows on from Mervi Pantti's earlier *Media and the Ukraine Crisis: Hybrid Media Practices and Narratives of Conflict* (2016) principally focused on Russia's 2014 annexation of Crimea. This latest volume and its contributing authors provide a range of chapters based on original empirical research, all of which demonstrate the increasingly multifaceted nature of war communications when plied and played out in today's panoply of available communication technologies, diverse media platforms and world news ecology. War has always been fought on communication fronts as well as geographic fronts, and understandably so. Historically and to this day, the communication front remains the principal means by which warring protagonists seek to legitimise their respective war aims, promulgate righteous claims and mobilise support at home and further afield, as well as delegitimise their opponents' claims, often by demonising 'the enemy' and so moving them symbolically closer to the killing zone. Information, disinformation, misinformation and strategic and tactical silences as well as deliberate censorship are all found at work in today's various shades of propaganda, which now also includes the latest technological developments whether the manufacture and circulation of deepfakes or reliance on algorithmic designs and use of artificial intelligence (AI).

Media and the War in Ukraine, then, not only provides one of the first detailed scholarly examinations of the diverse ways in which media and communications have performed and entered into the war in Ukraine, but also provides an insight into the changing nature of communication war in the twenty-first century. The editors bring pedagogical clarity to what may appear at first sight an increasingly chaotic communications environment, an environment long noted for its contribution to the 'fog of war'. They do so by organising their approach under four productive themes. These explore, respectively, (1) how media infrastructures and the interplay between platforms, technologies, institutions and civic actors condition knowledge of the Ukraine war; (2) how open-source intelligence increasingly contributes (dis)information about the war; (3) how the everyday life of war has been performed and documented on social media; and (4) how wider concerns of geopolitics and the different interplays between the local and the global have been enacted in reporting the war in Ukraine and with what possible implications or consequences. In this way, *Media and the War in Ukraine* offers the reader a series of acute discussions on the multifaceted nature of communications and warfare in the contemporary era.

As I write this, the Russian invasion of Ukraine looks set to become a protracted war of attrition with no immediate end in sight and only the prospect of further untold destruction, human misery and death. How communications variously stoke, tame, enact or decry the barbarism of this and other wars in the early twenty-first century will require no less vigilance and acute examination in the years ahead. The editors and contributors to this excellent collection have provided a platform of studies that will undoubtedly help pave the way for this, regrettably, necessary endeavour.

Simon Cottle, Series Editor *Global Crises and the Media*.

CONTENTS

Series Editor's Foreword   v
Simon Cottle
Acknowledgements   xi

Introduction   1

Part One: Media Infrastructures

Chapter 1. Understanding the Ukrainian Informational Order in the Face of the Russian War   21
Göran Bolin and Per Ståhlberg

Chapter 2. Swarm Communication in a Totalising War: Media Infrastructures, Actors and Practices in Ukraine during the 2022 Russian Invasion   37
Kateryna Boyko and Roman Horbyk

Chapter 3. Social Media Platforms Responding to the Invasion of Ukraine   57
Mervi Pantti and Matti Pohjonen

Part Two: The Use of Open-Source Intelligence

Chapter 4. Open-Source Actors and UK News Coverage of the War in Ukraine: Documenting the Impacts of Conflict and Incidents of Civilian Harm — 79
Jamie Matthews

Chapter 5. Faking Sense of War: OSINT as Pro-Kremlin Propaganda — 97
Marc Tuters and Boris Noordenbos

Part Three: Everyday Media in War

Chapter 6. TikTok(ing) Ukraine: Meme-Based Expressions of Cultural Trauma on Social Media — 119
Tom Divon and Moa Eriksson Krutrök

Chapter 7. 'Grandma Warriors' on YouTube: Negotiating Intersectional Distinctions and De/legitimisations of the War in Ukraine — 137
Marja Lönnroth-Olin, Satu Venäläinen, Rusten Menard, Teemu Pauha and Inga Jasinskaja-Lahti

Part Four: News and Geopolitics

Chapter 8. The Emotional Gap? Foreign Reporters, Local Fixers and the Outsourcing of Empathy — 157
Johana Kotišová

Chapter 9. Indian Press Coverage of Russia's Invasion of Ukraine — 175
Antal Wozniak and Zixiu Liu

Chapter 10. Reporting the War in Ukraine: Ecological Dissimulation in a Dying World — 195
Simon Cottle

Participative War: The New Paradigm of War and Media — 215
Andrew Hoskins
Notes on Contributors — 221
Index — 229

ACKNOWLEDGEMENTS

We are grateful to the authors of all chapters who made this book possible. We would especially like to thank the Global Crises and the Media Series Editor, Professor Simon Cottle for his continuous support and Professor Andrew Hoskins for generously sharing his insight and time to write the Afterword for this collection. We are grateful to Photographer Rio Gandara and *Helsingin Sanomat* for the permission to use the poignant photo of the war in Ukraine on the cover of this book.

This book was supported by the Academy of Finland under grant No. 332751.

INTRODUCTION

Media perspectives on Russia's war in Ukraine: Infrastructures, practices and everyday life

As we are writing this in March 2023, no end is in sight for the horrendous war in Ukraine despite the motivated Ukrainian resistance supported by Western arms and the 'unexpected' weakness of the Russian military. This war has been defined as 'the most connected' in history (Ford and Hoskins 2022), echoing how every war from the twentieth century into the twenty-first has been represented, shaped and defined by the prevailing media technologies at the given point in history. Since the invasion in February 2022, we have seen how popular social media platforms have become crucial arenas for information warfare but also for mobilising support and narrating the war. For example, at the outset of the war, Ukrainian President Volodymyr Zelensky appealed directly for international help through selfie videos taken on the war-ridden streets of Kyiv. More mundane social media forms are also proliferating. For example, as 'part of modern folklore', memes using playful and dark humour are circulated to comment on the hardship of the Ukrainian people and Russia's atrocious conduct (Antoniuk 2022).

We have also seen how disinformation, augmented by platforms and their algorithmic designs, has become an integral and systematic part of war propaganda. This takes the form of, for instance, conspiracy theories claiming that there is no war in Ukraine or that the Ukrainian government is infiltrated by Neo-Nazis (OECD 2022). And we have seen how generative AI tools are deployed by both state actors and citizens to verify information, detect locations and identify individuals; for example, software from the controversial company Clearview has been used to identify fallen Russian soldiers (Hagerty 2023). At the same time, examples abound of attempts to control and tame 'the most connected war': State censorship has intensified, and regulations such as the Digital Services Act (DSA) have been implemented to ensure a more accountable online environment.

Media and the Ukraine Crisis: Hybrid Media Practices and Narratives of Conflict was the title of our first volume on media and the conflict between Russia and Ukraine (Pantti 2016). It was published in 2016, following events that shook the foundations of the European security order. The annexation of Crimea in March 2014 and the involvement of the Russian military on Ukrainian territory brought back military aggression, which Europeans had thought was a thing of the past. The aggression was seen as a breach of international law and was followed by a series of economic sanctions against Russia by the EU and the United States, as well as Russia's expulsion from the G7. European news media aligned with the frames of the EU and brought the term 'new cold war' into the lexicon (Boyd-Barrett 2017; Ojala and Pantti 2017). This new volume examines media and the war in Ukraine in the rapidly changing media ecology and the reordered geopolitical context.

The ten chapters and the afterword included in this volume address a wide range of media forms, platforms and content as well as a new set of media practices and actors that have entered the field of contemporary war. Taken together, chapters investigate the war in Ukraine as it is framed, responded to and enacted in and through various media in different national and transnational settings. In this introduction, we first present the information war that has been amplified with Russia's invasion of Ukraine, before introducing four key themes that are studied throughout the book: (1) media infrastructures and the interplay between platforms, technologies, institutions and civic actors; (2) open-source intelligence contributing to (dis)information about the war; (3) the everyday life of war performed and documented on social media; and (4) a critical revisiting of a classical issue in scholarship on war and media, namely how news coverage of conflict is framed and conditioned by different interplays between the local and the global.

Information war

During the first year of the war, claims of Ukraine winning the information war, the battle for (Western) hearts and minds, continuously made the headlines of international news media (see e.g. Aral 2022; Butler 2022). Since the invasion, Ukraine's self-defence has dominated the information space in the West, not only gaining political, economic and military help but also mobilising moral support and wide compassion. The invasion has united Western democracies, at least temporarily. The European Council, in a statement at the outbreak of the war on 24 February 2022, strongly condemned Russia's 'unprovoked and unjustified military aggression against Ukraine' with which 'Russia is grossly violating international law and the principles of the UN Charter and undermining European and global security and stability' (EC 2022). Following up on this stance, the EU has introduced expanded economic and individual sanctions against Russia, and many EU and North American countries have supplied arms to Ukraine. In the Western governments' framing, the war has been seen as defending democratic values against actions taken by an authoritarian regime. This framing echoed President Zelensky's (2023) narrative of Russia's war against Ukraine being between evil and good, with his country protecting democracy and freedom.

It is not surprising that the Russian narratives used to build an enemy-image and legitimate the invasion, including Kyiv being overrun by 'Nazis' or Ukraine threatening ethnic Russians (Grigor and Pantti 2021; Splidsboel Hansen 2016), have not gained ground in Europe, as they defied observable reality. A further justification of the invasion purported by Russia has been that the West is to blame for the start of the war due to its hostility towards Russia. Moreover, despite great human and material losses in the war, the Russian narrative has enduringly been that Russia's victory is inevitable. For example, President Vladimir Putin delivered a televised state of the nation address on 21 February 2023, three days before the one-year anniversary of Russia's invasion of Ukraine, in which he expressed confidence that Russia would prevail on the battlefield. Yet all these communicative and political attempts at winning the war narrative have failed to stop Western support to Ukraine's effort to fight the Russian aggression. In the West, the war has unanimously been regarded as an unjustified and unprovoked military aggression against a sovereign state.

Since the invasion, disinformation has increased on social media platforms (OECD 2022). War propaganda has proliferated by using digital platforms such as Facebook, Twitter, Telegram and TikTok to misrepresent the war in Ukraine. TikTok became a dominant channel for disinformation, partly because of its inadequately resourced moderation policies (Frenkel 2022). While for many Ukrainian TikTok users the platform provided an arena to narrate the reality of war, out-of-context video manipulations and disinformation seeking attention or profit also proliferated. The current information war points to the ongoing development of forms of disinformation and tactics such as fake debunking videos, social media influencers being paid to promote propaganda and audio misinformation on TikTok (reusing audio tracks on top of unrelated videos).

At the same time, Ukraine has made a substantial and systematic effort to counter malign narratives and disinformation, while also promoting its own narrative. Ukraine's 'winning' of the information war is partly due to various actors' preparation for Russian interference. Since the 2014 annexation of Crimea, Ukrainian civil society organisations, such as the fact-checking website Stopfake (Bolin et al. 2016; Khaldarova and Pantti 2016), the Disinformation Coordination Hub and the Ukraine Crisis Media Center, have attempted to battle disinformation and sustain Ukraine's resilience to Russian information campaigns with the help of international funding and collaboration with international civil society organisations that specialise in fact-checking, media literacy and governmental agencies (NED 2023). Moreover, the Ukrainian IT Army, composed of international and Ukrainian volunteer hackers, work in collaboration with officials from Ukraine's Ministry of Defence to target Russian infrastructure and websites.

Media infrastructures and the shaping of connected war

It is a continuing and critical task for scholars from different disciplines to examine how media and information technologies create the infrastructures that shape how wars are represented and played out. Studies of the relationship between media and war have investigated the impact of broadcast and print journalism on public opinion and, consequently, policymaking (e.g. Cottle 2009; Hallin 1986; Robinson 2002; Thussu and Freedman 2003; Taylor 2003). Starting with Harold D. Lasswell's (1927, 1938) pioneering propaganda research in the interwar period, scholars have paid attention to how media framings of war have been conditioned by states' efforts to control and curate information from the frontline. Media serve as tools of war in the hands of a wide array of state and non-state actors. They constitute a channel for making conflicts knowable and visible for local and global audiences and as one of the environments in which war is waged and shaped – as understood in scholarly discussions concerning 'mediatized conflicts' in reference to media as an entity that is actively involved in co-structuring conflict (Cottle 2014; Eskjær et al. 2015; Hoskins and O'Loughlin 2010).

Over the past decade, scholars have focused on how social media platforms have set new conditions for disseminating and receiving communication from war (e.g. Patrikarakos 2017; Ford and Hoskins 2022; Mortensen and McCrow-Young 2023). Such platforms play a great role in information warfare, but they are largely driven by commercial interests rather than concern for public good or for facilitating fact-checked, nuanced and balanced information from areas of war. Importantly, the digital ecology and algorithm-driven platforms impact the epistemological framework for understanding war. They affect what we see and what we know about the war. Recommendation algorithms generate different images and experiences of the war depending on users' feeds: For some, the war appears brutally violent, while others may experience it as a flow of comedy clips (Tiffany 2022). In this light, it is crucial to understand the infrastructures that determine how the war in Ukraine is presented to users.

When Russia invaded Ukraine in 2014, only 4 per cent of Ukrainians were covered by at least 3G networks. By contrast, 89 per cent of Ukrainians have access to them today (OECD 2022). The war has also been referred to as 'the first TikTok war'. Even though this epithet is simplified and misleading (other wars have also been narrated on TikTok, and this platform is connected to other platforms and to the larger media ecology), it still captures the importance of viral social media videos drawing global attention – through distinct social media aesthetics and logics – to the war in Ukraine. Matthew Ford and Andrew Hoskins note in *Radical War* (2022) that perceptions of war are increasingly shaped through individualised informational feeds: The war is also fought among civilians who participate in the war by reporting and engaging in public diplomacy with their mobile phones.

The past effectiveness and large volume of Russian propaganda has not been disregarded by scholars or decision-makers (OECD 2022). Accordingly, the war has accentuated the demand for more effective platform regulation and accelerated the political will to hold social media platforms accountable for spreading disinformation and hate speech. In addition to economic sanctions, the EU blocked Russian media channels. The regulation of the Council of Europe (EU 2022/350) to suspend broadcasts from Russian state-sponsored media outlets RT and Sputnik in the EU was implemented on 1 March 2022. This regulation was justified as a response to the security threat that Russian propaganda and disinformation pose to the EU. At the same time, the EU put pressure on social media companies to use their power to take down Russian disinformation and other forms of propaganda. The time was ripe for rendering social media platforms more responsible, as they were increasingly criticised for their failure in responding to human rights challenges (HRW 2022). As a result of political pressure from the EU and Ukraine, social media platforms took new measures in countering disinformation by, for instance, blocking Russian state-affiliated media channels.

The first three chapters of this volume add substantially to scholarly literature on how media infrastructures condition our knowledge of the war in Ukraine. In Chapter 1, Göran Bolin and Per Ståhlberg propose that the Ukrainian 'networked informational state' surfacing after the start of the Russian invasion in February 2022 builds on the networks between state, civil society and market actors established during the Euromaidan Revolution in the winter of 2013–14. Based on their ethnographic fieldwork spanning several years on information management, nation branding and soft power in Ukraine, Bolin and Ståhlberg argue that these networks became reactivated and had to rebuild their structures after Russia's invasion. In Ukraine, communicative resources are dispersed and yet, at the same time, seem to be coordinated through these networks. This, the authors contend, invites us to rethink the relationship between state, military and media during armed conflicts.

In Chapter 2, Kateryna Boyko and Roman Horbyk similarly address how interplays between institutions, platforms and individual actors form the wartime media ecology and frame media presentations of the war in Ukraine. Adopting mixed methods, Boyko and Horbyk offer an empirical overview of how Ukrainian media organisations adapted to the situation following the invasion. At the beginning of the war, the Ukrainian government required all television channels to broadcast through one platform to control information about the war. However, on par with the findings presented by Bolin and Ståhlberg, this chapter points to how information flows were mainly decentralised and networked in a 'swarm tactic' parallel to the one deployed by the Ukrainian military. While the war damaged the Ukrainian media sector, a *levée en masse* (mass mobilisation) still took place through this dense entanglement between top-down and bottom-up forms of communication.

In the final chapter on infrastructure, Chapter 3, Mervi Pantti and Matti Pohjonen study how social media platforms have responded to the invasion of

Ukraine. Such platforms, as Pantti and Pohjonen demonstrate, tried to curb disinformation by blocking media affiliated with the Russian state. They argue that the Russian war in Ukraine represents the first time social media platforms and governments have been aligned against a major geopolitical player such as Russia. This, however, was a retroactive act, prompted by a public demand for these platforms to muster greater responsibility in shielding the public from Russian information warfare. Through a case study of blog posts from social media companies, the authors analyse how these platforms followed the course set by the EU to intervene in Russian disinformation and worked to enhance their own credibility and legitimacy by positioning themselves as humanitarian actors, promoting their cybersecurity expertise and active role in fostering democratic values.

Informed and disinformed by open-source intelligence

The next theme concerns how open-source intelligence contributes to informing and disinforming about the war. As the most serious attack on a sovereign state in Europe since the Second World War, the Russian invasion of Ukraine captured the attention of news audiences around the globe (Eddy and Fletcher 2022). Moreover, this war has gathered an unprecedented volume of visual content (Hoskins and Shchelin 2023).

Much of this footage is available online as open-source intelligence (often referred to as OSINT), that is, information that can be harvested from publicly available sources (Glassman and Kang 2012; Stottlemyre 2015; Pastor-Galindo et al. 2020). Open-source intelligence has created an unprecedented hub for visual information about the war in Ukraine. While all social media platforms host open-source intelligence, Russia-based Telegram constitutes the 'single most important repository of data during the war' (*Economist* 2023), which is noteworthy given this platform's frequent association with disinformation. A forewarning of the great role played by open-source intelligence came at the onset of the war on 24 February 2022, when an employee at the Middlebury Institute in California tweeted 'Someone's on the move' after having observed a traffic jam on the Russian side of the border on the Google Maps reports of road traffic. The invasion came less than three hours later (Ibid.).

Images acquiring status as open-source intelligence have been created for various purposes; they may be operational, such as surveillance by satellites or drones, or mundane, such as social media images taken to document occurrences. When entering investigations, this material is decontextualised from its original use and recontextualised as open-source intelligence. However, the evidence – hints, indications, traces – of locations, people, material, incidents, etc., can in most cases not simply be lifted from open-source intelligence. Evidence from open-source intelligence is to be constructed as much as it is to be collected. As Kelly Gates argues:

> We tend to think of recordings as evidentiary simply by nature of being captured and stored, but if recordings are not made use of, they never become evidence. And making use of recordings as evidence is not so simple. The status of recordings as evidence takes shape in the forms of analysis, or recounting of events, that leverage the evidentiary potential of those recordings. Turning media records into evidence is an analytical, interpretive activity, and, inescapably, a media production process. (Gates 2020: 404)

Open-source intelligence, despite being readily available, normally requires expertise, whether acquired professionally or informally, as well as access to digital tools and software, such as reverse image search and AI-based automated facial recognition. This means that intermediaries, for instance specialised teams of journalists or crowdsourcing groups, have often been involved when open-source intelligence enters the news media.

Two chapters deepen our knowledge of how open-source intelligence enters streams of information and disinformation in relation to the war in Ukraine. In Chapter 4, Jamie Matthews studies how mainstream media coverage of the Russian invasions of Ukraine is drawing on 'open-source actors', that is, collectives such as Bellingcat and Forensic Architecture that engage in gathering and investigating open-source intelligence. Through an exploratory content analysis of online UK news media, Matthews maps the types and uses of open-source actors that were featured in their coverage during the initial six months of the invasion of Ukraine. He finds that open-source practices and tools reconfigure war coverage since open-source actors provide evidence of war crimeswar crimes. This includes revealing how Russian forces targeted the the civilian population and identifying perpetrators in the massacre in Bucha on 1 April 2022. Moreover, this study also points to frequent metacoverage of how the news media can use open-source information to debunk Russian disinformation.

While the chapter by Matthews emphasises the constructive potential of open-source intelligence in delivering evidence and verifying information, the darker aspect of this format is explored in Chapter 5 by Marc Tuters and Boris Noordenbos. Through a study of WarFakes, a website and cluster of channels on Telegram, they examine how fabricated open-source intelligence is used strategically to spread disinformation. WarFakes proclaims to be devoted to debunking alleged 'fake news' on the Russian invasion in Ukrainian, Western and critical Russian outlets. However, WarFakes, which has ties to the Russian government, in reality weaponises and 'hijacks' the distinctive 'investigative aesthetics' (Fuller and Weizman 2021) of open-source intelligence to create the illusion of crowdsourced knowledge. The Bucha massacre is also studied in Tuters and Noordenbos's chapter: WarFakes created distorted crowdsourced evidence to support the Kremlin narrative that this massacre was a Ukrainian false flag operation backed by the West.

The everyday of war on social media platforms

The emergence of social media and mobile media has dramatically changed the production, dissemination and mobilisation of citizen images from areas of war and conflict during the last fifteen years (e.g. Andén-Papadopoulos and Pantti 2011; Allan 2013; Chouliaraki 2015; Mortensen 2015). As a result, news media no longer enjoy a monopoly on conflict reporting, and state/military are not able to manage the image flow in the same way and to the same extent as they did during the analogue media era. This marks a ground-breaking change from how images from conflicts were controlled, curated and censored in interplays between legacy news media and states throughout the twentieth century (Perlmutter 1998; Hariman and Lucaites 2007). While this development was initially lauded for its democratising potential in empowering citizens to document their everyday in war zones or human rights violations (e.g. Gregory 2015; Ristovska 2021), the more ambivalent or even detrimental effects have since surfaced. They include the risks that these images carry disinformation, especially due to the difficulties often involved in fact-checking and verifying such images. Moreover, attention is increasingly attuned to how the commercial imperatives of platforms and regulatory policies shape which visual narratives become dominant, and questions are raised about the character of the labour and the security for citizens witnessing war (e.g. Mitra and Witherspoon 2023; Mollerup and Mortensen 2020).

Scholars have also started to turn their attention to how the everyday of war is performed through social media and how different performative modes enter the everyday communication of conflict through social media – for instance, the playfulness of memes and the performativity of influencers and other social media personas contributing to narrating war (e.g. Della Ratta 2021; Mortensen and Neumayer 2021; Wiggins 2016). In Chapter 6, Tom

Divon and Moa Eriksson Krutrök engage in a case study of @valerisssh (Valeria Shashenok), one of the most prolific Ukrainian 'war influencers', a role in between citizen journalist at the frontline, voluntary witness to existential insecurity, microcelebrity activist and online content creator. Through memes and humorous content on her preferred platform, TikTok, @valerisssh has engaged in what Divon and Krutrök refer to as 'performances of trauma narratives', conveying stories of the life that she led with her family in a bomb shelter and her flight from the war-torn country. Performing the everydayness of war has provided @valerisssh with a platform of a million followers, who, almost in real time, have been able to experience the influencer's story as an entry point to understanding the human consequences of the war. War influencers such as @valerisssh challenge the norm that cultural trauma is narrated in mournful ways; indeed, it possibly attracts larger and younger audiences by creating a juxtaposition between the grimness of the situation and the playfulness of cheeky and quirky memes.

In Chapter 7, Marja Lönnroth-Olin, Satu Venäläinen, Rusten Menard, Teemu Pauha and Inga Jasinskaja-Lahti examine the 'weaponization of grandmotherhood' on social media. Analysing YouTube videos that feature elderly women, defined in the videos and user comments as 'grandmothers' (babushkas), they discuss how gender, age and ethnicity are mobilised for both resistance and justification of the war. Grandmothers become symbols of endurance and strength; they are 'all-seeing' and 'all-knowing'. While the Ukrainian government has stressed the unity of Ukrainians – and implemented a 'unified information policy' by combining all national television channels into one platform (Reuters 2022) to secure a unified war narrative and silence oppositional views – this chapter shows that the views of the war are not homogeneous and that politicised cultural discourses such as the discourse of 'grandmotherhood' function to legitimate both pro-Russian and pro-Ukrainian stances.

The geopolitics of news coverage

The Russian invasion of Ukraine has attracted massive and lasting media attention. This has provoked fears that the reporting of the war in Ukraine may cause other wars, conflicts and disasters around the world to slip from public attention. The global reverberations of the war in Ukraine put into perspective the scant media coverage and decreasing funding towards ongoing conflicts and humanitarian disasters in, for instance, Yemen, Ethiopia, Syria and Afghanistan. Accordingly, Western news reporting has been blamed for different treatment of the suffering of Ukrainians suggesting that they are more worthy of sympathy than displaced and suffering people coming from outside Europe. This reminds us once again that news coverage contributes to the production of global humanitarian hierarchies by crafting interpretations of security and threats and drawing boundaries between 'us' and 'others' (Ojala and Pantti 2017; Pantti et al. 2012). It also reminds us, as Mary Kaldor (2012) has stated, that global economic interdependency, global cultural interconnectedness and the dependence of conflicts on transnational networks for mobilising support are crucial to understanding the logics and practices of contemporary wars.

For understanding reporting on war and conflicts, we similarly need to consider the local-global relationship within international news reporting as codependent. Foreign reporters bring news to international audiences in their native languages – and by reporting on humanitarian needs and war crimes, they not only make them knowable but also participate in mobilising support. At the same time, they are dependent on localised understanding and practical help. The war in Ukraine is the largest armed conflict in Europe since the Second World War and a dangerous assignment for journalists. According to Journalists without Borders (RSF 2023), a total of 12,000 Ukrainian and foreign journalists have been accredited to cover the war in Ukraine during the past year and several have been killed.

Scholars are increasingly trying to understand the emotional aspects of journalistic work, including the tensions concerning the involvement of local newsworkers in international news reporting. Previous research (e.g. Murrell 2015; Palmer 2019) has addressed the hierarchical relationship between foreign correspondents and local media workers, so-called 'fixers', but has so far focused on the Global South. In Chapter 8, based on interviews with foreign reporters and local Ukrainian newsworkers, Johana Kotišová studies the tensions involved in transnational collaboration, particularly concerning emotional distance and proximity. Her study shows that in addition to providing local context, language and knowledge, local media workers' emotional engagement may be beneficial to the production of war news. The study sheds new light on the importance of local newsworkers in building ethical and caring relationships with local news sources – and thus contributing to the framing of news – while at the same time pointing to the continuing underestimation of local fixers.

The Russian war against Ukraine has reordered the global geopolitical landscape, which is also reflected in the ways it is covered by legacy news media in different national contexts. In addition to the rift in Russia-EU relations, the war has had global political and economic ramifications. In the UN General Assembly, Russian aggression was condemned by a great majority. Powerful Asian countries China and India refused to take a side, and, in addition, seventeen African countries abstained from the vote condemning the invasion (UN 2022). India's decision, reflected in national news reporting, was shaped by the country's national interests concerning trade and security. Frames of war are highly significant in directing national policy and conditioning the ways in which the public perceives the conflict, as the coverage prescribes certain actions and limits others (Entman 1993). In Chapter 9, Antal Wozniak and Zixiu Liu examine the news coverage of the war in two leading English-language Indian newspapers. The chapter contributes to the long-standing research on the news media's alignment with national political elites' geopolitical interpretations, particularly how national media outlets legitimise (or contend with) foreign policy frames (Hallin 1986; Herman and Chomsky 2008). Less attention, however, has been paid to the news framing and foreign policy decision-making with respect to non-Western countries. Wozniak and Liu conclude that Indian newspapers domesticated the war by focusing on aspects relating to Indian national interests, including the consequences of the war for India's economy and diplomatic relations, even if they used less evasive language than the political elite for describing the Russian invasion.

Beyond the environment of immense human suffering lies another, often overlooked, casualty of warfare. Political attention and media attention given to the war in Ukraine have provoked fears about the disappearance of climate change from their agenda. Considering that wars in themselves carry a high carbon impact and environmental price, it is an important task for journalists and scholars to examine the ways in which climate crisis and wars interact. The Russian war in Ukraine shows different dimensions of these complicated war-environment linkages. For instance, fossil fuel revenues are a key enabler of Russia's military build-up, and oil and gas are accordingly referred to as 'patriotic hydrocarbons' in Russian propaganda (Tynkkynen 2023). Chapter 10, the final chapter of the volume, contributes to the research on how news media address climate, or fail to do so (e.g. Boykoff 2011; Lester and Cottle 2009; Lester and Hutchins 2013). As Simon Cottle states in his study on how BBC News covers the intersections between war and global climate change, the Russian war in Ukraine has illuminated the world's interdependencies in times of war regarding energy, food shortages and consumer prices as well as military (in)security and environmental despoilation. His chapter concludes that while the atrocious human consequences of war must always be witnessed by news media, concerns of global climate change cannot be left for when the fighting stops.

Andrew Hoskins in the afterword reflects on how the war in Ukraine is so thoroughly documented and datafied that it is on the brink of being intelligible to human cognition. He brings to the fore how this war is a combination of a traditional war fought on the battlefield with 'trenches, artillery and tanks', at the same time as it represents 'a new hyper-individualisation of war', in which war to an increasing extent is presented to us in personalised social media feeds, small and sometimes random slices of the information from the ongoing conflict. Hoskins terms this 'participative war', which, at first sight, might come across as the peak of de-centralised war. However, as he argues, participative war could result in the exact opposite, as the ownership and control of information infrastructure might in the future spur the re-centralisation of war.

References

Allan, S. (2013). *Citizen Witnessing: Revisioning Journalism in Times of Crisis*. Cambridge: Polity Press.

Andén-Papadopoulos, K., and Pantti, M. (eds) (2011). *Amateur Images and Global News*. Bristol: Intellect Press.

Antoniuk, D. (2022). 'Making Sense of Ukrainian War Memes: From Watermelons to Saint Javelin', *The Kyiv Independent*, 29 November.

Aral, S. (2022). 'Ukraine Is Winning the Information War', *Washington Post*, 1 March, https://www.washingtonpost.com/outlook/2022/03/01/information-war-zelensky-ukraine-putin-russia, accessed 9 March 2023.

Bolin, G., Jordan, P., and Ståhlberg, P. (2016). 'From Nation Branding to Information Warfare: Management of Information in the Ukraine-Russia Conflict'. In M. Pantti (ed.), *Media and the Ukraine Crisis: Hybrid Media Practices and Narratives of Conflict*, pp. 1–18. New York: Peter Lang.

Boyd-Barrett, O. (2017). *Western Mainstream Media and the Ukraine Crisis: A Study in Conflict Propaganda*. London: Routledge.

Boykoff, M. T. (2011). *Who Speaks for Climate? Making Sense of Media Reporting on Climate Change*. Cambridge: Cambridge University Press.

Butler, M. (2022). 'Ukraine's Information War Is Winning Hearts and Minds in the West', *The Conversation*, 22 May, https://theconversation.com/ukraines-information-war-is-winning-heartsand-minds-in-the-west-181892, accessed 18 March 2023.

Chouliaraki, L. (2015). 'Digital Witnessing in Conflict Zones: The Politics of Remediation', *Information, Communication & Society*, 18 (11), 1362–77.

Cottle, S. (2009). *Global Crisis Reporting: Journalism in the Global Age*. Maidenhead: Open University Press.

Cottle, S. (2014). 'Rethinking Media and Disasters in a Global Age: What's Changed and Why It Matters', *Media, War & Conflict*, 7 (1), 3–22.

Della Ratta, D. (2021). 'Shooting 2011–21: Violence, Visibility, and Contemporary Digital Culture in Post-Uprising and Pandemic Times', *Film Quarterly*, 75 (2), 68–75.

Economist, The. (2023). 'Open-Source Intelligence Is Piercing the Fog of War in Ukraine', *The Economist*, 13 January, https://www.economist.com/interactive/international/2023/01/13/open-source-intelligence-is-piercing-the-fog-of-war-in-ukraine, accessed 21 March 2023.

EC (2022). European Council Conclusions, 24 February, Press release, https://www.consilium.europa.eu/en/press/press-releases/2022/02/24/european-council-conclusions-24-february-2022/, accessed 1 October 2023.

Eddy, K., and Fletcher, R. (2022). 'Perceptions of Media Coverage of the War in Ukraine'. Reuters Institute, *Digital News Report*, 15 June.

Entman, R. M. (1993). 'Framing: Toward Clarification of a Fractured Paradigm', *Journal of Communication*, 43 (4), 51–8.

Eskjær, M. F., Hjarvard, S., and Mortensen, M. (eds) (2015). *The Dynamics of Mediatized Conflicts*. New York: Peter Lang.

Ford, M., and Hoskins, A. (2022). *Radical War: Data, Attention and Control in the Twenty-First Century. Radical War: Data, Attention and Control in the Twenty-First Century*. London: Hurst & Company.

Frenkel, S. (2022). 'TikTok Is Gripped by the Violence and Misinformation of Ukraine War', *The New York Times*, 5 March, https://www.nytimes.com/2022/03/05/technology/tiktok-ukraine-misinformation.html, accessed 2 April 2023.

Fuller, M., and Weizman, E. (2021). *Investigative Aesthetics: Conflicts and Commons in the Politics of Truth*. London: Verso.

Gates, K. (2020). 'Media Evidence and Forensic Journalism', *Surveillance & Society*, 18 (3), 403–8.

Glassman, M., and Kang, M. J. (2012). 'Intelligence in the Internet Age: The Emergence and Evolution of Open Source Intelligence (OSINT)', *Computers in Human Behavior*, 28 (2), 673–82.

Gregory, S. (2015). 'Ubiquitous Witnesses: Who Creates the Evidence and the Live(d) Experience of Human Rights Violations?', *Information, Communication & Society*, 18 (11), 1378–92.

Grigor, I., and Pantti, M. (2021). 'Visual Images as Affective Anchors: Strategic Narratives in Russia's Channel One Coverage of the Syrian and Ukrainian Conflicts', *Russian Journal of Communication*, 13 (2), 140–62.

Hagerty, A. (2023). 'In Ukraine, Identifying the Dead Comes at a Human Rights Cost', *Wired*, 22 February, https://www.wired.com/story/russia-ukraine-facial-recognition-technology-death-military, accessed 9 March 2023.

Hallin, D. C. (1986). *The Uncensored War: The Media and Vietnam*. New York: Oxford University Press.

Hariman, R., and Lucaites, J. L. (2007). *No Caption Needed: Iconic Photographs, Public Culture, and Liberal Democracy*. Chicago: University of Chicago Press.

Herman, E. S., and Chomsky, E. (2008). *Manufacturing Consent: The Political Economy of the Mass Media*. London: Bodley Head.

Hoskins, A., and O'Loughlin, B. (2010). *War and Media: The Emergence of Diffused War*. Cambridge: Polity Press.

Hoskins, A., and Shchelin, P. (2023). The War Feed: Digital War in Plain Sight. *American Behavioral Scientist*, 67 (3), 449–63.

HRW. (2022). 'Russia, Ukraine, and Social Media and Messaging Apps: Questions and Answers on Platform Accountability and Human Rights Responsibilities', *Human Rights Watch*, 16 March, https://www.hrw.org/news/2022/03/16/russia-ukraine-and-social-media-and-messaging-apps, accessed 9 March 2023.

Kaldor, M. (2012). *New and Old Wars: Organized Violence in a Global Era* (3rd edition). Cambridge: Polity Press.

Khaldarova, I., and Pantti, M. (2016). 'Fake News: The Narrative Battle over the Ukrainian Conflict', *Journalism Practice*, 10 (7), 891–901.

Lasswell, H. D. (1927). 'The Theory of Political Propaganda', *American Political Science Review*, 21 (3), 627–31.

Lasswell, H. D. (1938). *Propaganda Technique in the World War*. London: Kegan Paul, Trench, Trübner & Co.

Lester, L., and Cottle, S. (2009). 'Visualizing Climate Change: Television News and Ecological Citizenship', *International Journal of Communication*, 3, 920–36.

Lester, L., and Hutchins, B. (eds) (2013). *Environmental Conflict and the Media*. New York: Peter Lang.

Mitra, S., and Witherspoon, B. (2023). 'Relational Labour or Digital Resistance: Social Media Practices of Non-Western Women Photographers'. In M. Mortensen and A. McCrow-Young (eds), *Social Media Images and Conflicts*, pp. 16–32. London: Routledge.

Mollerup, N. G., and Mortensen, M. (2020). 'Proximity and Distance in the Mediation of Suffering: Local Photographers in War-Torn Aleppo and the International Media Circuit', *Journalism*, 21 (6), 729–45.

Mortensen, M. (2015). *Journalism and Eyewitness Images: Digital Media, Participation, and Conflict*. New York: Routledge.

Mortensen, M., and McCrow-Young, A. (eds) (2023). *Social Media Images and Conflicts*. London: Routledge.

Mortensen, M., and Neumayer, C. (2021). 'The Playful Politics of Memes', *Information, Communication & Society*, 24 (16), 2367–77.

Murrell, C. (2015). *Foreign Correspondents and International Newsgathering: The Role of Fixers*. New York: Routledge.

NED. (2023). 'Shielding Democracy: Civil Society Adaptations to Kremlin Disinformation about Ukraine', The National Endowment for Democracy, February, https://www.ned.org/wp-content/uploads/2023/02/NED_Forum-Shielding-Democracy.pdf, accessed 9 March 2023.

Ojala, M., and Pantti, M. (2017). 'Naturalising the New Cold War: The Geopolitics of Framing the Ukrainian Conflict in Four European Newspapers', *Global Media and Communication*, 13 (1), 41–56.

OECD. (2022). 'Disinformation and Russia's War of Aggression against Ukraine', OECD Policy Responses, 3 November, https://www.oecd.org/ukraine-hub/policy-responses/disinformation-and-russia-s-war-of-aggression-against-ukraine-37186bde, accessed 9 March 2023.

Palmer, L. (2019). *The Fixers: Local News Workers and the Underground Labor of International Reporting*. New York: Oxford University Press.

Pantti, M. (2016). *Media and the Ukraine Crisis: Hybrid Media Practices and Narratives of Conflict*. New York: Peter Lang.

Pantti, M., Wahl-Jorgensen, K., and Cottle, S. (2012). *Disasters and the Media*. New York: Peter Lang.

Pastor-Galindo, J., Nespoli, P., Marmol, F. G., and Perez, G. M. (2020). 'The Not Yet Exploited Goldmine of OSINT: Opportunities, Open Challenges and Future Trends', *IEEE Access*, 8, 10282–304.

Patrikarakos, D. (2017). *War in 140 Characters: How Social Media Is Reshaping Conflict in the Twenty-First Century*. New York: Basic Books.

Perlmutter, D. D. (1998). *Photojournalism and Foreign Policy: Icons of Outrage in International Crises*. Westport, CT: Praeger.

RSF. (2023). 'Ukraine: A Year of Information Warfare in Numbers', Reporters without Borders, https://rsf.org/en/ukraine-year-information-warfare-numbers, accessed 19 March 2023.

Ristovska, S. (2021). *Seeing Human Rights: Video Activism as a Proxy Profession*. Cambridge, MA: The MIT Press.

Robinson, P. (2002). *The CNN Effect: The Myth of News, Foreign Policy and Intervention*. London: Routledge.

Reuters. (2022). 'Citing Martial Law, Ukraine President Signs Decree to Combine National TV Channels into One Platform', 20 March, https://www.reuters.com/world/europe/citing-martial-law-ukraine-president-signs-decree-combine-national-tv-channels-2022-03-20, accessed 9 March 2023.

Splidsboel Hansen, F. (2016). 'Mediatised Warfare in Russia: Framing the Annexation of Crimea'. In M. Pantti (ed.), *Media and the Ukraine Crisis: Hybrid Media Practices and Narratives of Conflict*, pp. 89–106. New York: Peter Lang.

Stottlemyre, S. A. (2015). 'HUMINT, OSINT, or Something New? Defining Crowdsourced Intelligence', *International Journal of Intelligence and CounterIntelligence*, 28 (3), 578–89.

Taylor, P. M. (2003). *Munitions of the Mind: A History of Propaganda from the Ancient World to the Present Day*. Manchester: Manchester University Press.

Thussu, D. K., and Freedman, D. (eds) (2003). *War and the Media: Reporting Conflict 24/7*. London: Sage.

Tiffany, K. (2022). 'The Myth of the "First TikTok War"', *The Atlantic*, 10 March, https://www.theatlantic.com/technology/archive/2022/03/tiktok-war-ukraine-russia/627017, accessed 9 March 2023.

Tynkkynen, V.-P. (2023). 'Öljykulttuurin rohkaisema väkivaltainen Venäjä'. In S. Tengvall (ed.), *Kuinka Venäjän hyökkäyssota muuttaa maailmaa?*, pp. 148-63. Helsinki: Gaudeamus.

UN. (2022). 'Ukraine: UN General Assembly Demands Russia Reverse Course on "Attempted Illegal Annexation"', *United News*, 12 October, https://news.un.org/en/story/2022/10/1129492, accessed 9 March 2023.

Wiggins, B. E. (2016). 'Crimea River: Directionality in Memes from the Russia–Ukraine Conflict', *International Journal of Communication*, 10, 451–85.

Zelensky, V. (2023). President Zelensky's Address to U.K. Parliament, 8 February, https://www.youtube.com/watch?v=Sn0C-5wKVu8, accessed 14 March 2023.

Part One:
Media Infrastructures

· 1 ·

UNDERSTANDING THE UKRAINIAN INFORMATIONAL ORDER IN THE FACE OF THE RUSSIAN WAR

Göran Bolin and Per Ståhlberg

Although wars, uprisings, and conflicts have been affiliated with media technologies before – from classic war propaganda to television wars and twitter revolutions – the Russian war on Ukraine has arguably integrated the media to an elevated extent. Over the first months of the full-scale war, there has been a growing fascination with flows stemming from Ukraine of images, videos and memes about the war. Video clips with high production values accompany President Zelensky in international parliaments, the Cannes Film Festival, the Glastonbury music festival, the Grammy Awards, NATO and the World Bank. Various governmental ministries, NGOs and private individuals produce memes on Twitter and other social media to raise support for Ukraine's cause, and images captured by the body cameras of soldiers at the front show successful Ukrainian military operations and bear witness to Russian atrocities and war crimes.

Wars are often thought of as a combat between states in strategic and operational control of disposable means. States are, following Max Weber (1919/2004), defined by their monopoly of the resources of legitimised physical violence. However, as Pierre Bourdieu (2012/2020) has argued in his lectures on the state, they are also defined by their control of the resources of symbolic violence, that is, the power to control the representations of social realities. But what happens with the control of these symbolic resources in times of paradigmatic societal transformations, when the state functions are unstable and communication resources are dispersed? Ukraine makes an interesting example of precisely how communication resources are dispersed, yet seemingly coordinated in ways that are beyond the centralised organisational institutions that more stable states have at their disposal. To understand the dynamics behind this flow of images and messages from Ukraine, and how they prompt us to rethink the paradigmatic understanding of the military and informational dimensions of war, we need to go back to the events around the Euromaidan revolution in 2013–14.

The aim of this chapter is to discuss the informational order of the war on Ukraine and how this was established during the Euromaidan Revolution in the winter of 2013–14 when flexible organisational networks with blurred boundaries between state, civil society, and market actors became instrumental in forming the international image of Ukraine. First, we will give a short historical background to the Euromaidan Revolution. Second, we will describe the orchestration of communication that arose during the revolution: how it was formed during a few months in late 2013 and early 2014, and how it produced a network of relations that proved very effective for countering competing images of Ukraine, especially from Russia. Third, we are going to study how these networks have become reactivated and intensified since the escalation of the war, and how they make up what we will discuss in terms of a *networked informational state*. The discussion has its empirical background in our ethnographic work on information management, nation branding and soft power in Ukraine during the years 2013–18 (Bolin and Ståhlberg 2023). The material stems from fieldwork that includes observations and interviews with PR agents and representatives from branding agencies, NGOs, activists, politicians and political administration, journalists, and news providers. We have also visited symposia and branding conferences and events, analysed branding material (posters, video clips, brand books), and consulted secondary sources such as news features, interviews, press releases from news agencies and other forms of informational material and reports from NGOs (for more detail, see Bolin and Ståhlberg 2023).

The state in turmoil

Like many east European countries formerly under Soviet rule or influence, Ukraine does not have a long history of sovereignty. The country had a short period of independence as the Ukrainian People's Republic between 1917 and 1921, following the Russian Revolution, and modern independence came with the collapse of the Soviet Union in 1991 (Wolczuk 2000). On 1 December 1991, a national referendum took place, and an overwhelming majority supported The Act of Declaration of Independence – more than 90 per cent of the 82 per cent of the electorate that took part voted in favour (Magocsi 1996/2010: 724ff). While remaining careful in its relation towards Russia, the government of Leonid Kuchma took a few steps towards building a Ukrainian national identity, with, for example, decrees of 'decommunisation' of the Soviet past (Oliinyk and Kuzio 2021: 808).

In relation to the election in November 2004, the presidential candidate Viktor Yanukovych was found to have manipulated the results of the presidential elections to his favour, which led to massive protests. These protests were successful, and a new and fair election – as declared by international observers – resulted in a victory for the opposition candidate, Viktor Yushchenko. The Yushchenko government advanced the distancing of Ukraine from Russia and the building of a Ukrainian national history. A particular focus was put on Holodomor, the Great Famine of 1932–3 caused by Josef Stalin's decision to curb the farmers' resistance to his agricultural policy. A museum of Holodomor was built to commemorate the victims of this forced starvation, and an Institute of National Remembrance was launched (Kasianov 2021; Oliinyk and Kuzio 2021: 808).

However, Yushchenko became increasingly unpopular during his presidency, and in 2010 he lost the election to his predecessor Yanukovych, who thus regained the power to lead the country. The Yanukovych government's power base was the pro-Russian Party of Regions, the dominating party in Ukraine between 2006 and 2014 with a strong base in East Ukraine. Despite its pro-Russian stance, the president announced the signing of an association agreement with the European Union (EU). On 21 November 2013, just a few days before the signing of this agreement, President Yanukovych surprisingly changed his mind and announced that he would not sign. This unexpected move led to protest on Maidan Nezalezhnosti, the Independence Square in central Kyiv. Initially, the protests were peaceful, but they were eventually met by hard crackdowns by special police forces, resulting in escalated violence and the killing of protesters. This escalation of violence led to the ousting of Yanukovych. Petro Poroshenko, an oligarch from South-Western Ukraine who had made his fortune on chocolate factories, won the new election. Societal equilibrium was not restored, however, since Russia soon after annexed the peninsula of Crimea in March 2014, and at the same time initiated a war in Donbas together with local separatists.

The Euromaidan Revolution, or The Revolution of Dignity as it was also labelled, led to a change in political power, but it did not introduce any paradigmatic change to the Ukrainian political system – despite being called 'a revolution'. The trust in politics, politicians and the parliamentary institutions among the public continued to be very low, and the belief in the power of politics to instigate change was minimal (Åslund 2014). The general opinion was that the Ukrainian government was weak and lacked both the skills and resources to inform international audiences about the situation in the country. Instead, initiatives for managing information came from civil society as well as PR and communication businesses.

The rise of a new informational order

During the first days of the Euromaidan Revolution, several new communication platforms were formed that covered the growing protests and the clashes with the police. These platforms included non-governmental organisations such as Euromaidan Press, Hromadske TV and Espreso TV, which complemented state-controlled news agencies such as Ukrinform and the commercial and public service broadcasters. Since there were very few international journalists stationed in Kyiv at the outbreak of the protests (Dyczok 2016: 7), these news agencies and streaming outlets that continuously broadcasted online from centrally placed positions in Kyiv, provided international news media with unedited and uncommented images from happenings (Metzger and Tucker 2017). Social media such as Facebook and Twitter and Russian Odniklassniki and VKontake complemented the news coverage with information and commentary posted by ordinary citizens, but they also functioned as extended distribution channels for the new media platforms. All the above-mentioned news agencies and broadcasters plus several others had their own profiles on the social media platforms and much of the circulation of information occurred in those online spaces.

The somewhat disorganised flow of images during the first months of the protests eventually became more organised after the ousting of President Yanukovych and the sudden Russian interference through the annexation of Crimea and the war in Donetsk and Luhansk. In response to these events, several initiatives emerged that in various ways sought to deal with the management of information on Ukraine: the press briefing platform Ukraine Crisis Media

Center (UCMC), the fake news-debunking organisation StopFake, the television channel Ukraine Today (UT) and the governmental Ministry of Information Policy (MIP). Each of these illustrates the blurred boundaries between government, corporate business and civil society, and are thus examples of *the new informational order* as it has come to define Ukrainian information policy.

The Ukraine Crisis Media Center was launched in March 2014 with the aim of providing global media with 'accurate and up-to-date information on the events in Ukraine', as the organisation initially formulated itself on its web pages (uacrisis.org), especially from army spokespersons and representatives of civil society organisations. From their provisional location in the Hotel Ukraine, situated at the top of the Maidan Nezalezhnosti, they offered news briefings and information support to foreign correspondents reporting from Ukraine. The UCMC was eventually moved to the Ukrainian House, a conference hall a few hundred metres from the Maidan. The activities of UCMC included daily press briefings by the military to report on the happenings on the eastern front of Ukraine, where Russia-backed separatists were fighting the Ukrainian army for the regions of Donetsk and Luhansk. In other countries, such a communication platform would be run and controlled by the state, but the UCMC was set up on the initiative of a couple of professionals from two PR agencies in Kyiv. As stated on their web pages, it was founded as an NGO with financial support from several European and North American organisations. The fact that they were organised as a civil society organisation and that their founders are from the branding business did, however, not distinguish their activities, and the way they operated communicatively from a governmental briefing platform.

Our second example is Ukraine Today, a broadcast and streamed television channel, founded in August 2014 by Ukrainian oligarch Ihor Kolomoyskyi and registered as an NGO. Despite its status as an NGO, it was run as a commercial station with advertising and user profiling as business model, combined with donation-based crowdfunding until its disorganisation in 2016. Such hybrid funding scheme combined a commercial business model with civil society aspirations. Ukraine Today's credo was 'to win the battle against the abuse of information within the informational war', according to the 'Our mission' statement on channel's website in 2015 (since many years defunct). Kolomoyskyi also owned other, purely commercial television channels. Ukraine Today, however, was different since it cooperated with state ministries, for example, the television programme *Reform Watch* was a collaboration with the Ministry of Economic Development and Trade. The channel also had a partnership with the Kyiv-Mohyla Business School in relation to the programme *Business Insight*.

The third example is StopFake, a news debunking organisation that was launched in March 2014 by faculty and students of journalism at the National University of Kyiv-Mohyla Academy. StopFake has worked to debunk news stories stemming from various international news outlets that were spreading speculative or false information about events in Ukraine. Most often news stories emanated from Russian media (e.g. the international television channel RT). By pointing to baseless claims, spotting inconsistencies, producing counter-stories and vetting images, StopFake has sought to counter or minimise the negative reporting of Russian news (Khaldarova and Pantti 2016: 896; Bolin, Jordan and Ståhlberg 2016). StopFake is funded by individual donations and grants from several international organisations, such as the International Renaissance Foundation (part of George Soros's Open Society Foundation), the National Endowment for Democracy (funded by the United States Congress), the Ministry of Foreign Affairs of the Czech Republic, the Sigrid Rausing Trust and the Embassy of the United Kingdom. StopFake is directed towards an international audience and was initially published in five languages: Ukrainian, Russian, Romanian, Spanish and English. In 2021, this has expanded to include Serbian, French, German, Dutch, Czech, Italian, Bulgarian and Polish. The organisational model of StopFake is similar to other civil society organisations, marked by a high degree of voluntary work and crowdsourcing. However, it also continuously and regularly cooperates with state institutions such as Ukrinform and the Ministry of Foreign Affairs.

The fourth example is the Ministry of Information Policy (MIP), which was launched by the Ukrainian government under President Poroschenko and Prime Minister Arseniy Yatsenyuk in December 2014. This launch of the ministry was quite controversial at the time: several journalists, including the international non-profit organisation Reporters Without Borders, raised voices against the formation of such an Orwellian 'Ministry of Truth' (Grytsenko 2014). This criticism was also shared by some diplomats, including the United States Ambassador to Ukraine. The Ministry of Information Policy persisted, however, and was active until 2019. Afterwards, some of its activities became relaunched within the Ministry of Culture and Information Policy.

As can be understood by its name, a Ministry of Information Policy is naturally responsible for formulating and communicating the state's informational policy, and hence also the instrument by which the state exercises control over its symbolic resources, including 'to combat biased information against Ukraine' (Interfax Ukraine 2014). The Ministry's communication strategy included arrangements for the embedding of international journalists in the war zones in Eastern Ukraine, the restoration of the communication infrastructure in the same area (e.g. television and mobile phone masts), nation branding campaigns and the iArmy, which was a small unit within the Ministry responsible for managing its social media accounts. The Ministry was also in charge of the state-owned online television channel UATV, although the channel had a certain degree of editorial freedom. More tightly connected to the ministry was the National News Agency of Ukraine – Ukrinform (ukrinform.net) – equipped with photo archives and a press centre and with international correspondents.

The composition of the staff of the Ministry of Information Policy was interesting. One of its deputy Ministers was Tetyana Popova, previously a high-profiled media professional. Popova, however, eventually resigned due to disagreements with the Ministry's policy, but remained active with the Ministry for several months after her resignation through her engagement in her own NGO called 'Information Security'. One state secretary with a background in the PR business managed the Ministry's nation branding campaigns, that is, orchestrated campaigns that aim to produce a favourable image of a nation state directed to an international audience of investors, tourists and politicians (Bolin and Ståhlberg 2010). The iArmy had a Facebook account 'Інформаційні війська України' [Information Forces of Ukraine], which defined it as a 'community organisation'. iArmy's web address '@i.army.org' further signals its civil society status.

As these four examples show, the management of information in post-Euromaidan Ukraine was executed by a mixture of governmental, civil society and corporate PR business organisations, which all cooperated in various combinations with one another. Some people, like Tetyana Popova, moved effortlessly between different organisations, and thus contributed to the blurred boundaries between societal spheres in their cooperation. She was, however, not alone in so doing. People in the PR sector worked together with government officials, and NGOs cooperated with state institutions. All in all, this makes up a complex networked structure that operated in conjunction with each other across societal spheres. In the next section, we will examine how these organisational networks that were formed in Ukraine in the wake of the change of power and Russia's increased military interference currently impact Ukraine's communicative efforts.

Networked information management and the grammar of the internet

As Sandra Braman (2006: 28ff) has pointed out in her historical overview of different types of state formations, *the informational state* historically succeeds the bureaucratic state and the bureaucratic welfare state. The informational state is networked, and it integrates state ministries and administrations with non-state actors in a system characterised by 'multiple interdependencies [...] in ways that largely require use of the global information infrastructure for information creation, processing, flows, and use' (ibid.: 36). This is in line with how Ned Rossiter (2006: 36) argues that an organised network 'must engage, by necessity, other institutional partners who may often be opposed to their interests'. Rossiter's definition appears as an accurate description of the interrelation between the actors described above (i.e. Ministry of Information Policy, Ukraine Crisis Media Center, StopFake and Ukraine Today), and can be seen as a type of multi-stakeholderism were it not for the fact that the activities lack the 'degree of centralization and hierarchization [...] essential for a network to be characterized as organized' (ibid.: 49). Rather than an organised network, it is in the Ukrainian case a few loosely coupled nodes that are adaptive enough to become activated at certain moments in time. This does not constitute an outsourcing of state functions, since it lacks the control over information flows that usually characterises consorted information efforts. It is rather a type of 'barely controlled chaos', as anthropologist Akhil Gupta (2012: 14) has called this form of un- or semi-regulated cooperative efforts that we can see in Ukraine at the intersection of the state, market and civil society.

This barely controlled chaos in the management of information also produces a specific type of text, and a very special kind of audience address. Nadia Kaneva (2022) has usefully pointed out that what can be seen in Ukraine after February 2022 is 'the first use of brand communication as part of a nation's war effort'. Usually, branding by nation-states is orchestrated to attract tourists or investors. A lesser observed function of nation branding is to gain support for the country at hand. This aspect of branding stands out much clearer in this case, as Ukraine is using the technologies of attraction common in marketing and branding to gain support for defending itself by humanitarian as well as military means (see also Bolin and Ståhlberg 2022). And indeed, the combination of video clips and smart web design used by the agents involved in communicative efforts in Ukraine speaks the persuasive language of advertising and PR – sometimes with a sombre tone to it, and sometimes with irony, schadenfreude, trolling or other communicative styles and forms characteristic of social media communication. In the remainder of this section, we will give some examples of this, arguing that these textual expressions are the result of the organisational mix in the moment of 'encoding', to use the terminology of Stuart Hall (1973).

Among the many different features of the Ukrainian communication efforts since the Russian invasion has been the informational campaigns executed to gain financial, humanitarian and military aid as well as general international support for Ukraine (Jardine 2022). Although we cannot know the nature of the support given to Ukraine without these activities, one can conclude that support has been given, foremost from countries in Western Europe, North America, and Australia. In that sense, the communication efforts can be considered successful. The tools used for these communication initiatives have mainly been online media: YouTube videos, websites, PR campaigns, social media presence on Twitter, and other platforms, but also less obvious media such as stamps, T-shirts and socks. Many of these are the result of co-operations between governmental departments and PR agencies.

An example of such cooperation between PR business and government is the official website of Ukraine (Ukraine.ua), verified by the Ministry of Foreign Affairs. Until the full-scale invasion in February 2022, it had the design of a rather typical nation branding platform, promoting the country to foreign investors and tourists. It was designed and crafted by professionals in the PR business making use of aesthetics familiar in the international promotion industry. Ukraine was marketed as an attractive country with beautiful sights, friendly people and exciting events. 'Ukraine Now' was the country's slogan before the invasion and the war in the Eastern parts of Ukraine was carefully avoided. Soon after the Russian full-scale invasion, the website was refashioned to raise international support during the escalated war. The opening page now states that 'On February 24, 2022, the ordinary life of Ukraine stopped, as did this website'. The visitor then has two options. One button leads to a page with information on the war, the other to the previous website. Each web page gives a drastically different image of Ukraine: One shows images of festivities, leisure and beauty, aimed to attract tourists to the country. Slogans such as 'Dynamic Ukraine Now', 'Innovative Ukraine Now' and 'Diverse Ukraine Now' are still alive on this page. The other alternative depicts a dark version of the world map with Ukraine in yellow at the centre, dwarfed by a gigantic Russia in red colour. The visitor to the web page then has the options of taking part in stories from the front, scrolling through a photo gallery, seeing documentation about Russian war crimes or following the latest developments in a continuously updated news feed. The design and aesthetic of the war website are similar to the tourist branding page regarding colours, fonts and layout. It is also designed by the PR agency Banda – a Ukrainian PR bureau that previously has worked with promoting Ukraine in more entertaining contexts, such as the Eurovision Song Contest held in Kyiv in 2017.

Two features of this campaign stand out. First, presenting Russia as Ukraine's 'other' is explicit in that the site highlights the horrors of 'Russian war crimes'. In a powerful feature on the site, visitors are allowed to hear air raid signals warning Ukrainians across the country of an imminent Russian attack. Second, the war site portrays Ukrainians and their experience as defenders, heroes and victims. In contrast, the former site presented Ukraine as a pleasant experience for others (visitors and investors). People and organisations that were working with a particular type of meaning management (such as promoting Ukraine to investors and tourists) could within weeks shift to a different form of managing meaning (promoting the Ukrainian view of the war), thus entering a tighter cooperation with governmental departments, in this case the Ukrainian Ministry of Foreign Affairs.

Another clear example of the cooperation and relations between the Ukrainian government and the PR business is the campaign 'Brave like Ukraine'. According to an interview in *Wired* (Meaker 2022), the idea and initiative for this campaign came from the Kyiv-based advertising bureau Banda. The managing team at Banda brought the idea to the Minister of Digital Transformation, Mykhailo Fedorov, in mid-March 2022 and met approval, and the campaign was then launched in early April. That campaigns such as this originate among the branding business rather than among politicians is fully in line with similar campaigns in which governments are involved, be they nation branding campaigns or domestic opinion formation. This is in fact the way the PR business works: demand for PR services does not arise out of nowhere but needs to be produced. As we have discussed elsewhere, advertisers simply need to convince their potential customers about the need to execute campaigns (Ståhlberg and Bolin 2016; Bolin and Ståhlberg 2021). On the website, it can be learned that the Office of the President, the Cabinet of Ministers, and the Ministry of Digital Transformation are the 'senders' of the campaign (brave.ua), and that the site is 'Created by Banda'. The campaign has included the use of billboards at public transport hubs across the world, but it also features an online shop (shop.brave.ua) where clothes, merch, jewellery, artwork, food and other consumer goods are displayed for purchase, many of which are designed in the Ukrainian national colours of blue and yellow or feature other signifiers of Ukraine, such as the trident, sunflowers and national embroidery. Profits from the marketplace commission go to the reconstruction of Ukraine.

The Ukrainian ministries are also very active on social media, where they have their own profiles. The tone and audience address on these sites often differ from the more official language that can be found on corresponding profiles of ministries and governmental agencies in other countries. An example is the Twitter profile 'Defense of Ukraine', which is the 'Official page of the Ministry of Defense of Ukraine' (https://twitter.com/DefenceU). The Twitter feed is a mix of daily statements of losses on the part of Russia (how many dead soldiers, destroyed tanks, ships and aircrafts), images of destroyed enemy equipment and soldiers, commemorations of Ukrainian soldiers killed in action, combat sequences, but also TikTok videos of dancing soldiers, soldiers with kittens or dogs, and more stylish video clips which are skilfully edited and accompanied by up-tempo music.

There are, furthermore, other communication efforts related to the war, which strike different communicative tones and use other modes of audience address. One such effort is the more confrontative campaign centred on the postal stamp 'Russian warship – Go fuck yourself!', which has received international recognition. The stamp commemorates the resistance proven by the coast guards at the strategically placed Snake Island, outside of the coast of mainland Ukraine in the southwest at the very beginning of Russia's full-scale attack. Upon a call to surrender by the Russian flagship of the Black Sea fleet Moskva, the coast guard defiantly responded with the already mentioned profanity, and it was for some time believed that they had been killed. This was not the case, but the video with their clearly heard exchange of words had received widespread international attention, and the coast guard who uttered the famous words became decorated after having been freed in a prisoner exchange in late March (Sauer 2022).

The competition for the design of the stamp was announced on 1 March by Ukrposhta, the Ukraine Post Office, with the aim of celebrating Ukraine's determination to defend itself. A public vote was held online (McCarty 2022). The winner was announced already on 12 March, and the winning motive by the Ukrainian artist Boris Groh was chosen above other contestants (Michael 2022). The sinking of the warship by Ukrainian Neptune anti-ship missiles on 12 April was followed by gloating memes. The warship stamp was succeeded in June 2022 by a stamp depicting the image of Ukrainian farmers towing away enemy tanks with their tractors (Starr 2022), and yet a new one directly after the strike on the Kerch Bridge in early October (Koshiw 2022). This stamp was issued on Russia's Unity Day on 4 November, a national holiday instituted in 2005 by Vladimir Putin to replace the previous commemoration of the Russian Revolution.

The issuing of these stamps, and their timing with the Russian national commemoration day, can be considered a kind of 'trolling' that has set its mark on the communication strategies adopted by Ukraine. Trolling is a typical 'tactic' of the subordinated part in a power struggle if we follow the distinction between the strategies of the dominator and the tactics of the weak made by Michel de Certeau (1984/1988: 34ff). de Certeau theorised this 'art of the weak' (ibid.: 37) with inspiration from Claus von Clausewitz's treatise *On War* (Clausewitz 1832/1976), where he compared tactics with 'wit', an act of sudden reversal of perspective that has the effect of taking the audience by amused surprise. Such trolling can be seen in many of the earlier communication efforts by Ukraine during the low-scale war. It was, for example, also activated in a promotional video for Eurovision Song Contest (ESC) in Kyiv in 2017, subtly titled 'We won't give up', where a young girl can be seen dancing and singing through various picturesque landscapes in Ukraine, ultimately including recognisable images from Crimea, and anchored with the final lyrics 'let's celebrate – come to Ukraine'.[1] The same tactic was used by the Ukrainian national soccer team, which appeared in newly designed shirts with a map of Ukraine including Crimea for the European soccer championship in 2021 (Bolin and Ståhlberg 2023: 113–17). On both occasions – the ESC 2017 and European soccer championship – Russia filed protests to the organising institutions (EBU and UEFA respectively), but as in all successful acts of trolling, these protests were in vain and in fact further contributed to the humiliation. Importantly, all instances of 'trolling' were dependent on networks of collaborating actors from civil society as well as government authorities and PR agencies.

Braman (2019: 149) usefully argues that nation branding is a specific form of information policy, a part of the 'continuing evolution of the informational state'. What can be learned from the examples above is that branding has become an integral part of the networked activities of the informational state of Ukraine. The groundwork of the organisational structure for this was gradually established in the wake of the Euromaidan Revolution, and this structure has been further consolidated since the outbreak of the full-scale war with Russia since February 2022. This has resulted in a very specific type of informational order, that is also clearly visible in the consorted audience address and the signifying practices adopted at the intersection of government, civil society and market.

Conclusion: War communication and the informational state

Previous takes on the external communication of nation states have, following Weber (1919/2004) and Bourdieu (2012/2020), often emphasised the state's control over symbolic resources. Our research has pointed to the fact that what might appear as a consorted voice directed towards international audiences has a more complex structure of communicative interrelations between the state and agents outside of it.

In this chapter, we have discussed the ways in which the Ukrainian state has nurtured its communication policy at the intersection between government, market-oriented corporate power and civil society since the Euromaidan Revolution. The alliances made during the revolution have paved the way for the short distances between these societal spheres, and the individual actors moving between them with ease – one day working for a PR agency, while another day working for a governmental ministry or for an NGO. This mixes their roles and renders the boundaries between societal spheres porous. In the face of an outer enemy, such integration of societal spheres is understandable and logical. Whether these alliances and cooperation will continue also during times of peace, and whether the informational state will continue in such a post-war scenario, remains to be seen in future research.

Note

1 The video can be found on YouTube: https://www.youtube.com/watch?v=Ggem1JBNc0w, accessed 23 January 2023.

References

Åslund, A. (2014). 'Oligarchs, Corruption, and European Integration', *Journal of Democracy* 25 (3), 64–73.

Bolin, G., and Ståhlberg, P. (2010). 'Between Community and Commodity: Nationalism and Nation Branding'. In A. Roosvall and I. Salovaara Moring (eds), *Communicating the*

Nation: National Topographies of Global Media Landscapes, pp. 79–101. Gothenburg, Sweden: Nordicom.

Bolin, G., and Ståhlberg, P. (2021). 'The Powerpoint Nation: Branding an Imagined Commodity', *The European Review*, 29 (4), 445–56.

Bolin, G., and Ståhlberg, P. (2022) 'Nation Branding vs. Nation Building Revisited: Ukrainian Information Management in the Face of the Russian Invasion'. *Place Branding & Public Diplomacy*, https://doi.org/10.1057/s41254-022-00277-z, accessed 23 January 2023.

Bolin, G., and Ståhlberg, P. (2023). *Managing Meaning in Ukraine: Information, Communication and Narration since the Euromaidan Revolution*. Cambridge, MA: MIT Press.

Bolin, G., Jordan, P., and Ståhlberg, P. (2016). 'From Nation Branding to Information Warfare: Management of Information in the Ukraine–Russia Conflict'. In M. Pantti (ed.), *Media and the Ukraine Crisis: Hybrid Media Practices and Narratives of Conflict*, pp. 3–18. New York: Peter Lang.

Bourdieu, P. (2012/2020). *On the State: Lectures at the Collège de France 1989–1992*. Cambridge: Polity.

Braman, S. (2006). *Change of State: Information, Policy, and Power*. Cambridge, MA: MIT Press.

Braman, S. (2019). 'Trumpean Nation Branding. Strange Attractions and Information Policy'. In P. Jakobsson and F. Stiernstedt (eds), *Fritt från fältet: Om Medier, Generationer och Världen – Festskrift till Göran Bolin*, pp. 149–67. Huddinge: Södertörn University.

Certeau, M. de (1984/1988). *The Practice of Everyday Life*. Berkeley: University of California Press.

Clausewitz, C. von (1832/1976). *On War*. Princeton, NJ: Princeton University Press.

Dyczok, M. (2016). *Ukraine's Euromaidan: Broadcasting through Information Wars with Hromadske Radio*. Bristol, UK: E–International Relations Publishing.

Grytsenko, O. (2014). 'Journalists, Free Speech Activists Protest Against "Ministry of Truth"', *Kyiv Post*, 4 December, https://www.kyivpost.com/article/content/reform-watch/journalists-media-rights-activists-demand-abolishing-of-newly-formed-ministry-of-truth-374003.html, 3 May 2021, accessed 23 January 2023.

Gupta, A. (2012). *Red Tape: Bureaucracy, Structural Violence, and Poverty in India*. Durham, NC: Duke University Press.

Hall, S. (1973). *Encoding/Decoding in the Television Discourse*. CCCS Occasional Paper 7. Birmingham: Birmingham University/CCCS.

Interfax Ukraine. (2014). 'Poroshenko: Information Ministry's Main Task is to Repel Information Attacks Against Ukraine', 8 December, https://en.interfax.com.ua/news/economic/238615.html. 26 March 2021, accessed 23 January 2023.

Jardine, A. (2022) 'This Campaign Is Celebrating Ukrainian Bravey Around the World', *AdAge* 31 May, https://adage.com/creativity/work/campaign-celebrating-ukrainian-bravery-around-world/2418766?adobe_mc=MCMID%3D132995253949787612980481454%E2%80%A6, accessed 23 January 2023.

Kaneva, N. (2022). '"Brave Like Ukraine": A Critical Discourse Perspective on Ukraine's Wartime Brand', *Place Branding and Public Diplomacy*, https://doi.org/10.1057/s41254-022-00273-3, accessed 23 January 2023.

Kasianov, G. (2021). 'Holodomor and the Holocaust in Ukraine as Cultural Memory: Comparison, Competition, Interaction', *Journal of Genocide Research*, 24 (2), 216–27.

Khaldarova, I., and Pantti, M. (2016). 'Fake News: The Narrative Battle over the Ukrainian Conflict', *Journalism Practice*, 10 (7), 891–901.

Koshiw, I. (2022). 'Ukraine Issues Crimean Bridge Strike Stamp on Russia's Union Day', *The Guardian*, 4 November, https://www.theguardian.com/world/2022/nov/04/ukraine-issues-crimean-bridge-strike-stamp-on-russias-unity-day, accessed 23 January 2023.

Magocsi, P. R. (1996/2010). *A History of Ukraine: The Land and Its Peoples*. Toronto: Toronto University Press.

McCarty, D. (2022). 'Winner in Ukraine Stamp-Design Contest Sends Russia a Message', *Linn's Stamp News*, 14 March, https://www.linns.com/news/world-stamps-postal-history/winner-in-ukraine-stamp-design-contest-sends-russia-a-message, accessed 23 January 2023.

Meaker, M. (2022). 'How Ukraine Is Winning the Propaganda War', *Wired*, 22 June, https://www.wired.com/story/ukraine-propaganda-war/, accessed 23 January 2023.

Metzger, M. M., and Tucker, J. A. (2017). 'Social Media and EuroMaidan: A Review Essay', *Slavic Review*, 76 (1), 169–91.

Michael, C. (2022). 'Ukraine Reveals "Russian Warship, Go Fuck Yourself!" Postage Stamp', *The Guardian*, 12 March, https://www.theguardian.com/world/2022/mar/12/ukraine-reveals-russian-warship-go-fuck-yourself-postage-stamp, accessed 23 January 2023.

Oliinyk, A., and Kuzio, T. (2021). 'The Euromaidan Revolution: Reforms and Decommunisation in Ukraine', *Europe-Asia Studies*, 73 (5), 807–36.

Rossiter, N. (2006). *Organized Networks: Media Theory, Creative Labour, New Institutions*. Rotterdam: NAi Publishers.

Sauer, P. (2022). 'Ukraine Gives Medal to Soldier Who Told Russian Officer to "Go Fuck Yourself"'. *The Guardian*, 29 March, https://www.theguardian.com/world/2022/mar/29/ukrainian-soldier-russian-warship-medal-snake-island, accessed 23 January 2023.

Ståhlberg, P., and Bolin, G. (2016). 'Having a Soul or Choosing a Face? Nation Branding, Identity and Cosmopolitan Imagination', *Social Identities*, 22 (3), 274–90.

Starr, M. (2022). 'Ukraine Issues Postal Stamps of Tractor Towing Away Russian Tank', *The Jerusalem Post*, 19 June, https://www.jpost.com/omg/article-709853, accessed 23 January 2023.

Weber, M. (1919/2004). 'Politics as Vocation'. In D. Owen and T. Strong (eds), *The Vocation Lectures*, pp. 32–94. Illinois: Hackett Books.

Wolczuk, K. (2000). 'History, Europe and the "National Idea": The "Official" Narrative of National Identity in Ukraine', *Nationalities Papers*, 28 (4), 671–94.

· 2 ·

SWARM COMMUNICATION IN A TOTALISING WAR: MEDIA INFRASTRUCTURES, ACTORS AND PRACTICES IN UKRAINE DURING THE 2022 RUSSIAN INVASION

Kateryna Boyko and Roman Horbyk

During the first weeks of the Russian invasion of Ukraine, part of the Russo-Ukrainian War continuing since 2014, the Ukrainian resistance and victories fascinated external observers. One of these unforeseen victories has been successful communication. This chapter aims to give an empirical overview of shifts in the Ukrainian mediascape during the first year of the invasion, focusing on three principal sites of analysis: media infrastructures, actors and practices. We observe collaborative communication between different actors, involving a synergy of top-down, bottom-up and horizontal actions, where hyperlocal reporting, lobbyism via social media, media activism, folklore and art have played important roles. Ukrainian society compensated for its lack of resources through the media and communication equivalent of a *levée en masse* (mass mobilisation), yet in a decentralised, networked way based on swarm communication paralleling the swarming tactics used by the Ukrainian military.

Our analysis is based on three kinds of data obtained in the following ways: a systematic review and scraping of war-related hashtags on Facebook, Twitter and YouTube; following official, professional and semi-professional Telegram channels (the primary source of information for Ukrainians since the invasion [Opora 2022]); and episodic monitoring of Ukrainian news media, TV channels and publications about the media. The data collection lasted from 24 February 2022 until February 2023, accumulating an archive of 15,000 social media postings as the documentary basis for our analysis. The authors also conducted interviews with six Ukrainian media professionals: a deputy chief editor of an online news media publication, a journalist covering the media market, two media experts, a military administration press officer and a strategic communication professional. Unstructured online interviews in Ukrainian occurred between March 2022 and December 2022. Two follow-up sessions with those interviewed during this period were organised in December 2022, focusing on editorial work during power outages. We also used supplementary interviews with five civilian refugees, conducted in March–April 2022 onsite in Lviv.

From limited to total(ising) war

We follow Käihkö (2021) in interpreting the 2014 annexation of Crimea and war in Donbas as examples of limited war, where adversaries set a smaller military aim to which they do not commit all their resources. The 2022 invasion marked an expansion towards total war, whereby (ideally) all resources are committed to the adversary's defeat. Total war also legitimises targeting civilian infrastructure and populations. It is possible to apply the perspective of total war to this war, but with some reservations. While Russia has used the principles of total war (attacking Ukrainian civilians and infrastructure), the characteristic full mobilisation has been lacking. Simultaneously, Ukraine has involved its civilians more than Russia, but it has never attacked civilian targets on Russian territory. There have also been certain restrictions on how weapons have been used. Russia may have started the invasion as another limited war, albeit with a grand aim (regime change or occupation); however, upon the initial failure, it required expansion towards total war. Certainly, we can observe that the principles of total war are being asymmetrically employed by the belligerents. At most, we can speak of a new type of war, occupying the middle ground between limited and total. We call this a 'totalising war', as it is transitioning from a limited to a total war, although the total aims are still constrained by the belligerents' limited military capacity.

Another fundamental aspect is the role of technology. Recently, modern warfare has been defined as *digital war* (Merrin 2018), as it is increasingly reliant on digital technologies, and even participatory war (Boichak and Hoskins 2022). It is possible to speak of a rollback to pre-industrial forms of total war, conceptualised by Clausewitz based on the *levée en masse* during the French Revolution:

> Suddenly war again became the business of the people – a people of thirty millions, all of whom considered themselves to be citizens. (...) The people became a participant in war; instead of governments and armies as heretofore, the full weight of the nation was thrown into the balance. (Clausewitz 2008: 238)

What makes this current iteration special is its networked, mediatised character, whereby mobilisation and its consequences are wired by communication that combines both legacy and networked media in a hybrid media system (Horbyk 2023). Here, the concept of mediascape as a combination of infrastructure and content (Appadurai 1990) is especially productive. The concept of collaborative communication also appears important in explaining the mechanics of participatory war. This concept, which originated in marketing studies, is characterised by high frequency, reciprocal feedback, mutually beneficial information sharing and the use of rationality in persuasion (Joshi 2009: 134; Mohr and Nevin 1990).

The three periods of war communication: Mobilisation, plateau and blackout

We cannot approach the Ukrainian mediascape during the first year of the invasion as a static snapshot. Since 24 February 2022, it has been changing rapidly at the levels of infrastructure capacities, practices of media outlets and media consumption patterns. We suggest the following mediacentric periodisation of the first year of the war:

1. *Total mobilisation* (from 24 February to the de-occupation of Northern Ukraine in early April). The Russian offensive from multiple directions and missile strikes all over the country led to shock, the destruction of everyday routines and massive displacement of Ukrainians around the country and abroad as well as mobilisation and resistance. According to representative polls, 81 per cent of Ukrainians donated to the Armed Forces of Ukraine (AFU), 63 per cent provided refugees with clothes, and 60 per cent donated to humanitarian efforts (NDI 2022). Thus, we

can state that most of Ukrainian society became participants in the war effort. This period was characterised by the media system's transition to martial law conditions, obsessive news consumption (largely on social media) and robust content production and circulation. It ended with Ukraine's victory in the Battle of Kyiv and the revelation of the atrocities committed by Russian military personnel in the occupied territories.
2. *Plateau* (early April to October). War became an established part of life. New war-induced media practices and rituals became routine, including air raid smartphone alerts, daily publication of Russian losses, minutes of silence and crowdfunding initiatives in the media. Many businesses reopened, some people returned from evacuation, and children restarted school offline. This period also saw frontline victories and losses, from the sinking of the cruiser *Moskva* and the liberation of the Kharkiv region to the tragic fall of Mariupol and Russia's limited success in Donbas.
3. *Blackout* (starting on 10 October and ongoing as of February 2023). Russian strikes on critical energy infrastructure throughout the country led to massive power outages as well as mobile. and internet disconnection. This disrupted the already established media production and consumption routines. The gaps in content posting after strikes became noticeable for smaller outlets, and consumption was restricted by blackouts (evident from the sharp drop in YouTube channel views, according to one interviewee). TV viewing decreased significantly, down by 44 per cent during the week of 31 October in Kyiv (Biloskurs'ky and Serhienko 2022). During the blackouts, analogue and non-electronic media, such as books, have become more popular.

Summing up, we identify three periods between February 2022 and February 2023: total mobilisation, plateau and blackout. Each can be characterised by radical changes in media production and consumption, from the breaking of established routines to the formation of new routines to a new disruption. These changes have been shaped by, on the one hand, the external logic of the totalising war and, on the other hand, by infrastructural turmoil. What, then, have been the key developments in media infrastructures?

Media infrastructures: Ravage and resilience

Media and communication are determined by their underlying materiality. In particular, broadcast media and digital communication depend on the network of transmitting and receiving devices and the power grid that feeds them. In this section, we focus on the infrastructural transformations since the invasion. While Ukraine has a historically weak newspaper culture, its television network is robust, with up to 30 channels via digital TV and hundreds via over-the-top (OTT) services. Internet penetration is also rather high: 71 per cent of Ukrainians used the web in 2019 (Ukrinform 2019), and 60 per cent were registered on social media platforms (Kondratenko 2021). The country is covered with dense mobile networks of varying quality: 3G and 4G from six GSM and two CDMA operators are available in major population centres and along important roads, while connection in the countryside can be poor.

This infrastructure, which is vital for Ukrainian society's cohesion, already came under attack during the annexation of Crimea and the limited invasion of Donbas in 2014, when Russia aimed at securing control first over TV transmitters and later over mobile towers and internet cables. The occupied territories were severed from the Ukrainian grid, and new physical networks were created, wired via Russian traffic nodes (Horbyk 2022). When the Russian armed forces invaded Ukraine in 2022, they sought to destroy infrastructure. On 1 March, the main TV centre in Kyiv was targeted by a missile killing five people and causing (ostensibly limited) damage to the equipment (Zharovs'ky 2022). In this context, the destruction of many television transmitters in the contested areas and deep inside the country can also be considered deliberate.

Thus, TV channels were forced to reorganise their production routines and move studios to secure compounds. This became a factor in the TV centralisation and the establishment of the United News (*Yedyni novyny*) broadcast. In the occupied areas, such as Kherson, occupation administrations took control of broadcasting facilities and replaced Ukrainian TV channels with Russian ones. Before 24 February, Ukrainian TV channels were present on commercial satellites, but they were made available for free thereafter – partly to mitigate this forced disconnection.

Russian forces similarly attacked mobile communication infrastructure. As previous research has shown (Horbyk 2022), the AFU have been using regular mobile telephony since 2014 to compensate for gaps in their communication systems. This arguably motivated the Russian Army to disrupt mobile communication. According to the interviewed civilian refugees from Bucha, Irpin, Kherson, Mariupol and Sumy, mobile connection was lost during the Russian attacks, partly due to damage to power supplies, but also to the physical destruction of masts that some witnessed. Russians actively employed radio electronic warfare, particularly Leer-3 devices designed to jam mobile signals.

This imposed a communication blackout on people in the frontline and occupied areas. Both receiving information from the outside world and providing information about local developments became hard or even impossible.

By the plateau phase, Starlink satellite internet terminals became a vital infrastructure element, and 22,000 terminals were operative in Ukraine by September (Markquardt 2022). Initially, these entered military use as relatively secure frontline communication options. As Ukraine reclaimed more ground at the places where mobile sites had been destroyed, the military provided their Starlinks to civilians (who had to come to designated sites with a terminal installed). Ukraine also established domestic mobile roaming, whereby a user can connect to the network of an operator other than their own. Due to increasing damage to the electricity and communication infrastructure, more civilians and businesses invested in Starlink, power generators, industrial batteries and other support devices. These developments also elevated the role of radio as a source of information, especially in the blackout phase.

The government and local authorities started developing a network of the so-called "Invincibility Points" (*punkty nezlamnosti*), which are heated shelters with electricity, television broadcasts and mobile and internet connections. This pinpoints an interesting infrastructural centralisation/decentralisation dynamic. As the communication hardware is decimated, the media texture thins out, and media use – previously compartmentalised and privatised via individual devices – becomes locally centralised at nodes where the texture of signals and connectivities is thicker. By virtue of this, media use also becomes a shared, communal activity.

Actors and their practices

In this section, we explore the entanglement of practices by the state, media and audiences that are the main actors in the wartime mediascape. These collective and individual actors have been collaborating according to a blended military/media logic. During the invasion's first days, trust between the state and society was the major asset contributing to mobilisation and resistance. The need for cohesion immediately posed two challenges for communicators. First, in terms of the balance of informing, how should they communicate to keep people updated and safe but not supply the foe with information that could be used to harm? Second, how could they prevent society from succumbing to panic or euphoria?

This blended logic implied constraining some information flows and amplifying others by way of information management (Bolin and Ståhlberg 2023). Unlike in peacetime, official content is generally accepted as truth during war, as our interviews with the journalists revealed. Because of the presence of fabricated news, misinformation and enemy psy-ops, searching for and disseminating alternative sources of information were not encouraged by the social contract.

The state institutions and support networks

The full-scale war increased the visibility of the state institutions, the military, their press-services and individual spokespersons. However, the Ukrainian state is far from a homogenous vertical apparatus: its system is very much decentralised, and content production is not very coordinated. As was evident from our research interviews, there is no single message box, and official spokespersons have a lot of autonomy.

Apart from President Volodymyr Zelensky, who is perceived in the West as the leader of Ukrainian resistance, other official voices are prominent in the wartime information field. These include presidential advisors such as controversial and eventually dismissed Oleksii Arestovych, who was notable during the total mobilisation period due to his outreach to Russian audiences and the use of his voice – commonly perceived as hypnotically soothing – in war update videos, and ministers such as Iryna Vereshchuk, who deals with prisoner-of-war exchanges and civilian evacuations. Local authorities, bestowed with more powers by the decentralisation reform of 2014, have also achieved prominence in cities and regions, such as Kyiv mayor and ex-boxer Vitalii Klychko and the head of the Mykolayiv region, Korean–Ukrainian Vitalii Kim, whose optimism and hipster socks have made him a protagonist in memes.

Apart from prominent individuals, there are also state agencies that all maintain their presence on social media, have press officers and regularly create newsworthy content. These include the Security Service of Ukraine, the Centre for Countering Disinformation and the State Emergency Service of Ukraine. They can be represented even by fictional and non-human characters (Horbyk and Orlova 2022). This was exemplified by Patron, the mine-sniffing Jack Russell terrier, which became a personification of Ukrainian deminers, and the Ukrainian Air Force's fictional Ghost of Kyiv. The military, of course, is represented first of all by the very real Commander-in-Chief of the AFU Valerii

Zaluzhny and Minister of Defence Oleksii Reznikov. However, most content is produced and disseminated at every level of the military structure: starting from the Ministry of Defence and Commander-in-Chief headquarters, then going down all the branches of the AFU, and ending with separate units' and even individual soldiers' milblogs.

However structured and well-coordinated the communication from the state appears, it is a network of institutions and groups of influence that communicate independently. A common denominator was often found at the level of intuition: 'There is a lot of improvisation and haste in the conditions of war (...). We just feel what needs to be done and how,' said a military administration press officer. Another important aspect is the collaboration between the state and civil society. Much official communication is outsourced to creative agencies and non-governmental organisations (NGOs), including the wartime nation branding campaign 'Brave', developed by the advertising agency Banda (Kaneva 2022). According to one interviewee from such an NGO, this is a two-way collaboration: sometimes NGOs approach state institutions with a project idea, and sometimes vice versa. Civil society engagement legitimises such projects and prevents power games within the state sector, as officials are more open to ideas from the outside than from other institutions because the latter raises issues of subordination. In general, state institutions conduct a policy of internal non-confrontation: even rivals are united in the face of the common threat and avoid opposing one another publicly. However, as our interviewee stated, the President's Office is very sensitive to competition and tries to influence other actors to limit their celebritisation potential.

Information management

What are the functions of the state with regard to wartime communication? The first function is the regulation of information flows. Ukraine never followed the same template as Russia, where censorship was de jure imposed in March 2022 (Gosudarstvennaya Duma 2022). Even if Ukrainian martial law legislation enables military administrations to regulate the work of internet providers, mass media and printeries (Verkhovna Rada 2015), no such restrictions were implemented during the total mobilisation phase; instead, the containment of information was based on a social contract with journalists and civilians. The government had recommended not disseminating addresses and photos of recent missile strikes and movements of Ukrainian military and foreign weapons supplies. However, as new missile strikes followed disclosures that were made despite this recommendation, penal legislation was later adopted.

The AFU likewise regulates journalists' access to the frontline. The presence of journalists on the frontline is not necessary for connecting the army and the rear, stated the military administration press officer, because content from the frontline nonetheless proliferates via soldiers' and locals' social media posts. Journalists' presence seems beneficial if instructions are followed – 'to film what is needed; not to film what is not' – since news can be used for reconnaissance and intelligence. A deputy editor-in-chief of a prominent online publication complained that the military reluctantly granted frontline accreditation to journalists, especially Ukrainian journalists. The interviewee explained this through the prevalence of military logic over media logic: 'It's less important what we will write in our publications than to win with the least losses,' including losses among journalists.

Direct official and military communication

The state has become an important source of exclusive information thanks to control over frontline access. State institutions frame the strategic narrative of national resistance by using professional and citizen content, formal and informal language, serious messages, and entertainment. Daily addresses by Zelensky, in which he talks to the 'free people of a free country', provide a point of stability. Other genres used by the state institutions are speeches to international organisations and democratic parliaments and appeals to Russian civilians (to protest the invasion) and soldiers (to surrender).

The official army sources provide systematic updates, appropriated by internet users to create memes and viral content. Yet not all information is disclosed, especially regarding Ukrainian losses. To avoid damaging morale, casualties are usually presented as individual stories of heroism but not in terms of numbers. Sometimes, as in the Kharkiv counter-offensive or the Crimea Bridge explosion, Ukrainian officials have kept a significant silence, letting unofficial versions from both sides fill in the vacuum.

Apart from official websites, social media platforms form important state communication channels. On these platforms, the AFU disseminates not only many drone videos of combat victories but also professional features about soldiers, semi-official milblogs, captives' interrogations and intercepted phone calls where Russians discuss their failures and atrocities. During the total mobilisation phase, when fierce resistance was crucial, the military disseminated videos and infographic manuals on the use of Molotov cocktails and Javelin/NLAW anti-tank missile launchers, as well as recommendations on what content should not be disclosed, how to be updated without a connection and how to act if the enemy seizes one's smartphone – in other words, wartime media literacy training.

Russian disinformation was countered by a combination of humour, debunking and prebunking (Lewandowsky and Linden 2021). Making people aware of upcoming disinformation and provocations proved to be a successful prevention technique. For example, deep fakes with Zelensky 'urging' Ukrainians to surrender were received with mockery after the warning from the Security Service of Ukraine (Mishchenko 2022). Another way to engage with the audience has been entertaining content, such as memes, dark humour jokes, music and songs. Given the outburst of grassroots participatory culture, the Ministry of Defence commissioned songs praising Ukrainian soldiers, new weapons and civilian resilience. Some of these songs became national hits, including the much-remixed and -covered 'Bayraktar' by Taras Borovok, which was named after Turkish-made attack drones successfully used by Ukrainian forces.

Apps, chatbots and gamification

The collaborative aspect of communication between the state and the public is reflected in multiple chatbots. Some of these were used for participatory reconnaissance, collecting information from locals about the position of enemy vehicles and troops, saboteurs, collaborators and explosive objects (e.g. *yeVoroh* [a pun on *eEnemy* and *here's the enemy*] and @stop_russian_war_bot). Some 433,000 Ukrainians had contributed to *yeVoroh* as of 7 December 2022 (ZN.UA 2022). Other bots were used for helping families find missing relatives, acquire information about Ukrainian POWs and gain advice about first aid or relocation. Some of the bots were used for collaboration between state institutions and the public against disinformation (Kravchenko 2022; Vogue 2022).

It is important to note that the Diya e-governance app, in particular, used daily by millions of Ukrainians to obtain state services, was partly converted to wartime use, hosting the chatbot *yeVoroh* along with a game. Computer games are well-known tools for civic engagement (Kahne et al. 2009). Several games commissioned by the Ukrainian state and military are simple shooters with a patriotic message that can be played offline or that use a small amount of internet traffic. One of these, *yeBayraktar*, was already developed by March 2022 for Diya by the Ministry of Digital Information. The gamer acts as an operator of the Bayraktar drone and prevents enemy tanks from breaching the checkpoint (Brovko 2022). Another game, *Azv vs Zombies*, was issued in the AppStore on behalf of the Azov Regiment – a symbol of resistance in the siege of Mariupol. In the post-apocalyptic landscape of the ruined Azovstal ironworks, the gamer–soldier shoots zombies who unequivocally resemble the Russian military (NoWorries 2022). These games are not only *digital sedatives* (Brovko 2022) and time killers for people in bomb shelters; they are also digital tools for performing a shared media ritual (Couldry 2005). By enabling people to be together when spatially separated and to feel involvement in the common fight, these games ultimately maintain an imagined community.

Media outlets and media professionals

In May, Ukrainian journalists received a collective Pulitzer Prize. However, such appraisal has come at a price: 39 local and foreign journalists were killed during the first seven months of the full-scale invasion (Antonyuk 2022).

The changes in the media market and work conditions for reporters have been unprecedented. Before the invasion, the main Ukrainian media, particularly the commercial TV channels, were directly or indirectly associated with certain oligarchs, such as Renat Akhmetov, Viktor Pinchuk, Dmytro Firtash and Valerii Kolomois'ky, who used media ownership to gain political weight and further their economic interests (Riabinska 2017; Dutsyk and Dyczok 2021). None of the major TV channels were profitable. After February 24, Ukrainian TV sank into crisis because of the advertisement market collapse and the losses that the oligarchs suffered. This and anti-oligarch legislation led to the closure of Akhmetov's large Media Group Ukraine, with the subsequent dismissal of all the employees (Dan'kova 2022d). Other TV channels were also cutting losses at the expense of staff. According to our journalist interviewee, some channels initiated layoffs, while others reduced salaries by 50–70 per cent or sent staff on unpaid leave. Regional media were on the verge of extinction because of the advertisement breakdown, infrastructural damage and paper price increase. Newspapers sought survival strategies such as the integration of editorial teams, slashing page numbers or completely going online (Dan'kova 2022a).

On the invasion's first day, TV channels changed their programming, abandoning entertainment shows and turning to the format of marathons, where newscasts alternated with interviews (Dan'kova and Zhuk 2022). In late

February, five TV channels from three media groups united with Public TV (*Suspil'ne*) to launch the United News marathon, where every editorial team received a several-hour slot to broadcast news around the clock. It is unclear who initiated this – the authorities or the TV channels themselves. It may have been a common initiative because it solved certain challenges for both sides by creating a unified official information flow and easing the burden of 24-hour news broadcasting for the channels that had not previously been news channels per se. United News became 'the point that assembled all information systems of the state, that conveys Ukraine's stance (...) [through the] unity of media, authorities and the army', as one of the marathon hosts stated (Dan'kova 2022c).

This centralisation did not occur without controversy. Three oppositional channels – 5 Channel, Pryamy and Espreso TV – from the orbit of ex-president Petro Poroshenko were not invited to United News despite expressions of interest. Instead, they launched their own marathons and were subsequently excluded by the regulator from the digital television package. Although they continued to broadcast on YouTube and via satellites, this case raised concerns regarding the independence of United News. While the journalists involved in the marathon denied any allegations of pressure from the authorities, they mentioned self-censorship when reporting unofficial information that could potentially harm the cause (Dan'kova 2022c). Avoidance of political debates led to the prevalence of guests from Zelensky's party (70.4 per cent of all guests in May–September) (Kulyas 2022).

United News has become a powerful tool for demonstrating the unity of the nation, but it is simultaneously hazardous for freedom of speech and pluralism. It also undermines the successful reform of the formerly state-owned TV into a public service broadcaster. As the journalist interviewee said, '[a]lthough its existence is justified during the war, the marathon creates a temptation for the authorities; they get used to owning a media resource. The question is how the authorities will act afterwards.'

Personal anecdotes about journalists sleeping on the sofa in the office (Dan'kova 2022c) or broadcasting radio from the bathroom during air raid alerts (University of Manitoba Archives 2022) are indicative of the drastic changes in working conditions for the media. Reporting and thus contributing to the war effort has been a coping strategy. 'On the first morning, I stayed restless in bed, didn't know what to do. So, I went to our website and started to post news', recalled a journalist from a Kyiv-based online publication. Editorial teams became virtual since the journalists were dispersed in space: some stayed in their cities, while others evacuated to Western Ukraine or abroad. This imposed technical challenges, but it made the teams resilient to wartime disruptions such as air raid alerts and electricity outages. In a virtual newsroom, journalists are backing each other up, substituting for those who cannot perform their duties. However, when Russia's missile strikes started to cause massive outages, this approach started to unravel. Sometimes no Ukraine-based journalist in the team could work, and the flow of news remained uninterrupted only because of those colleagues who had evacuated abroad.

War questions journalistic standards. The journalists we spoke to stated that the invasion had not changed editorial policy: they continued to report on events important to society. However, they also mentioned the priority of civic and military logic over the urge to recount everything. This applied to recent missile strikes, leaks from the military, filming Russian victims and government critique. As a military photographer said, '[m]y filter is not to harm Ukraine and not to harm my people. I am Ukrainian; I want us to win as soon as possible with minimum victims' (Dan'kova 2022b).

Despite the crisis induced by economic and infrastructural challenges, Ukrainian media outlets proved resilient and capable of adjusting to the new circumstances. Media communities, traditionally parallel to different political camps, demonstrated unprecedented solidarity, mutual assistance and collaboration between journalists, state institutions and civil society. The war increased the consolidation of information flows due to United News and journalists prioritising military logic, but at the same time, it introduced decentralising trends with virtual editorial teams. A new and long-debated media law was adopted in December 2022 and went into effect on 31 March 2023. This law is seen as simultaneously overdue and controversial by the public and our interviewees, as it expands the state regulator's powers, particularly with respect to online media. Most agreed that much will depend on its application and that amendments may be needed.

Audiences and their media practices

The war has led to tectonic shifts in content consumption and media practices. United News is watched by 32 per cent of media consumers, according to a representative poll from late 2022, and it is vastly trusted as an information source (USAID-Internews 2022). The consumers are also satisfied with the decreased pluralism, which is perceived as overcoming polarisation and media manipulation. About 13 per cent still use Russian sources, mostly to check on the Russian narrative, and only 2 per cent are unhappy with the available Ukrainian sources (Opora 2022). While the audience of United News is older (it is the main information source for people above 60), younger audiences are flocking to social media. Overall, 59 per cent receive information mainly from social media, whereas TV is the number one source for 43 per cent (Opora 2022), compared to 67 per cent before the invasion (Detektor media 2022).

Social media are the main sources of information for most Ukrainians today. This can be explained not only through technological and generational changes but also through increased mobility. While TV consumption is homebound, social media cater for news on the move, and moving is what millions of Ukrainians have been doing since 24 February. As the interviews showed, most consumers valued social media for speed, short news and videos.

The leading platforms are Telegram and YouTube: Ukrainians spend about 40 per cent of their social media time on each, followed by Facebook with 12 per cent (Opora 2022). Use of Telegram has exploded in particular during the invasion. Another poll showed that 60 per cent of respondents used Telegram as a news source in 2022, compared with only 20 per cent in 2021 (USAID-Internews 2022). The most popular channels include the news channels Trukha (2.7 million followers), TSN (932,000) and UNIAN (876,000), but there are also smaller channels with audiences in thousands. The media market has completely transformed, with an extremely fragmented and niche audience, for whom a host of smaller Telegram channels has replaced several of the most-watched TV channels. However, established media organisations tend to have a strong presence on Telegram too (e.g. UNIAN and TSN).

This restructuring has completely redrawn the map of audience media practices. First, news consumption has moved from TV to smartphones, becoming more personalised. Second, it has become more intimate because of the public/private ambiguity built into the app's design as a messenger-cum-news channel. News consumption is combined in one app with private conversations with friends and family, and sharing information in a private chat becomes easier. News consumption is thus integrated into networking and organising. As over 80 per cent of Ukrainians participate in the war effort in some form, social media and messenger apps are key platforms for the creation and coordination of robust horizontal networks. This has ushered in a new type of active audience, for whom news forms only some of the building blocks necessary for their own social practice. The shift from consumption to media participation has been especially pronounced.

It is because of this greater emphasis on smartphone-mediated information and participation that the Russian attacks on mobile and power infrastructure have been so disruptive. Another disruption has come from the Western tech giants, especially Meta, which, in March 2022, softened its moderation policy for Ukrainians by allowing calls for the destruction of the Russian military (Vengattil and Culliford 2022) before limiting this three days later and decisively ruling out any anti-Russian statements (Vengattil 2022). In practice, social media companies often ban posts and block users and news organisations for violation of rules and hate speech when they share photographic evidence of Russian massacres or express outrage at them. The major mainstream online media publication, *Ukrainska Pravda*, received five red status warnings, which automatically meant an end to monetisation and decreased organic reach (Mel'nyk 2022). The Ukrainian government sent an official letter to Meta, urging it to stop censoring Ukrainians, ostensibly to no avail (Media Sapiens 2022). As one example among thousands, in February 2023, Facebook deleted a post by the mayor of Kramatorsk, Oleksandr Honcharenko, telling about a Russian artillery strike on a local cemetery; it contained no hateful or graphic content, only pictures of destroyed graves and a brief matter-of-fact condemnation of the deed without any slurs (Espreso 2023). This has led the Ukrainian public to condemn social media policies as censorship or even foul play in Russia's favour. It raises issues of what community standards are or should be, especially for a nation resisting an invasion. This situation has also contributed to Telegram's success (where moderation is minimal).

Decentralised strategic communication at the sites of production and circulation is complemented by participatory communication merged with activism, often in a non-binding, hop-on/hop-off form that we call 'hop-on/hop-off activism'. Such activism does not always require systematic commitment. One example is condo chats in messengers, where neighbours inform one another about important developments in their area. This spontaneous hyperlocal citizen journalism is vital in the frontline and occupied areas.

Social media have become spaces for informing, speaking out, coordination, recording history and creating myths, and the shift between an ordinary citizen and an activist is as easy and instant as the shift between two chats in Telegram. Possible activities include sharing memes and jokes, launching petitions, informing foreign audiences through Twitter storms and hashtag fights, blocking malicious groups and trolls, and creating and disseminating songs and artworks (Boyko forthcoming). Users collaborate on complex tasks such as fundraising, coordination of DDoS attacks, logistics, etc., or even on illegal (i.e. in peacetime) activities such as false bomb warnings about Russian infrastructure or scamming Russians online to donate to the AFU. New and unusual audiences are often involved: children ridicule Russian propaganda on TikTok and participate in troll blocking or DDoS attacks.

We propose the concept of 'swarm communication' to capture this and similar future situations. This also parallels the apparent use of combat swarming tactics by the Ukrainian military. Like a swarm, Ukrainian civilian participatory networks are non-vertical and fluid (albeit not completely without a central core and a vague, diffuse hierarchy). They can quickly disengage from issues that are solved or lose relevance and reassemble around new problems; and they are characterised by individual chaotic movements that nonetheless have the same vector – victory – on the larger scale.

Conclusions

The Russian invasion changed the Ukrainian mediascape instantly and dramatically, yet this process has been far from homogenous, as can be seen in the three stages we have identified. The mediascape saw contradictory tendencies, both centralising and decentralising. On the one hand, the ownership of large media holdings by financial–political groups (oligarchs) was undermined, and the dominance of TV was shaken by a constellation of Telegram channels and other social media, blurring public and private communications and meshing them together in participatory media practices. On the other hand, the state claimed a much larger role than ever before, managing and controlling information flows, especially around combat. Yet the state itself is a diffused actor, a networked rhizome of institutions whose interests can often overlap and contradict one another. This networked state is augmented by the robust support of NGOs that have situationally collaborated with the government during the war. Even though chaotic at first sight, this system is guided by a common goal and is flexible due to the autonomy it provides.

This makes Ukraine's strategic communication collaborative and allows for the creation of open-ended transmedia narratives (cf. Bolin and Ståhlberg 2023) that can include contributions from all sorts of actors – state, non-state, private and even the enemy – whose communications are recontextualised as an element of Ukraine's own story. Such diffusion and decentralisation challenge the presumption of a systematic and centralised process that is at the heart of all definitions of propaganda from Lasswell (1928) to Jowett and O'Donnel (2019). From a traditional perspective, the lack of a single communication centre and voice is seen as a weakness. For example, Lasswell attributed the German defeat in the First World War to such disorganisation. In a mediatised society, however, centralisation seems less applicable. The diffusion of actors and production also questions the utility and adequacy of applying the concept of propaganda to Ukraine's wartime communication. Instead of this centralised activity, it can rather be characterised as strategic collaborative communication founded on the dialogical and symmetrical public relations models.

Apart from disruption, the work of media organisations also saw the decentralisation of work routines. Simultaneously, the constraints on journalistic work often led to internal contradictions. While journalists tried to follow both military logic and media logic, the two often conflicted. As a result, media logic often finds itself overridden by military logic. When the opposite happens, the triumph of media logic often creates security vulnerabilities.

Finally, the audience's consumption also underwent simultaneous decentralisation and personalisation via smartphones, as well as a new recentralisation thanks to the communicative nodes of connected shelters during the blackout phase. Overall, the audience experienced a greater integration of public information and personal communication, which enhanced networks of solidarity and mutual support. Collaborative communication between the state, the media and citizens acquired the characteristics of a swarm, as the audience's media practices were determined by hop-on/hop-off activism and swarm communication. These are the principal tools of civilians' self-mobilisation in a totalising war, and they fit well with Ukraine's swarming military tactics and diffused state hierarchies.

References

Antonyuk, N. (2022). 'Zhurnalisty, yaki zahynuly . . .', *Glavkom*, 15 September, https://glavcom.ua/country/society/za-chas-vijni-zahinulo-39-ukrajinskikh-medijnikiv-spisok-875419.html, accessed 9 December 2022.
Appadurai, A. (1990). 'Disjuncture and Difference in the Global Economy', *Theory, Culture & Society*, 7, 295–310.
Biloskurs'ky, O., and Serhienko, I. (2022). 'Yak vidklyuchennya . . .', *Detektor media*, 8 November, https://detector.media/blogs/article/204649/2022-11-08-yak-vidklyuchennya-elektro energii-vplynuly-na-telepereglyad-u-kyievi/, accessed 9 December 2022.
Boichak, O., and Hoskins, A. (2022). 'My War: Participation in Warfare', *Digital War*, 1–8, https://link.springer.com/article/10.1057/s42984-022-00060-7, accessed 6 February 2023.

Bolin, G., and Ståhlberg, P. (2023). *The Management of Meaning in Turbulent Times: Information Policy, Agency and Media in Ukraine*. Cambridge: MIT Press.

Boyko, K. (forthcoming). 'Valkyries and Madonnas: Constructing Femininity during the Russo-Ukrainian War'. In A. M. Sätre, Yu. Gradskova, and V. Vladimirova (eds), *Post-Soviet Women – New Challenges and Ways to Empowerment*. London: Palgrave MacMillan.

Brovko, L. (2022). 'Nove zaspokiilyve ...', *Apostrof*, 21 March, https://apostrophe.ua/ua/news/society/2022-03-21/novoe-uspokoitelnoe-ot-d-v-prilojenii-poyavilas-funktsiya-upravleniya-bayraktarom/263374, accessed 9 December 2022.

Clausewitz, C. von (2008). *On War*. Oxford: Oxford University Press.

Couldry, N. (2005). *Media Rituals: A Critical Approach*. London: Routledge.

Dan'kova, N. (2022a). 'Yak vyzhyvayut ...', *Detektor media*, 28 May, https://detector.media/rinok/article/199558/2022-05-28-yak-vyzhyvayut-gazety-i-zhurnaly-pid-chas-viyny-sim-istoriy-iz-riznykh-kintsiv-ukrainy/, accessed 9 December 2022.

Dan'kova, N. (2022b). 'Voyenna korespondentka ...', *Detektor media*, 6 June, https://detector.media/community/article/199893/2022-06-06-voienna-fotokorespondentka-yuliya-kochetova-miy-filtr-ne-nashkodyty-ukraini-i-ne-nashkodyty-svoim-lyudyam/, accessed 9 December 2022.

Dan'kova, N. (2022c). 'Vadym Karp'yak: ...', *Detektor media*, 8 June, https://detector.media/community/article/199943/2022-06-08-vadym-karpyak-meni-zdaietsya-shcho-pro-viynu-mozhna-govoryty-vidvertishe-i-chesnishe/, accessed 9 December 2022.

Dan'kova, N. (2022d). 'Shcho vidbuvayetsya ...', *Detektor media*, 12 July, https://detector.media/rinok/article/200916/2022-07-12-shcho-vidbuvaietsya-z-mediabiznesom-rinata-akhmetova/, accessed 9 December 2022.

Dan'kova, N., and Zhuk, O. (2022). 'De marafony ...', *Detektor media*, 24 February, https://detector.media/oglyad-i-zmi/article/196865/2022-02-24-de-marafony-de-serialy-shcho-ukrainski-telekanaly-pokazuyut-pid-chas-rosiyskogo-vtorgnennya/, accessed 9 December 2022.

Detektor media. (2022). 'Mediaspozhyvannya v ...', 15 February, https://detector.media/infospace/article/196442/2022-02-15-mediaspozhyvannya-v-ukraini-zmina-mediapotreb-ta-progrash-rosiyskoi-propagandy/, accessed 9 December 2022.

Dutsyk, D., and Dyczok, M. (2021). 'Ukraine's Media: A Field Where Power is Contested'. In M. Kasianov, G. Minakov, and M. Rojansky (eds), *From 'the Ukraine' to Ukraine*, pp. 169–206. Stuttgart: Ibidem.

Espreso. (2023). 'Mer Kramators'ka povidomyv ...', 1 February, https://espreso.tv/mer-kramatorska-povidomiv-shcho-facebook-vidaliv-yogo-post-pro-obstril-mista, accessed 6 February 2023.

Gosudarstvennaya Duma. (2022). 'Vvoditsya otvetstvennost ...', 4 March, http://duma.gov.ru/news/53620/, accessed 9 December 2022.

Horbyk, R. (2022). '"The War Phone": Mobile Communication on the Frontline in Eastern Ukraine', *Digital War*, 1–16, https://link.springer.com/article/10.1057/s42984-022-00049-2, accessed 6 February.

Horbyk, R. (2023). 'Mediatisation of War and the Military: Current State, Trends, and Challenges in the Field'. In G. Bolin and R. Kopecka-Piech (eds), *Contemporary Challenges in Mediatization Research*, pp. 111–28. London: Routledge.

Horbyk, R., and Orlova, D. (2022). 'Transmedia Storytelling and Memetic Warfare: Ukraine's Wartime Public Diplomacy', *Public Diplomacy and Place Branding*: online first, https://link.springer.com/article/10.1057/s41254-022-00283-1, accessed 6 February.
Joshi, A. W. (2009). 'Continuous Supplier Performance: Effects of Collaborative Communication and Control', *Journal of Marketing*, 73 (1), 133–50.
Jowett, G. S., and O'Donnell, V. (2019). *Propaganda & Persuasion* (7th ed.). Thousand Oaks: Sage.
Kahne, J., Middaugh, E., and Evans C. (2009). *The Civic Potential of Video Games*. Cambridge: MIT Press.
Käihkö, I. (2021). 'A Conventional War: Escalation in the War in Donbas, Ukraine', *Journal of Slavic Military Studies*, 34 (1), 24–49.
Kaneva, N. (2022). '"Brave Like Ukraine": A Critical Discourse Perspective on Ukraine's Wartime Brand', *Place Branding and Public Diplomacy*, 1–5, https://doi.org/10.1057/s41254-022-00273-3, accessed 8 February 2023.
Kondratenko, M. (2021). 'Za rik . . .', *DW*, 17 March, https://www.dw.com/uk/za-rik-karantynu-kilkist-ukraintsiv-u-sotsmerezhakh-zrosla-na-sim-milioniv/a-56899697, accessed 9 December 2022.
Kravchenko, A. (2022). 'Top-7 chat-botiv . . .', *ArmyInform*, 23 August, https://armyinform.com.ua/2022/08/23/top-7-chat-botiv-yaki-nablyzhayut-peremogu-ukrayiny-u-vijni-z-rf/, accessed 9 December 2022.
Kulyas, I. (2022). 'Pidsumky monitorynhu . . .', *Detektor media*, 26 September, https://detector.media/shchodenni-telenovini/article/203137/2022-09-26-pidsumky-monitoryngu-telemarafonu-iedyni-novyny-za-piv-roku-berezen-veresen-2022-roku-persha-chastyna/, accessed 9 December 2022.
Lasswell, H. D. (1928/2015). *Propaganda Technique in World War I*. Greenville: Coachwhip Publications.
Lewandowsky, S., and van der Linden, S. (2021). 'Countering Misinformation and Fake News through Inoculation and Prebunking', *European Review of Social Psychology*, 32 (2), 348–84.
Markquardt, A. (2022). 'Exclusive: Musk's SpaceX Says It Can No Longer Pay for Critical Satellite Services in Ukraine', *CNN*, 14 October, https://edition.cnn.com/2022/10/13/politics/elon-musk-spacex-starlink-ukraine/index.html, accessed 9 December 2022.
Media sapiens. (2022). 'Mintsyfry prosyt Meta . . .', 30 July, https://ms.detector.media/sotsmerezhi/post/29949/2022-07-30-mintsyfry-prosyt-meta-poyasnyty-pravyla-moderatsii-ukrainskogo-kontentu-u-facebook-ta-instagram/, accessed 6 February 2023.
Mel'nyk, T. (2022). 'Sotsmerezhi Tsukerberga banyat . . .', *Forbes*, https://forbes.ua/innovations/moderatsiya-16122022-10561, accessed 6 February 2023.
Merrin, W. (2018). *Digital War: A Critical Introduction*. London: Routledge.
Mishchenko, T. (2022). 'Rashysty namahayutsya . . .', *Mezha*, 16 March, https://mezha.media/2022/03/16/rashysty-nezmogly-dipfeyk-z-zelenskym/, accessed 9 December 2022.
Mohr, J. J., and Nevin, J. R. (1990). 'Communication Strategies in Marketing Channels: A Theoretical Perspective', *Journal of Marketing*, 54 (4), 36–51.
NDI. (2022). 'Mozhlyvosti ta . . .', https://www.kiis.com.ua/materials/pr/20220920_o/August%202022_wartime%20survey%20Public%20fin%20UKR.pdf, accessed 9 December 2022.

NoWorries. (2022). 'Rozrobnyky NFT . . .', 15 September, https://noworries.news/rozrobnyky-nft-zapustyly-gru-na-pidtrymku-geroyiv-azovu/, accessed 9 December 2022.

Opora. (2022). 'Demokratiya, prava i svobody . . .', July, bit.ly/3W0fSmu, accessed 9 December 2022.

Riabinska, N. (2017). *Ukraine's Post-Communist Mass Media: Between Capture and Commercialization*. Stuttgart: Ibidem.

Ukrinform. (2019). 'V Ukraini . . .', 10 October, https://www.ukrinform.ua/rubric-technology/2797152-v-ukraini-kilkist-internetkoristuvaciv-zrosla-do-23-miljoniv.html, accessed 9 December 2022.

University of Manitoba Archives. (2022). '29th Annual J.B. Rudnyckyj Lecture – Dr. Marta Dyczok and Andriy Kulykov', *YouTube*, 17 March, https://www.youtube.com/watch?v=dg7IyBRKw3o, accessed 9 December 2022.

USAID-Internews. (2022). 'Ukrayinski media...', November, https://internews.in.ua/wp-content/uploads/2022/11/Ukrainski-media-stavlennia-ta-dovira-2022.pdf?fbclid=IwAR3HW8VIA0k-9KvpxWnNG50MDFx7vVbqnX-xnTkwTseT7WzsxeHr4j67Gbs, accessed 9 December 2022.

Vengattil, M. (2022). 'Meta Narrows Guidance to Prohibit Calls for Death . . .', *Reuters*, 14 March, https://www.reuters.com/technology/meta-narrows-guidance-restrict-calls-death-head-state-2022-03-14/, accessed 6 February 2023.

Vengattil, M., and Culliford, E. (2022). 'Facebook Allows War Posts . . .', *Reuters*, 11 March, https://www.reuters.com/world/europe/exclusive-facebook-instagram-temporarily-allow-calls-violence-against-russians-2022-03-10/, accessed 6 February 2023.

Verkhovna Rada. (2015). Pro pravovy . . ., 12 May, https://zakon.rada.gov.ua/laws/show/389-19#Text, accessed 9 December 2022.

Vogue. (2022). '11 korysnykh chat-botiv . . .', 11 March, https://vogue.ua/article/culture/lifestyle/11-korisnih-chat-botiv-u-telegram-u-period-viyni-47862.html, accessed 9 December 2022.

Zharovs'ky, Ye. (2022). 'P"yatero lyudei . . .', *NV.ua*, 1 March, https://nv.ua/ukr/kyiv/raketniy-udar-po-kijivskiy-televezhi-p-yat-zagiblih-novini-ukrajini-50221376.html, accessed 9 December 2022.

ZN.UA. (2022). '"Narodna rozvidka" . . .', 7 December, https://zn.ua/ukr/TECHNOLOGIES/narodna-rozvidka-chat-botom-jevorih-skoristalisja-ponad-430-tisjach-ukrajintsiv.html, accessed 9 December 2022.

· 3 ·

SOCIAL MEDIA PLATFORMS RESPONDING TO THE INVASION OF UKRAINE

Mervi Pantti and Matti Pohjonen

Disastrous events, such as wars and catastrophes, have been theorised as 'focusing events' that can bring about abrupt changes in policies and institutional arrangements (Birkland 1998; Tierney, Bevc and Kuligowski 2006). These events can generate new conceptions and actions or, alternatively, reinforce the prevailing politics and structures of power (Lukes 2006). Russia's invasion of Ukraine seized political and media attention, raising urgent public discussions about the responses and responsibilities of different actors in Europe. This question of responsibility also concerns the role of social media platforms, which wield notable power in shaping political and civic processes today. However, as multinational private companies, they are principally driven by commercial interests, not by public good (Gillespie 2018; Helberger et al. 2018).

Digital platforms have played an important role in global crises, conflicts and war in the twenty-first century. Humanitarian organisations, activists and ordinary people have used them to document human rights violations, appeal to the international community for solidarity and organise relief efforts (Pantti et al. 2012). Although digital platforms offer an immense amount of information about wars, they are also used by various participants in conflicts to muster support or discredit the opposing side. Today, platforms have come under growing global criticism for not being able to prevent the spread of harmful content, as recently seen in the criticism of their failure to control hate and extreme speech in countries such as Myanmar and Ethiopia (Pohjonen 2019; Sablosky 2021; Udupa, Gagliardone and Hervik 2021).

In times of conflict, digital platforms become the tools for information warfare, which is understood here as the use of communication and information technology to achieve influence in digital information space, often through 'particularly unethical forms of communication' (Szostek 2020: 2740), such as disinformation, fake accounts, propaganda, cyberattacks and hacking. During conflicts and war, information warfare intensifies with magnified propaganda and disinformation campaigns for national and international audiences. Since the beginning of the Russian invasion of Ukraine, disinformation channels and users known to spread disinformation about the COVID-19 pandemic pivoted towards supporting pro-Russian disinformation (EDMO 2022).

In the context of the Russian war in Ukraine, digital platforms have taken a wide array of steps to counter disinformation, predominantly by blocking Russian state-affiliated media locally or globally (HRW 2022). These actions are not unseen in previous conflicts and wars, but their scale and consistency have been unprecedented. Historically, digital platforms have tried to balance the conflicting demands of governments and civil society groups to moderate and remove illicit content by positioning themselves as neutral intermediaries who are not legally liable or socially responsible for the published content (Gillespie 2010; Napoli and Caplan 2017). Platforms have also previously been seen supporting the foreign policy interests of the United States (US) and the European Union (EU). For instance, during the various 'social media revolutions' (Iran 2009, Egypt 2011, Tunisia 2011 and EuroMaidan in Ukraine 2014), digital platforms were actively promoted by Western democracies as tools to bring about democratic change in authoritarian regimes. These examples of platform and government interests visibly aligning towards similar geopolitical aims, however, have so far been mostly regional in scale. One exception is the relative global consensus that emerged in response to the use of social media by jihadi groups such as Al-Qaeda and ISIS (Conway et al. 2017). Within a relatively short time, these platforms acted to remove violent content through collaborations, such as the Global Internet Forum for Counter-terrorism (GIFCT). These collaborative efforts between social media companies and governments were later expanded in the Christchurch Call following the Christchurch Mosque attacks in New Zealand in 2019 to control other types of terrorist content on social media (Hoverd, Salter and Veale 2021).

This chapter argues that the Russian war in Ukraine represents the first time where such geopolitical alignment between platforms and governments has extended to major geopolitical players, such as Russia. A qualitative reading of social media companies' blog posts in the aftermath of the Russian invasion shows how the platforms responded to public demands for greater responsibility against Russian information warfare. This chapter studies how the war in Ukraine opened a new horizon of action that compelled the platforms to actively side with EU policy to 'intervene' and how this intervention, in turn, informed major digital platforms' responses to the war.

Digital platforms in the information war

The regulation of the Council of Europe (EU 2022/350) to suspend broadcasts from Russian state-sponsored media outlets RT and Sputnik was implemented on March 1, five days after Russia invaded Ukraine. Some national authorities in the EU acted even before the regulation to crack down on Russian propaganda. Although the securitisation of disinformation in various EU documents had started following the annexation of Crimea in 2014 (e.g. European Council 2015), such restrictions had not previously been used to regulate social media platforms in times of crisis, at least at such scale and scope against another major geopolitical player.

Blocking the Russian state-backed media was an attempt to block Russia's expected aggression and interference on social media, as previously seen in Russian disinformation campaigns to influence Western elections. The regulation was justified as a response to the security threat that Russian disinformation poses to the EU: 'The Russian Federation has engaged in continuous and concerted propaganda actions targeted at civil society in the Union and neighbouring countries, gravely distorting and manipulating facts' (EU 2022/350: 7). Disinformation was interpreted as 'part of a hybrid warfare strategy Russia was using against the EU', requiring extraordinary measures 'to defend all citizens and infrastructure, as well as their democratic systems', as stated by the 'Special Committee on Foreign Interference in all Democratic Processes in the European Union, including Disinformation' (INGE) (European Parliament 2022). The committee concluded that the EU should tighten control on platforms as a part of this new strategy of defence to protect European citizens and democracy.

Even before these events, there was growing interest and policy pressure in Europe to confirm intermediary responsibility for platforms. At the core of this aspiration is the question of whether and in which situations social media platforms are accountable for their users' online actions. The Digital Services Act (DSA), launched in April 2022, sets out new standards for the accountability of platforms regarding harmful content. In this regulatory framework, platforms are required to mitigate risks, such as disinformation and hate speech. As stated by the Commissioner for the Internal Market, Thierry Breton, who is responsible for strengthening EU tools for countering disinformation, '[w]ith the DSA, the time of big online platforms behaving like they are "too big to care" is coming to an end' (European Commission 2022). The changing nature of the relationship between digital platforms and governments in times of serious crises is written in the DSA's 'crisis response mechanism' (DSA 2022, Art. 27a), which allows the European Commission to intervene in content moderation decisions and requires 'very large' platforms to limit any urgent threats to public security.

In this context, which is characterised by both a growing political will to hold platforms accountable and an unprecedented sense of urgency in the face of the Russian attack, the EU put pressure on social media companies to use their power and take down Russian disinformation and other forms of propaganda. Other parties, including the Ukrainian government, several national governments and the prime ministers of countries bordering Russia or Ukraine (Poland, Estonia, Latvia and Lithuania), added to the pressure by making public statements demanding a crackdown on Russian disinformation on platforms. In particular, Mykhailo Fedorov, Ukraine's Minister of Digital Transformation, launched a shame and guilt eliciting campaign on social media that pressured all main social media and tech companies to cut ties with Russia. For instance, Tim Cook, Apple's CEO, was tagged in a tweet: 'Now @tim_cook let's finish the job and block @AppStore access in Russia. They kill our children, now kill their access!' (March 2, 2022). These high publicity requests placed digital platforms at the centre of the information war and geopolitical conflict, in which they were forced to pick sides and put their preferred impartial stance aside.

Platforms adopted similar policy changes one after another in response to the pressure because these platforms tend to closely watch each other's actions (Gillespie et al. 2020). As Caplan and boyd (2018) stated, platforms create joint normative visions by unifying their policies of what is 'harmful' and 'how and when they should intervene'. Facebook (Meta) and the Chinese video platform TikTok took the lead and blocked access to RT and Sputnik across Europe, along with barring Russian state media from running ads. Twitter followed with a similar ban. The actions extended to information technology companies: Microsoft blocked downloads of the RT app worldwide and Google did the same in Ukrainian territory. In addition, Google-owned YouTube blocked RT and Sputnik channels in Europe and barred their ad revenue on YouTube. Apple blocked RT and Sputnik from the Apple App Store outside Russia and suspended all product sales in Russia. As a distinct measure, Meta platforms Facebook and Instagram issued a change in their regular hate speech policy to allow users in Ukraine to call for death against Russian leaders and troops in the context of the Russian invasion of Ukraine. This decision led to global controversy about the alleged double standards adopted by platforms and critics pointing out that 'Facebook's human rights and free speech rules tend to match up with US policy preferences' (Biddle 2022).

In response to these policies, commentators have argued that the actions adopted by platform companies potentially represent a paradigm shift in how tech companies operate in the context of war and conflict. Scott and Kern (2022) stated that these decisions to take a stand against Russia could 'fundamentally change the companies' relationships with governments that are being forced, in real time, to acknowledge the power that social media wields in a time of war'. From an alternative perspective, however, these decisions show that the EU and European governments had the power to direct how platforms responded to the Russian invasion of Ukraine. As we argue, the geopolitical crisis added more momentum to efforts in Europe to demand greater accountability from platforms and, in practice, force them to pick a side.

Platforms in times of armed conflicts

As international corporations, platforms have not been known to be proactive in self-regulating harmful content, arguably because disinformation and extreme content attract users' attention, here according to the logic of the algorithmic recommender systems of the platforms. For instance, since 2014, the Ukrainian government has urged, without success, platform companies to improve their efforts to stop Russia from spreading disinformation and promoting support of Russia's occupation of parts of Ukraine (HRW 2022). The usual criticism on social media platforms has been that they act on problems too late and do too little (Wagner, Deutch and Zuidijk 2022). Historically, internet platforms have argued that they only host content produced by other parties and, therefore, unlike media companies, should not be seen as responsible for what is published on their platforms (Gillespie 2010; 2018).

However, in recent years, following heated debates around privacy breaches, political interference and disinformation, platforms have increasingly been subject to political scrutiny; accordingly, scholars have identified a 'responsibility turn' in their public communication (Flew 2018; Mager and Katzenbach 2021). Following the COVID-19 pandemic, social media platforms have collaborated with governments and public health authorities and introduced, 'at an unprecedented speed and scale' (Baker et al. 2020), new tools and policies to combat the spread of harmful content related to global crises, such as COVID-19 and climate change (e.g. Gadde and Derella 2020; Meta 2022).

Content moderation inevitably has geopolitical implications (Banchik 2021; Hallinan et al. 2021). As Roberts (2019) noted, the content moderation decisions of social media platforms 'point to the ideological preferences' embedded in the platform companies' global policies and systems of moderation. Social media platforms have also been criticised for not meeting human rights responsibilities in wars and crises globally (e.g. DeCook et al. 2022; HRW 2022). A common view among human rights activists and scholars is that platform companies lack an understanding of the societies and political environments in which they operate (Brown 2020). Particularly in developing countries, social media companies have failed to invest in content moderators who are fluent in local languages and familiar with local contexts. On the other hand, governmental pressure to remove 'extremist' content has led to situations in which platforms remove content documenting human rights violations or legitimate protests (Banchik 2021).

Accountability demands targeted at platform companies have generally been divided into global civil society organisations' campaigns for better content moderation of harmful content and demands by different governments to control the information circulating on social media platforms in their countries. Civil society organisations have actively campaigned against platforms in an effort to prevent hateful and misleading content. Critics have argued that these companies have been too slow to respond to the spread of harmful or misleading content, which, in some cases, has led to widespread unrest and violence amplified by content circulated online (De Gregorio 2019; Stremlau and Marchant 2020; Suzor 2019).

Conversely, the relationship between governments and platforms has historically been contentious. Examples of this antagonistic relationship include India banning TikTok in 2020 because of a geopolitical dispute with China.

Facebook has been temporarily or partially banned by 30 countries globally. In China, for instance, Facebook was blocked following the 2009 riots in Urumqi. According to the Chinese government, Facebook was used to coordinate the protests. YouTube has been temporarily or partially banned in 23 countries and remains permanently banned in five countries. Twitter also remains blocked in seven countries, including China, and was temporarily banned in Egypt, Nigeria and Turkey in response to government demands to remove content. As these examples show, blocks and restrictions typically result from the censorship of nondemocratic governments or relate to government relations with the company. De Gregorio and Stremlau (2020) argued that the content moderation practices by the major digital platforms should be seen as one among the many tactics that different global actors have available to control information circulating online. One tactic that is used especially in times of political unrest and in nondemocratic regimes is to use internet shutdowns – usually without the complicity of platforms – to remove access to social media.

Within this context, we can position the actions taken by digital platforms during the Ukraine War. Although the requests to remove content by governments are not unique globally, the actions taken in the aftermath of the Russian invasion nonetheless represent the most comprehensive efforts by platform companies to respond to government demands for removing content. Thus, the actions taken by Facebook, YouTube, Twitter and other platforms in response to Russian state-owned media's propaganda campaigns represent the most significant and wide-reaching open campaign so far to explicitly deal with online disinformation and hate speech on social media or to align with the foreign policy interests of the EU.

Social media company blogs

Platforms are under constant pressure to respond to the growing accountability demands from governments and civil society actors, as well as communicate their policies to wider audiences. One forum where such public communication takes place is the public blogs of these social media companies, such as the Newsroom for Meta/Facebook or the official blogs by Twitter and YouTube. Although these blogs represent the official public relations and brand-building messages made by corporations to directly address their various stakeholders (Colton and Poplovski 2019), they also allow researchers to explore how the platforms themselves articulate their position and activities in response to major crises and conflicts. In the case of the war in Ukraine, the platforms have used their blogs strategically to explain what their policies and actions have been following the Russian invasion.

To explore the narratives found in the corporate communication of platforms during the Ukraine War, we collected all the blog posts of the major social media companies and their owner companies available from their websites. This included all the blog posts published between the Russian invasion at the end of February until the end of October 2022. The keyword 'Ukraine' was used to identify and subset all the blog posts specifically mentioning Ukraine for the analysis. The final corpus consisted of 40 blog posts collected from Google, Meta (Facebook, Instagram), Twitter and YouTube. The material is not evenly distributed between the platforms. Google produces blogs very actively and, therefore, has by far the most blogs in our data set (27), followed by Meta (8), Twitter (3) and YouTube (2). Our initial aim was also to include TikTok, the only non-Western company. However, what was noteworthy in the data was the absence of posts from TikTok that directly addressed the Russian invasion of Ukraine. In general, TikTok's corporate communication rarely discusses political issues. Based on the available data, we then carried out a qualitative analysis to identify how these platforms narrated their stance and activities during the war.

Blog narratives and credibility building

Unsurprisingly, the corporate blogs did not directly address their companies' shortcomings regarding the circulation of disinformation and hate speech or the accountability demands placed on platforms. Instead, they stressed their objectives of keeping their users and workers safe and helping Ukrainians, both in their immediate needs when faced with a violent invasion and in rebuilding their future. For the platform companies, the war represented an opportunity to rehabilitate their reputations and highlight their key values after facing accusations of not having done enough to prevent the spread of harmful content. The literature on disasters and humanitarian communication has shown that involvement in humanitarian projects represents excellent branding and public relations opportunities for companies with 'further potential benefits, such as increased visibility, access to new markets, access to data, and opportunities to pilot new technologies' (Madianou 2019: 5).

One of the key functions of corporate blogs is to build and maintain corporate credibility (Colton and Poplovski 2019). In credibility building, manifesting responsibility, trustworthiness and caring, as well as demonstrating expert knowledge, are key qualities. Reading blog posts against these authority-building strategies, we identified three broad *social roles* through which the social media platforms narrated their response to the war in Ukraine: (1) humanitarian actors; (2) cybersecurity experts; and (3) guardians of democracy through technology and innovation.

Platforms as humanitarian actors

Amidst the accountability pressure targeted at the platforms by Ukraine and the EU, a key theme that the blogs highlighted was the multiple humanitarian missions the companies were engaged with to help Ukrainians by collaborating with several governmental and non-governmental agencies. These partnerships with authoritative organisations and various philanthropic practices effectively communicated that the company/platform was socially responsible. Reporting acts of social responsibility are usually aimed at demonstrating a moral responsibility that goes beyond profits (Colton and Poploski 2019). Through blogs, the platforms publicly expressed empathy towards the plight of Ukrainians, as seen in the opening sentence of the Twitter blog post entitled 'Our ongoing approach to the war in Ukraine': 'Like so many around the world, we're disturbed and deeply saddened by the Russian invasion of Ukraine and the humanitarian crisis unfolding there' (Twitter 16 March).

The companies engaged in charitable giving in various ways. Google, for instance, focused on Ukrainian refugees and supporting education in Ukraine. Accordingly, it described collaboration with UNESCO, the International Rescue Committee, the Ukrainian Ministry of Education and Science and others. Similarly, Meta stressed collaboration with leading global humanitarian organisations and detailed its own humanitarian foci, including supporting journalists and human rights activists in Ukraine:

> We're committing $15 million to support humanitarian efforts in Ukraine and neighboring countries. This includes $5 million in direct donations to UN agencies and more than a dozen nonprofits, including International Medical Corps who will be using these funds to deploy mobile medical units to Ukraine and Internews to support at-risk journalists and human rights defenders in the region. We're also donating to UNICEF to scale up lifesaving support for children and families in Ukraine and the region. (Meta 3 March)

This narrative of involvement in the humanitarian responses to the Ukraine War demonstrates platforms' efforts in reclaiming public accountability, providing them with an excellent opportunity to create a positive perception of their social responsibility and caring for people in need. In CEO of Google and Alphabet Sundar Pichai's words, responsibility towards refugees is 'embedded in Google's DNA' (Google 19 September). The blog narrates Pichai's personal experiences as an immigrant and his encounters with Ukrainian refugees after he received a Global Citizen Award from the Atlantic Council, which recognised Google's response to the Russo–Ukrainian War and the support of refugees. In Google's narrative, its products and services, employees and Googlers of different nationalities were bringing relief:

> I'm also thinking of 10-year-old Yana, who left Ukraine with her family and enrolled in school in Poland. With the help of Google Translate, she's made a new best friend, despite the language barrier. Yana and her family are among the 7 million refugees from Ukraine in Europe today. The need is unprecedented. So is the response. When I was in Warsaw last spring, I was struck by how many Google employees were hosting multiple families in their homes. (Google 19 September)

A well-known critique of corporate social responsibility (CSR) is that a moral discourse offers companies a cover for profit making. In her research on 'technocolonialism' in disaster response, Madianou (2019) argued that, by engaging in humanitarianism, corporations have been extending their authority over social life. In other words, companies can reframe social problems and solutions in line with their own objectives – for instance, by stressing the role of technology in the rebuilding of the refugees' lives (Madianou 2019). Such an attempt can be seen in Google's persistent emphasis on its products' role in crisis relief:

> To help teachers keep teaching, Google is working with the Ukrainian Ministry of Education and Science, UNESCO, and partners from around the world to provide hardware, software, content and training. To help education continue for both remaining and displaced students, Google is giving 43,000 Chromebooks to Ukrainian teachers – helping them to connect with their students, wherever they are now based. To ensure those devices make the best possible impact, Google is partnering with local organisations to train around 50,000 teachers – and providing our Chrome Education Upgrade so that schools can set-up and manage devices remotely. (Google 24 May)

Although the above quote illustrates a generous contribution to the assistance of the Ukrainian people, it could also be interpreted as an example of how private companies work to make themselves indispensable to key public sectors, including education. As van Dijck, Nieborg and Poell (2019) stated, platform power is based on making diverse societal institutions dependent on the infrastructure and services of major platform companies.

Platforms as cybersecurity authorities

The stress placed on technological expertise and innovation in corporate blogs reflects what Keller and Aaker (1998) have called the expertise dimension of corporate credibility. In this narrative, details about the verifiable proficiencies of companies, their employees and technology help demonstrate the benefits that such companies possess for society more broadly. Besides positioning themselves as humanitarian actors, the platforms' communication stressed their role as leading cybersecurity actors during (and preceding) the war in Ukraine. The blogs portrayed platforms as actors whose technological expertise can be used to support Ukraine in the information war and cyber war, but, more broadly, defend democracies against various cyber threats, often originating from authoritarian countries such as Russia.

The platforms stressed how they were taking measures to both support Ukraine by removing misleading and harmful content and, just as importantly, by providing the technological support needed to protect the Ukrainian government from cyberattacks such as phishing, malware campaigns, espionage and malign information operations. One such measure was Twitter's new 'crisis misinformation policy' announced on 19 May, supposedly sped up by the public pressure following Russia's invasion. According to the post, their crisis misinformation policy is as follows:

> ... a global policy that will guide our efforts to elevate credible, authoritative information, and will help to ensure viral misinformation isn't amplified or recommended by us during crises. In times of crisis, misleading information can undermine public trust and cause further harm to already vulnerable communities. [--] While this first iteration is focused on international armed conflict, starting with the war in Ukraine, we plan to update and expand the policy to include additional forms of crisis. (Twitter 19 May)

What is interesting about this framing is that such technological expertise has also been linked explicitly to the broader geopolitical implications of the Russo–Ukrainian War. Defending cybersecurity is not only a necessary corporate strategy for digital platforms, but it is also linked to the security of Western democracies. Thus, the technological expertise the companies provide, in conjunction with work done by governments and academics, can help defend openness, transparency, free access to information – and democracy – more broadly in a new global situation.

Platforms as cybersecurity actors have perceived themselves as active participants in the information war – not as neutral players as might have been the case before – whose interests are aligned with the geopolitical interests of the Western world. In this narrative, the platforms had gained their authority through persistent technological development and sharing their knowledge with others – platform companies, governments and other societal actors. The emphasis on the long-time efforts to create technologies and policies to safeguard online safety aims to rehabilitate their reputations after facing demands in recent years to take responsibility for spreading harmful content. In this way, Ukraine's proclaimed winning of the information war, in some sense, was owed to these companies' long-standing efforts in the region:

> In recent months, we have witnessed a growing number of threat actors – state actors and criminal networks–using the war as a lure in phishing and malware campaigns, embarking on espionage, and attempting to sow disinformation. But this time, we were ready with a modern infrastructure and a process for monitoring and responding to threats as they happened. [---] And we helped the Ukrainian government modernize its cyber infrastructure, helping fortify it against attack. We are proud that we were the first company to receive the Ukrainian government's special peace prize in recognition of these efforts. Online security is extremely important for people in Ukraine and the surrounding region right now. (Google 19 July)

Thus, platforms' technological expertise – and the values these companies embody – are articulated as a crucial force helping defend the democratic world against external actors and the dangers related to cybersecurity. The above-cited Google blog post titled 'Transparency in the shadowy world of cyberattacks' summarises this in the following way:

> And, looking beyond Russia and Ukraine, we see rising threats from Iran, China, and North Korea. Google is a proud American company, committed to the defense of democracy and the safety and security of people around the world. And we believe cybersecurity is one of the most important issues we face. (Google 19 July)

Guardians of democracy

If the platform companies' expertise in cybersecurity is articulated as a positive force helping defend Western democracies against external threats, another shared narrative in the blogs positioned the platforms as guardians of democracy. Whereas the cybersecurity narrative focused more on sharing technological expertise to fight against cyber threats, this narrative addressed the role technology companies can have in defence of Western values more broadly. As such, it echoed the earlier debates about Silicon Valley as a 'force for good' globally, as exemplified by the rhetoric around 'liberation technology' during the so-called 'social media revolutions' (Meijas 2012; Morozov 2011). The role of the guardian of democracy was articulated as a response to the criticism that the platforms have been a target of in recent years, especially for their inaction and ineptitude for moderating hate speech and disinformation. The war seems to have offered an opportunity for platforms to redeem themselves and regain their role as defenders of democratic values. In his remarks at the Copenhagen Democracy Summit, Google's President of Global Affairs Kent Walker summarised this relationship between technology and democracy:

> I'd like to speak today about the debt technology owes democracy, and how technology can work with democracy to repay that debt. But first, let's talk about why that partnership is so critically important . . . democratic values of openness and pluralism allow cooperation and scientific inquiry to flourish . . . but technology can also benefit democracy itself, by proving that democracies can deliver for citizens, expanding choice and raising living standards. (Google 6 October)

Beyond the Ukraine War, technology – and technological innovation in particular – can help defend democracies from attacks from authoritarian countries through supporting values and processes such as democratic deliberation, open access to reliable information and a free press. Walker remarked in the same Google blog post:

> Technology and innovation can also be a force for democratic procedural legitimacy: Supporting democratic institutions, increasing transparency and accountability in governance, and protecting and promoting human rights. When developed and used responsibly, technology can foster the essential exchange of ideas and broaden civic engagement in the democratic process. (Google 6 October)

Thus, the Ukraine War provided an opportunity to show how technology companies can, once again, be the solution rather than the cause of the problems that democracies face. In particular, the technological innovation represented by these companies can also provide the necessary resources to respond to future crises and defend the free exchange of ideas necessary for democracies to function.

Accordingly, a Meta post titled 'Meta's Ongoing Efforts Regarding Russia's Invasion of Ukraine' explicitly positioned Meta's policies in defence of Ukrainian 'rights to speech as an expression of self-defence in reaction to a military invasion of their country' (Meta 26 February). This included the actions taken by Meta to block propaganda from state-led media outlets run by Russia, such as RT and Sputnik. However, although this ideal of defending democracy from external threats and state propaganda by authoritarian countries can be seen in how the social media companies' public relations communication tried to explain their role during the war, in practice, the actions taken by the companies represent, as has been the case in other crises, more *ad hoc* decisions taken in response to the changing political situation and growing public and political pressure. As critics have argued, Meta's Facebook and Instagram, for instance, have made more than a dozen policy revisions since the start of the invasion, leading to internal confusion, especially among content moderators working on the front lines of deciding what content is acceptable and what is not (Mac, Isaac and Frenkel 2022). What these narratives nonetheless show is how the policies of social media platforms often work reactively in relation to changing political environments and public opinion, trying to find a suitable position in an increasingly strict regulatory environment, especially in the EU.

Conclusion

The Ukraine War provided an opening during which the platforms were compelled to take government demands for more accountability seriously. The war has become an accelerator of existing trends and challenges, turning tech companies and platforms into major battlefields at a critical geopolitical moment. It also represented a shift where the political and public demand to support Ukraine brought social media platforms to closer alignment with the Western government's concerns. This represented a break from previous cases globally, where the relationship between platforms, content moderation and freedom of speech has been historically more antagonistic and contested.

This new kind of geopolitical alignment can be seen in the corporate communication of the major platforms. The blogs explicitly positioned the platforms in support of Ukraine against Russia and, more broadly, in support of democratic nations against attacks from authoritarian governments, here in a system where tactics such as cyberattacks have become commonplace.

In our exploratory analysis of the blog posts, we can see similar attempts to communicate this new positionality to the broader public and other stakeholders. It shows that the interests of the platform's narratives aligned, even if temporarily, with the geopolitical interests of the EU in three ways: through positioning them as humanitarian actors; through a focus on their cybersecurity expertise; and through the promotion of democratic values. Whether this geopolitical alignment was temporary, however, or whether the war was indeed a focusing event in the sense that the major social media platforms and the Western governments become aligned more permanently remains to be seen. The corporate communication of the major social media companies during the beginning of the war in Ukraine seems to suggest that digital platforms would prefer to, once again, see themselves as collaborating – rather than being in an adversarial relationship – with Western governments, which has long been the case in contested debates on platform accountability focusing more on hate speech and mis/disinformation.

Platforms' decisions following the invasion and governmental pressure in Europe also led to criticism from civil society activists for disregarding the ideals of freedom of speech and platforms' uneven application of human rights across global conflicts. A petition signed by 31 civil liberties organisations rightly argued that other crisis situations where lives are at stake have not received the same amount of support:

> While we recognize the efforts of tech companies to uphold democracy and human rights in Ukraine, we call for long term investment in human rights, accountability, and a transparent, equal and consistent application of policies to uphold the rights of users worldwide. *Once platforms began to take action in Ukraine, they took extraordinary steps that they have been unwilling to take elsewhere.* (EFF 2022; our italics)

In conclusion, the corporate communication of social media platforms suggests a new kind of geopolitical alignment between social media platforms and democratic governments, especially the EU, in response to the Ukraine War. This fits the broader narrative the EU has been promoting, which increasingly sees digital platforms as important players in geopolitical security and protecting European values, such as human rights, democracy and freedom of speech (Ringhof and Torreblanc 2022).

References

Baker, S. A., Wade, M., and Walsh, M. J. (2020). 'The Challenges of Responding to Misinformation During a Pandemic: Content Moderation and the Limitations of the Concept of Harm', *Media International Australia*, 177 (1), 103–7.

Banchik, A. V. (2021). 'Disappearing Acts: Content Moderation and Emergent Practices to Preserve At-Risk Human Rights–Related Content', *New Media & Society*, 23 (6), 1527–44.

Biddle, S. (2022). 'Facebook's Ukraine-Russia Rules Prompt Cries of Double Standard', *The Intercept*, 14 April, https://theintercept.com/2022/04/13/facebook-ukraine-russia-moderation-double-standard/, accessed 30 December 2022.

Birkland, T. A. (1998). 'Focusing Events, Mobilization, and Agenda Setting', *Journal of Public Policy*, 18 (1), 53–74.

Brown. D. (2020). 'Big Tech's Heavy Hand Around the Globe', *Foreign Policy in Focus*, 8 September, https://www.hrw.org/news/2020/09/08/big-techs-heavy-hand-around-globe, accessed 21 October 2022.

Caplan, R., and boyd, d. (2018). 'Isomorphism through Algorithms: Institutional Dependencies in the Case of Facebook', *Big Data & Society*, 5 (1), https://doi.org/10.1177/2053951718757253, accessed 21 October 2022.

Colton, D., and Poploski, S. (2019). 'A Content Analysis of Corporate Blogs to Identify Communications Strategies, Objectives and Dimensions of Credibility', *Journal of Promotion Management*, 25 (4), 609–30.

Conway, M., Khawaja, M., Lakhani, S., Reffin, J., Robertson, A., and Weir, D. (2017). 'Disrupting Daesh: Measuring Takedown of Online Terrorist Material and Its Impacts', *Studies in Conflict & Terrorism*, 42 (1-2), 141–60.

DeCook, J. R., Cotter, K., Kanthawala, S., and Foyle, K. (2022). 'Safe from "Harm": The Governance of Violence by Platforms', *Policy & Internet*, 14, 63–78.

De Gregorio, G. (2019). 'From Constitutional Freedoms to the Power of the Platforms: Protecting Fundamental Rights in the Algorithmic Society', *European Journal of Legal Studies*, 11 (2), 65-103.

De Gregorio, G., and Stremlau, N. (2020). 'Internet Shutdowns and the Limits of Law', *International Journal of Communication* 14, 1–19, https://ssrn.com/abstract=3622928, accessed 1 October 2023.

DSA. (2022). Regulation (EU) 2022/2065 of the European Parliament and of the Council of 19 October 2022 on a Single Market for Digital Services and Amending Directive 2000/31/, https://eur-lex.europa.eu/legal-content/EN/TXT/?uri=CELEX%3A32022R2065&qid=1666966938325, accessed 2 April 2023.

EDMO. (2022). 'How Covid-19 Conspiracy Theorists Pivoted to Pro-Russian Hoaxes', European Digital Media Observatory, 30 March, https://edmo.eu/2022/03/30/how-covid-19-conspiracy-theorists-pivoted-to-pro-russian-hoaxes/, accessed 2 April 2023.

EU. (2022/350). Council Regulation (EU) 2022/350 of 1 March 2022, https://eur-lex.europa.eu/legal-content/EN/TXT/PDF/?uri=CELEX:32022R0350, accessed 2 April 2023.

European Commission. (2022). 'Digital Services Act: Commission Welcomes Political Agreement on Rules Ensuring Safe and Accountable Online Environment', Press release 23 April, https://ec.europa.eu/commission/presscorner/detail/en/ip_22_2545, accessed 21 September 2022.

European Council. (2015). European Council Conclusions, 19–20, https://www.consilium.eur opa.eu/media/21888/european-council-conclusions-19-20-march-2015-en.pdf, accessed 21 September 2022.
European Parliament. (2022). European Parliament Resolution of 9 March 2022 on Foreign Interference in All Democratic Processes in the European Union, Including Disinformation (2020/2268(INI)), https://www.europarl.europa.eu/doceo/document/TA-9-2022-0064_EN.html, accessed 21 September 2022.
EFF. (2022). 'Civil Liberties Groups Urge Social Media Platforms to Better Protect Free Flow of Information in Crisis Zones', *Electronic Frontier Foundation*, 12 April, https://www.eff.org/press/releases/human-rights-groups-urge-social-media-platforms-better-protect-free-flow-information, accessed 2 October 2022.
Gadde, V., and Derella, M. (2020). 'An Update on Our Continuity Strategy during COVID-19', Twitter blog, 16 March, https://blog.twitter.com/en_us/topics/company/2020/An-update-on-our-continuity-strategy-during-COVID-19.html, accessed 21 December 2022.
Gillespie, T. (2010). 'The Politics of "Platforms"', *New Media & Society*, 12 (3), 347–64.
Gillespie, T. (2018). *Custodians of the Internet: Platforms, Content Moderation, and the Hidden Decisions That Shape Social Media*. New Haven, CT: Yale University Press.
Gillespie, T., Aufderheide, P., Carmi, E., Gerrard, Y., Gorwa, R., Matamoros-Fernández, A., Roberts, S. T., Sinnreich, A., and Myers West, S. (2020). 'Expanding the Debate about Content Moderation: Scholarly Research Agendas for the Coming Policy Debates', *Internet Policy Review*, 9 (4), https: https://policyreview.info/articles/analysis/expanding-debate-about-content-moderation-scholarly-research-agendas-coming-policy, accessed 21 September 2022.
Hallinan, H., Scharlach, R., and Shifman, L. (2022). 'Beyond Neutrality: Conceptualizing Platform Values', *Communication Theory*, 32 (2), 201–22.
Helberger, N., Pierson, J., and Poell, T. (2018). 'Governing Online Platforms: From Contested to Cooperative Responsibility', *The Information Society*, 34 (1), 1–14.
Hoverd, W., Salter, L., and Veale, K. (2021). 'The Christchurch Call: Insecurity, Democracy and Digital Media –Can It Really Counter Online Hate and Extremism?', *SN Social Sciences*, 1 (2), https://doi.org/10.1007/s43545-020-00008-2, accessed 29 September 2022.
HRW. (2022) Human Rights Watch. *Russia, Ukraine, and Social Media and Messaging Apps. Questions and Answers on Platform Accountability and Human Rights Responsibilities*, https://www.hrw.org/news/2022/03/16/russia-ukraine-and-social-media-and-messaging-apps, accessed 21 September 2022.
Keller, K. L., and Aaker, D. A. (1998). 'The Impact of Corporate Marketing on a Company's Brand Extensions', *Corporate Reputation Review*, 1 (4), 356–78.
Lukes, S. (2006). 'Questions about Power: Lessons from the Louisiana Hurricane', *Items. Insights from the Social Sciences*, https://items.ssrc.org/understanding-katrina/questions-about-power-lessons-from-the-louisiana-hurricane/, accessed 21 September 2022.
Mac, R., Isaac, M., and Frenkel, S. (2022). 'How War in Ukraine Roiled Facebook and Instagram', *New York Times*, 30 March, https://www.nytimes.com/2022/03/30/technology/ukraine-russia-facebook-instagram.html, accessed 17 January 2023.

Madianou, M. (2019). 'Technocolonialism: Digital Innovation and Data Practices in the Humanitarian Response to Refugee Crises', *Social Media + Society*, 5 (3), https://doi.org/10.1177/2056305119863146, accessed 21 September 2022.

Mager, A., and Katzenbach, C. (2021). 'Future Imaginaries in the Making and Governing of Digital Technology: Multiple, Contested, Commodified', *New Media & Society*, 23 (2), 223–36.

Marchant, E., and Stremlau, N. (2020). 'Internet Shutdowns in Africa. The Changing Landscape of Internet Shutdowns in Africa – Introduction', *International Journal of Communication*, 14 (8), https://ijoc.org/index.php/ijoc/article/view/11490, accessed 2 October 2022.

Meijas, U. A. (2012). 'Liberation Technology and the Arab Spring: From Utopia to Atopia and Beyond', *Fibreculture*, 20, 204–17, https://twenty.fibreculturejournal.org/2012/06/20/fcj-147-liberation-technology-and-the-arab-spring-from-utopia-to-atopia-and-beyond/, accessed 5 October 2022.

Meta. (2022). 'Sharing Our Progress on Combating Climate Change', Meta blog, 6 November, https://about.fb.com/news/2022/11/metas-progress-on-combating-climate-change/, accessed 21 September 2022.

Morozov, E. (2011). *The Net Delusion: The Dark Side of Internet Freedom*. Perseus Books, USA.

Napoli, P., and Caplan, R. (2017). 'Why Media Companies Insist They're Not Media Companies, Why They're Wrong, and Why It Matters', *First Monday*, 22 (5), 1–16.

Pantti, M., Wahl-Jorgensen, K., and Cottle, S. (2012). *Disasters and the Media*. New York, NY: Peter Lang Publishing.

Pohjonen, M. (2019). 'A Comparative Approach to Social Media Extreme Speech: Online Hate Speech as Media Commentary', *International Journal of Communication*, 13, 3088–103.

Ringhof, J., and Torreblanc, J. I. (2022). 'The Geopolitics of Technology: How the EU can Become a Global Player', Policy Brief, European Council of Foreign Relations, 17 May, https://ecfr.eu/publication/the-geopolitics-of-technology-how-the-eu-can-become-a-global-player/, accessed 20 December 2022.

Roberts, S. T. (2019). *Behind the Screen: Content Moderation in the Shadows of Social Media*. New Haven, CT: Yale University Press.

Sablosky, J. (2021). 'Dangerous Organisations: Facebook's Content Moderation Decisions and Ethnic Visibility in Myanmar', *Media, Culture & Society*, 43 (6), 1017–104.

Scott, M., and Kern, R. (2022). 'Social Media Goes to War', *Politico*, 2 March, https://www.politico.eu/article/social-media-goes-to-war/, accessed 21 December 2022.

Suzor, N. (2019). *Lawless: The Secret Rules that Govern our Digital Lives*. Cambridge: Cambridge University Press.

Szostek, J. (2020). 'What Happens to Public Diplomacy during Information War? Critical Reflections on the Conceptual Framing of International Communication', *International Journal of Communication*, 14, 2728–48.

Tierney, K., Bevc, C., and Kuligowski, E. (2006). 'Metaphors Matter: Disaster Myths, Media Frames, and Their Consequences in Hurricane Katrina', *The Annals of the American Academy of Political and Social Science*, 604 (1), 57–81.

Udupa S., Gagliardone, I., and Hervik, P. (2021). *Digital Hate: The Global Conjuncture of Extreme Speech*. Bloomington: Indiana University Press.

van Dijck, J., Nieborg, D., and Poell, T. (2019). 'Reframing Platform Power', *Internet Policy Review*, 8 (2), https://doi.org/10.14763/2019.2.1414, accessed 21 September 2022.

Wagner, K., Deutsch, L., and Zuidijk, D. (2022). 'Social Media Companies Crack Down on Russian Misinformation', *Government Technology*, 4 March, https://www.govtech.com/security/social-media-companies-crack-down-on-russian-misinformation, accessed 2 October 2022.

Part Two:
The Use of Open-Source Intelligence

· 4 ·

OPEN-SOURCE ACTORS AND UK NEWS COVERAGE OF THE WAR IN UKRAINE: DOCUMENTING THE IMPACTS OF CONFLICT AND INCIDENTS OF CIVILIAN HARM

Jamie Matthews

Open-source intelligence (OSINT) describes the gathering and analysis of public online data sources. The collective endeavours of digital volunteers and investigations conducted by actors such as Bellingcat produce evidence that provide a valuable perspective on events. Open-source investigations verified the culpability of pro-Russian separatists in the downing of Malaysian Airlines MH17 over Donetsk, Ukraine in 2014 by tracking the movements of the Russian Buk missile launcher (Bellingcat 2014). They also corroborated the use of chemical weapons by the Syrian military in Douma in 2018 by using satellite imagery, architectural details and images from the ground to produce 3D models of the attack sites and cannisters (Forensic Architecture 2018). Increasingly, the use of these research techniques is an important tool and practice for journalists when researching their stories. Open-source intelligence practices, and the actors that conduct investigations, are now also valuable sources for journalists, shaping the meanings and understanding of significant events.

In a confused and contested media space, these open-source practices and actors are a vital resource in documenting the war in Ukraine. This includes the use of social media geolocation and online data sources to confirm military losses and to map incidents of civilian harm. While existing research has considered the changing practices of journalism that are facilitated by open-source intelligence techniques (Müller and Wiik 2021) and the contribution of investigations by Bellingcat to conflict reporting (Cooper and Mutsvairo 2021), less is known about how open-source actors are shaping the contours of mainstream news coverage.

This chapter documents how open-source actors contribute to mainstream news media accounts of the Russian invasion of Ukraine and its impacts. Through an exploratory content analysis of online news coverage of the initial six months of the war in UK news media, it seeks to map the types and use of open-source actors by UK news organisations. The guiding research questions for the study are as follows:

1. What open-source actors have featured prominently in UK news media coverage of the Russian invasion of Ukraine and its impacts?
2. What prominent stories, events and issues that have occurred during the war feature open-source actors as sources?
3. How are these actors used within news accounts? Are they used as a source, to corroborate or challenge different perspectives on an issue or event, or to introduce readers to open-source intelligence techniques, resources and the different actors?

While it is established that open-source intelligence practices offer new opportunities for newsgathering and verification, the findings from this study suggest that as sources these actors enable coverage that underline the impacts of conflict and presents it in different ways. In news accounts of Russia's invasion of Ukraine, open-source actors provide another layer of access, enabling news accounts to highlight and evidence incidents of civilian harm.

As has followed wider transformations in digital journalism, I argue in this chapter that the insights provided by open-source actors, and the embedding of open-source practices and tools into in-depth investigations, are reconfiguring news organisations' coverage of war and conflict.

OSINT practices, tools and actors

The war in Ukraine is characterised by information manipulation tactics and disinformation propagated by various actors (OECD 2022). While propaganda has long existed as a weapon of war, the evolution in the production and dissemination of information, illustrated by the breadth of online sources, have both simplified its creation and amplified its potential. Russia, in particular, has deployed a complex and multi-layered strategy to 'introduce, amplify, and spread false and distorted' narratives about the war and its intentions (NewsGuard 2022: 1). These are capabilities that Russia has developed since the annexation of Crimea in 2014 and deployed through state media sources, such as RT, anonymous websites and social media platforms (NewsGuard 2022). Trolls and bots on these platforms are a further established feature of pro-Kremlin disinformation (Aro 2016). The Ukrainian government has also sought to influence the information and narratives about the war, a strategy that is necessary to counter disinformation, galvanise the morale of its own people and enhance support for its cause amongst western publics (Serafin 2022).

The collection, analysis and use of publicly available or open-source data, alongside new techniques and tools for data analysis, afford new opportunities for sourcing and verifying information. These sources of data, practices and tools are diverse. In addition to monitoring social media and searching for data published online, the field has expanded to include specialised software that enhances the speed and breadth of sources that can be accessed and enables the visualisation of information (Bellingcat 2022b). Commercial platforms such as Maltego (2022) allow users to connect to different data sources and identify relationships between people or organisations. Tools such as Google Earth Pro, which enable users to search and access satellite imagery and geolocate devices used to capture images and video content, are amongst the most frequently used by researchers (Bellingcat 2022b).

These practices, which have been variously described as internet sleuthing and open-source intelligence, are used by activists, researchers, volunteers and journalists to investigate, provide evidence, corroborate and make sense of the war. The crowdsourced 'digital labour' of volunteers and advocacy groups contributed to the geolocation and verification of the BUK video that proved Russia's involvement in the targeting of MH17, enabling Ukraine to bolster its own discursive reach by presenting a 'credible and externally vetted' account that counteracted Russian claims (Sienkiewicz 2015: 215).

Alongside citizen volunteers and activists, there are also the collective endeavours of non-profit groups such as Bellingcat, Forensic Architecture and Airwars that conduct open-source investigations and publish their findings. Some scholars describe these organisations as an interpreter tier, working at the interface between amateur investigations and mainstream news organisations, drawing on the expertise of both volunteers and paid interpreters

(Sienkiewicz 2016). As actors, they have become authoritative voices in the context of ongoing wars and conflict (Müller and Wiik 2021).

Since the annexation of Crimea and Russia's support of separatists in Ukraine, these actors have played a crucial role in the conflict. Their research was cited in January 2022, warning of Russian troop mobilisations on Ukraine's border (Looft and Adib 2022). Following Russia's full-scale invasion, they published evidence to corroborate the massacre of civilians in the city of Bucha (Bellingcat), the use of cluster munitions (Airwars and Bellingcat) and attacks perpetrated by Russian forces on civilian communication infrastructure and sites of cultural significance (Forensic Architecture). These investigations bring together teams with complementary expertise to comb through online data sources, using methodologies, tools and software to verify and triangulate videos and online, public databases, amongst other resources, to piece together and present accounts of events but to also refute Russian claims and disinformation.

In addition to these collectives, there are other open-source actors that use these same methodologies and techniques. New approaches of mining and processing data are transforming responses to humanitarian crises, enabling remote volunteers to monitor social media and map crisis response (Chernobrov 2018). OSINT techniques are also integrated into the investigative work of prominent human rights organisations and by United Nations investigative bodies[1] (Murray, McDermott and Koenig 2022). In the war in Ukraine, Human Rights Watch employ OSINT techniques to map the use of cluster munitions (Human Rights Watch 2022) and Amnesty International's Crisis Evidence Lab collects audio and visual material, such as satellite imagery, video footage and images of spent munitions as evidence of violations of international law (Amnesty International 2022).

In parallel, news organisations are expanding their capabilities to integrate these techniques into their newsgathering practices and approaches to their in-depth investigations, establishing open-source hubs or allowing journalists to develop their own expertise to conduct open-source research. Reese (2022: 262) argues that the application of OSINT to newsgathering enhances the range of participants that contribute to 'accountable journalism' and enables 'greater credibility, legal protection and resilience against authoritarian intrusion'. *The New York Times* established its own visual investigations team in 2017 that produces powerful investigative journalism drawing on open-source visual evidence. They published the 'Killing Khashoggi' video investigation that reconstructed the movements of the Saudi hit team that killed the Saudi dissident and journalist Jamal Khashoggi (Botti et al. 2018). Research has explored how their visual investigations through eyewitness images can serve as a platform for voice in Western news coverage of global wars and conflict (Ristovska 2022).

There are also recent examples where open-source actors collaborated with major news outlets to present their investigations to a wider audience. Bellingcat, for example, worked with the BBC on investigations into political assassinations in Russia (BBC 2022) and its Africa Eye team to expose atrocities in Cameron (Scott 2018). *The Guardian* published an award-winning investigation in cooperation with Forensic Architecture detailing the circumstances of a police shooting in the UK (Siddique et al. 2020). These partnerships reflect the increasingly collaborative and international approach, which bring together a breadth of expertise, to investigative journalism that would otherwise go unreported (Sambrook et al. 2018).

Alongside the security apparatus of states, open-source actors also include policy research centres, such as the Centre for Emerging Technology and Security (CETaS), established at the Alan Turning Institute (UK) to develop and use expertise outside of government in using open-source intelligence (Corera 2022). OSINT, in particular when used by state authorities, does raise issues of privacy protection and intellectual-property enforcement. While open-source data are publicly available, they include private and sensitive information, such as data sourced from social media accounts, and can comprise leaked user data. Moreover, the reuse of online audio and video content may infringe their terms of use and breach copyright (Koops, Hoepman and Leenes 2013).

While it has been acknowledged that open-source actors are becoming important and frequently cited sources in conflict and crisis journalism and that journalism practices are evolving to incorporate source intelligence techniques, in particular for investigative journalism (Cooper and Mutsvairo 2021; Müller and Wiik 2021), less is known about how these actors shape the contours of mainstream news coverage. This is of particular significance during a war that scholar Matthew Ford (cited in Nast 2022) describes as the 'most digitally connected in history' and illustrative of the influence digital infrastructure has on conventional military conflicts (Ford and Hoskins 2022).

Study and method

To evaluate the presence and use of open-source actors, an exploratory content analysis of UK news outlets coverage of the first six-months of the war in Ukraine was conducted. The period for data collection were from 24 February

2022, the date that Russia launched its full-scale invasion, running up until 24 August 2022.

The study focuses on the presence of open-source actors, as defined by Müller and Wiik (2021) in four major UK online news outlets: *The Guardian* (www.guardian.com/uk); *The Telegraph* (www.telegraph.co.uk); *Mail Online* (www.dailymail.co.uk); and *the Daily Mirror* (mirror.co.uk). These selected outlets reflect the ideological spectrum of UK news, including left of centre (*The Guardian* and *the Daily Mirror*) and right-leaning outlets (*The Telegraph* and *Mail Online*). The four selected outlets include both quality news providers, which traditionally devote more space to current affairs foreign news coverage, and tabloid news outlets, which allocate more space to celebrity, human-interest and sport (Skovsgaard 2014). All are amongst the top twenty most frequently visited English-language news outlets by UK audiences (Ofcom 2022).

An initial search for articles in the four outlets reporting on the invasion of Ukraine and making reference to open-source actors was conducted using the text search function of the LexisNexis news database. Various combinations of search terms were used to identify relevant articles. All articles include a reference to 'Ukraine' and at least one of the additional search terms of 'open source', 'Bellingcat', 'Oryx' or 'Airwars'. The last three terms represent specific open-source actors, as non-profit collectives, as discussed above that collaborate with news organisations, conducted previous investigations into war and conflict zones and appeared as sources within news reports. No references to Forensic Architecture, which has conducted extensive investigations into the conflict in Syria, appeared in the initial text search and so was excluded as an actor for this study. Commercial providers of open-source intelligence, such as Janes were also excluded from the analysis. In addition, the generic search term 'open source' was used to identify the presence of other actors, such as NGOs, that are cited as providing information derived through open-source investigative techniques and that are identified as such in news articles. This search term also captures references to investigations conducted by other news organisations and identified in articles. Open-source databases, such as Dattalion, although valuable for journalists, providing access to verified eyewitness footage and accounts of the war, are resources rather than actors and were not captured by this study. All types of online articles, including news, analysis, comment and opinion, were included. A first sift was conducted to remove duplicates and irrelevant articles. This produced an initial sample of 267 articles from the four news outlets (*The Guardian*: 78, *The Telegraph*: 67, *Mail Online*: 90 and *the Daily Mirror*: 32).

The second stage of the analysis involved a close reading of the articles to identify the types of stories, events and issues where open-source actors feature as sources and the different actors cited in reports. To answer the third research question, notes were taken about how these actors are used within news accounts. This included identifying whether actors, their investigations or evidence they provide are the subject of the story, for example if reporting, commentary or analysis consider the use of open-source intelligence and its role in conflict. Conversely, if actors feature as sources, conveying information journalists draw on to develop a story or to support or challenge different perspectives on an issue or event (Fisher 2018). Other aspects also noted include whether primary source material, such as videos and images, from these actors were incorporated into reports and how sources are used, for example, to substantiate reports or provide alternative perspectives on events. The key findings emerging from this analysis are presented and discussed below.

Challenging disinformation and verifying incidents of civilian harm

The analysis shows that open-source actors were referenced more frequently in the quality news outlets, with a total of 145 articles or 54 per cent of the sample drawn from either *The Guardian* or *The Telegraph*. Across the four outlets, however, there were more articles from the *Mail Online* (90) than *The Guardian* (67) and *The Telegraph* (67). It is to be expected that the quality outlets would devote more coverage to the war in Ukraine and, as a consequence, there are more articles from these outlets citing open-source actors. It is also known that open-source actors, including Bellingcat, work in partnership with quality news providers to publish the outcomes of their research and investigations. In addition, it is the quality news outlets, those that have supported and promoted in-depth investigative journalism, that are recognising the value of open-source information and how it can be used to provide evidence to support reporting and analysis. This has included establishing dedicated open-source teams.

It is important to note that while the *Mail Online* featured more articles that made reference to open-source actors than other outlets, research has shown that the *Mail Online* reposts agency copy more often than other outlets (Nicholls 2019). Within the sample from the *Mail Online*, a number of articles reference open-source actors but quote other publications, including *The

Guardian and *The Times*. This was not evident in the articles sourced from the other three outlets.

Within the sample, there were articles from all four outlets that included references to the search term open-source. For the specific actors used as search terms, however, these were not present in all outlets. References to Bellingcat were the most prominent and were found in a significant proportion (51 per cent) of articles obtained from each outlet (137 of the 267 articles, 23 in the *Daily Mirror*; 33 in The *Telegraph* 37 in *The Guardian*, and 44 in the *Mail Online*). This shows that Bellingcat is the most frequently cited open-source actor in UK news accounts of the invasion of Ukraine. Oryx featured as an actor in all of the news outlets, except the *Daily Mirror*. It was a prominent actor in the *Mail Online*, cited in 23 articles included in the sample. References to Airwars were less frequent than other actors and only found in one article from *The Telegraph* and two from *The Guardian*. It was not present in any articles from the *Daily Mirror* or the *Mail Online*.

Other open-source actors identified in articles or that made reference to open-source information and practices in reporting on the war included, the Conflict Intelligence Team (CIT), an independent organisation based in Russia that conducts open-source investigations. It was a significant actor prior to the invasion, providing information about the movements of Russian troops, and has collaborated with others including Bellingcat. There were also references to the open-source intelligence used by Space Review, an online publication, in providing information about Russian hypersonic missiles (*Mail Online*, 12 July) and work carried out by independent Russian journalists to identify the perpetrators of war crimes (*Mail Online*, 6 August).

From the first day that Russian forces crossed the border into Ukraine, articles in the sample made reference to open-source actors. Reports from the 24 and 25 February cited 'open-source research group, CIT' (*The Guardian*, 24 February) and Bellingcat (*The Telegraph*, 24 February) as sources confirming the locations of missile strikes, including the targeting of residential apartment blocks in Kyiv and Kharkiv. References were also made to 'open-source data' in early reports, cited as evidence that Vladimir Putin's televised address announcing the start of a 'special military operation' in Ukraine was prerecord rather than delivered live (*The Telegraph*, 25 February). In this example, attribution was not made to a specific actor but to open-source data and *The Telegraph's* Moscow correspondent.

From the 28 February 2022, open-source actors started to appear in articles as providing or corroborating evidence of possible war crimes and human-rights abuses perpetrated by Russian forces. This is a recurring pattern in the use of open-source actors in the sample. The initial reports cited these actors as confirming cluster bomb attacks in populated areas of Ukraine, the use of which are prohibited by the 2008 convention[2] on cluster munitions, and their indiscriminate effects contravening the Geneva Conventions. Prominent actors were Bellingcat, with its founder Eliot Higgins quoted as having video footage and stills that provided evidence that Russia was bombing civilian areas with cluster munitions. These online reports embedded excerpts of dashcam, security camera and video footage captured by Ukrainians on their mobile phones showing bombing and missile strikes (*The Guardian*, 28 February; 2 March; *The Telegraph*, 28 February, *Mail Online*, 2 March).

Subsequent allegations of war crimes and the targeting of civilians emerged across the six-month period of the study. Most significant were the attacks on the Mariupol maternity hospital on 9 March and Mykolaiv hospital on 4 April and the massacre of civilians in Bucha, evidence that came to light on 1 April after Russian forces withdrew from the city, and the uncovering of mass graves and burial sites in former occupied areas of Ukraine. In articles reporting these events, all of which are significant episodes in the timeline of the invasion, open-source actors were prominent in articles from the four outlets. Harrowing pictures of the destruction of the Mariupol maternity hospital and the civilians caught up in the attack made headlines worldwide. It was an act that was widely condemned by the international community (Trevelyan 2022). Russian actors, including Russian embassies, however, released images through their Twitter accounts that claimed to show an image of a tank in front of the hospital to support their claim that the hospital was a legitimate military target occupied by the Ukrainian Azov battalion. Assertions were also made by the Russian state, and across conspiracy forums, that the attack was staged due to one of the injured women photographed by the Associated Press being a Ukrainian beauty blogger (Milmo and Farah 2022). In subsequent reports that condemned these accounts as further examples of Russian disinformation, open-source actors, in particular evidence and comments attributed to Bellingcat, were used to demonstrate that these were false claims. These included photos and links to earlier Instagram posts. They also reported comments by Elliot Higgins that called on Twitter to remove the 'propaganda-spewing accounts' from the platform (*The Guardian*, 10 March). This example shows how representatives of open-source actors were given a platform as sources to respond to claims. It also illustrates how open-source actors provide direct evidence that journalists use within their reports to challenge disinformation, through verifiable, clear evidence, much of which is linked to or embedded within online news articles.

Evidence of the killing of civilians in Bucha was attributed to open-source actors in a number of subsequent reports. Drone footage verified and shared by Bellingcat that showed a Russian tank opening fire on a civilian and satellite images featured prominently in reports (the *Mail Online*, 5 April; *The Telegraph*, 6 April; *The Guardian*, 5 April). This material was significant in disputing Russian claims that bodies found in the city streets were staged and left by the Ukrainian military after the withdrawal of Russian forces. *The Guardian* report made explicit reference to the analysis and publication of satellite images by *The New York Times*, and work conducted by its visual investigations team. This was not apparent in the other reports. However, all presented a detailed exposition of the processes employed in obtaining satellite and drone imagery and for substantiating images, for example, by matching locations with images available online. Importantly, the articles also noted the value of this evidence not only for journalists but in gathering and documenting evidence of the human rights abuses occurring in the war in Ukraine.

As a 40-mile-long Russian convey of military vehicles stalled on the outskirts of Kyiv in early March, in addition to citing British and US intelligence sources, open-source actors featured prominently in articles. They provided evidence of the poor state of repair of Russian military equipment, with assessments from Oryx highlighting the number of tanks destroyed, damaged or seized in the invasion and supported by images and videos embedded into articles (*The Guardian*, 10 March; *The Telegraph*, 3 March; the *Daily Mirror*, 11 March; the *Mail Online*, 11 March). Bellingcat was also cited in articles as verifying video footage of a drone strike on the convey through the use of geolocation techniques (*The Guardian*, 10 March). This example demonstrates how these open-source actors, in this instance and, in particular when referring to Oryx, can supplement and verify the accounts provided by state intelligence sources. Reports about the lack of progress by Russian forces often cited UK Ministry of Defence intelligence updates. OSINT actors, however, not only corroborated these accounts by confirming military losses from social media (Hambling 2022), but their multimedia content was embedded into online stories, enriching news accounts.

Across the 6-month period, other prominent stories where open-source actors featured included allegations reported in March that attendees of informal peace talks between Russian and Ukrainian delegates, brokered by Russian oligarch and former owner of Chelsea Football Club, Roman

Abramovich, suffered symptoms that were consistent with poisoning (*The Guardian*, 28 March; *The Telegraph*, 28 March; the *Mail Online*, 28 March). Claims that were attributed to investigations conducted by Bellingcat. As Russian losses in the war continued to mount, open-source actors were also cited naming senior Russian officers that had been killed in the invasion (the *Mail Online*, 8 and 9 March; *The Daily Mirror*, 12 March; *The Telegraph*, 11 March) and providing details of the losses of military hardware and equipment (*The Daily Mirror*, 30 May; the *Mail Online*, 12 August; *The Guardian*, 11 August).

The final point to note from the analysis of coverage is that while the majority of articles used open-source actors as sources to provide information that is cited within an article or to support a particular viewpoint, there was also space within reports to introduce readers to open-source intelligence techniques, resources and the different actors. Specifically, there was an emphasis on considering the role for this type of information in discrediting claims and disinformation shared by Russian actors and to gather evidence of possible war crimes. Articles in the sample detailed how open-source verification was used to identify the perpetrators of the massacre in Bucha by using social media (*Guardian*, 5 April; the *Mail Online*, 10 April) and approaches used by other news organisations to confirm the location of videos (the *Mail Online*, 5 May). There were also pieces, both news and comment, that discussed how open-source actors provided 'insights to rival state intelligence agencies' (*The Telegraph*, 1 March), its significance to contemporary warfare and ability to challenge disinformation (*The Telegraph*, 1 June; *The Guardian*, 4 April). In others, they reflected on how open-source intelligence and actors contribute to the conflict being defined as the first 'social media war' (*The Telegraph*, 5 March; *The Guardian*, 19 March) or discussed open-source approaches through an interview with Bellingcat founder, Eliot Higgins (*The Telegraph*, 17 April).

Discussion and conclusion

This chapter has evaluated how open-source actors contributed to UK online news coverage of the invasion of Ukraine. From the exploratory analysis presented here, it is evident that a range of different actors featured prominently as sources. They are used to illustrate the impacts of the conflict, in particular to provide evidence of war crimes and the targeting of civilians by Russian forces, but also dispute spurious claims made by the Russian state. The most common source cited in reports was Bellingcat, arguably the most well-known and established open-source actor.

These open-source actors offer another layer of access within news coverage of the invasion of Ukraine. While major news organisations have correspondents embedded in Ukraine, open-source actors are able to offer insights that would previously have been almost impossible to obtain without a significant number of researchers working within a conflict zone and the risks and restrictions this demands. The examples introduced above show how open-source actors, and the practices and tools that they deploy in their investigations, enable new possibilities for documenting war and conflict. Their value to the coverage of the war in Ukraine is their contribution to substantiating evidence of war crimes and human rights violations but also offering alternative perspectives on the impacts of the war, through video records and innovative visual presentations.

The sources that journalists use to inform story selection and the information that they report will have their own agendas (Grant 1999). Amid the chaos of war and conflict, with claims, counterclaims and fake news, functional truth is difficult to ascertain. This has been a feature of the war in Ukraine. Russian disinformation is well documented, but Ukraine has also engaged in its own propaganda. The use of open-source actors in reporting on the war, however, represents, not only a different type of source, able to verify and offer alternative perspectives, but one that may also offer greater transparency. There are various factors that contribute to this. First, for these actors, as organisations, collectives or teams of researchers, as they variously describe themselves, transparency in their methods is a guiding value of their work, one that is consistent with journalistic principles (Reese 2022). Airwars, for example, describes itself as a 'transparency organisation' (Airwars 2022) and transparency and its principles are set out in Bellingcat's editorial standards and practices (Bellingcat 2022a). Second, when cited in news reports, the approaches, tools and techniques that these actors use in their investigations are discussed alongside the information that they provide. Third, in many of the news accounts, as demonstrated from the sample of articles, still images and the original source video material, are embedded within online reports. This provides a degree of transparency and clarity for readers, and in turn accountability for sources and the information that they provide. It also offers insights into the processes and techniques for verifying content.

Recent research shows that digital sources, namely entities accessed from the internet but not identified as individuals are less likely to be cited in news reports (Barnoy and Reich 2021). One limitation of this study is that it is only identifying named open-source actors cited in news. The increasing use, however, of open-source actors may also be indicative of the shift towards enhanced transparency in news, enabling audiences to understand the process of source selection and to access materially directly through links and embedded content (Karlsson and Clerwall 2018; Phillips 2010). This principle is significant to the coverage of war and conflict, where alongside the professional norms of objectivity and impartiality, it can enable audiences to understand war, its impacts and the different actors and their interests (Somerville 2017).

As news organisations further integrate open-source tools and approaches into their own investigations, it is unclear whether this may hinder these transparent practices. The use of publicly available material from social media, satellite images, video content and databases and tools for cross-checking and verifying its provenance, will become an established approach to support in-depth investigative journalism (Elvery 2022). In UK mainstream media coverage of the war in Ukraine, alongside open-source actors, there were stories and material attributed to the work of other news organisations, most notably *The New York Times*, and its visual investigations unit, and *The Washington Post*. As these innovations become standardised and incorporated into investigative journalism practice, with a possible shift away from the open-source actors that are the focus for this chapter, then transparency in these approaches and their contribution to storytelling may reduce. It is important, however, that this transparency remains as it enables audiences to evaluate the authenticity of information and understand how these tools and publicly available resources are contributing to news production. This is even more significant to the coverage of war and conflict where there is a need to provide reliable information and assess truth claims amongst the flood of disinformation that circulates in the contemporary media environment. It enables journalism to maintain its authority and its status as a knowledge-producing practice (Carlson 2020).

Finally, as citizen journalism, user-generated content, and social media have now become integral to war and conflict reporting (Balabanova and Parry 2014), open-source actors and the digital tools and approaches that are being integrated into investigative practice, are enabling news accounts to enhance the breadth and depth of perspectives on war and conflict. As citizen journalism transformed the witnessing of conflict, enabling news to give voice to those affected by war and conflict (Chouliaraki 2015), and in turn contributing to more authentic representations (Pantti 2013), open-source actors and practices are shaping the contours of coverage of war and conflict. The actors highlighted in this chapter, alongside the new tools, data and practices they use, are empowering citizens, activists and journalists to document and challenge the dominant narrative to the war in Ukraine. Importantly, they are enabling rich and critical investigative insights that uncover and substantiate alleged war crimes, human rights abuses and the terrible toll of this war on civilians. This is of critical importance and why there is a need for further empirical research to consider how these actors and practices are leading to shifts in investigative journalism in the context of war and conflict.

Notes

1 The Commission of inquiry on the protests in the Occupied Palestinian Territory, the UN Independent Investigative Mechanism for Myanmar (IIMM) and the UN International, Impartial Independent Mechanism for Syria have all engaged open-source experts in these investigations (Murray, McDermott and Koenig 2022).
2 Both Russia and the United States are presently non-signatory states.

References

Airwars. (2022). https://airwars.org, accessed 28 November 2022.
Amnesty International. (2022). 'A Guide to How Amnesty Verifies Military Attacks in Ukraine', https://www.amnesty.org/en/latest/news/2022/03/a-guide-to-how-amnesty-verifies-military-attacks-in-ukraine/, accessed 15 December 2022.
Aro, J. (2016). 'The Cyberspace War: Propaganda and Trolling as Warfare Tools', *European View*, 15 (1), 121–32.
Balabanova, E., and Parry, K. (2014) 'Introduction: Communicating War', *Journal of War & Culture Studies*, 7 (1), 1–4.
Barnoy, A., and Reich, Z. (2021). 'The Familiarity Paradox: Why Has Digital Sourcing Not Democratized the News?', *Digital Journalism*, 1–20, https://doi.org/10.1080/21670811.2021.1937254.
BBC. (2022). Russian agent linked to assassination team was tracking Boris Nemtsov, investigation finds, https://www.bbc.co.uk/news/av/world-europe-60878664, accessed, 15 December 2022.
Bellingcat. (2014). 'Origin of the Separatists' Buk: A Bellingcat Investigation', https://www.bellingcat.com/news/uk-and-europe/2014/11/08/origin-of-the-separatists-buk-a-bellingcat-investigation/, accessed 13 December 2022.
Bellingcat. (2022a). 'Bellingcat-Standards and Practices', https://www.bellingcat.com/about/, accessed 28 November 2022.
Bellingcat. (2022b). 'These Are the Tools Open Source Researchers Say They Need', *Bellingcat*, https://www.bellingcat.com/resources/2022/08/12/these-are-the-tools-open-source-researchers-say-they-need/, accessed 15 December 2022.

Botti, D., Browne, M., Jordan, D., Singhvi, A., Kirkpatrick, D., Gall, C., et al. (2018). 'Video: Killing Khashoggi: How a Brutal Saudi Hit Job Unfolded', *The New York Times*, 16 November, https://www.nytimes.com/video/world/middleeast/100000006154117/khashoggi-istanbul-death-saudi-consulate.html, accessed 30 November 2022.

Carlson, M. (2020). 'Journalistic Epistemology and Digital News Circulation: Infrastructure, Circulation Practices, and Epistemic Contests', *New Media & Society*, 22 (2), 230–46.

Chernobrov, D. (2018). 'Digital Volunteer Networks and Humanitarian Crisis Reporting', *Digital Journalism*, 6 (7), 928–44.

Chouliaraki, L. (2015). 'Digital Witnessing in War Journalism: The Case of Post-Arab Spring Conflicts', *Popular Communication*, 13 (2), 105–19.

Cooper, G., and Mutsvairo, B. (2021). 'Citizen Journalism: Is Bellingcat Revolutionising Conflict Journalism?'. In Skare Orgeret, K. (ed.), *Insights on Peace and Conflict, Reporting*, pp. 106–20. Abingdon-on-Thames: Routledge.

Corera, G. (2022). 'New UK Centre Will Help Fight Information War', *BBC News*, 7 June, https://www.bbc.com/news/technology-61718097, accessed 22 November 2022.

Elvery, S. (2022) *What Should a 'Modern Reporter's Notebook' Include in the 21st Century*, https://reutersinstitute.politics.ox.ac.uk/what-should-modern-reporters-notebook-include-21st-century, accessed 22 November 2022.

Fisher, C. (2018) 'News Sources and Journalist/Source Interaction', *Oxford Research Encyclopaedia of Communication*, https://oxfordre.com/communication/view/10.1093/acrefore/9780190228613.001.0001/acrefore-9780190228613-e-849, accessed 24 November 2022.

Ford, M., and Hoskins, A. (2022). *Radical War: Data, Attention and Control in the Twenty-First Century*. London: Hurst and Company.

Forensic Architecture. (2018). 'Chemical Attack in Douma', https://forensic-architecture.org/investigation/chemical-attacks-in-douma, accessed 13 December 2022.

Grant, A. (1999). 'Reporters Wrestle with How to Use Sources', *Nieman Reports*, https://niemanreports.org/articles/reporters-wrestle-with-how-to-use-sources/, accessed 30 November 2022.

Hambling, D. (2022). 'How Heavy Are Russian Losses, And What Does It Mean for Their Offensive?', https://www.forbes.com/sites/davidhambling/2022/04/26/how-heavy-are-russian-losses-and-what-does-it-mean-for-their-offensive/, accessed 25 November 2022.

Human Rights Watch. (2022). 'Ukraine: Cluster Munitions Repeatedly Used on Mykolaiv', https://www.hrw.org/news/2022/03/17/ukraine-cluster-munitions-repeatedly-used-mykolaiv, accessed 30 November 2022.

Karlsson, M., and Clerwall, C. (2018). 'Transparency to the Rescue?', *Journalism Studies*, 19 (13), 1923–33.

Koops, B., Hoepman, J., and Leenes, R. (2013). 'Open-Source Intelligence and Privacy by Design', *Computer Law & Security Review*, 29 (6), 676–88.

Looft, C., and Adib, D. (2022). 'The Independent Investigators Tracking Russia's Military Buildup', *ABC News*, February 4, https://abcnews.go.com/Technology/independent-investigators-tracking-russias-military-buildup/story?id=82529068, accessed 15 December 2022.

Milmo, D., and Farah, H. (2022). 'Twitter Removes Russian Embassy Tweet on Mariupol Bombing', *The Guardian*, 10 March, https://www.theguardian.com/world/2022/mar/10/twitter-removes-russian-embassy-tweet-on-mariupol-bombing, accessed 30 November 2022.

Müller, N. C., and Wiik, J. (2021). 'From Gatekeeper to Gate-Opener: Open-Source Spaces in Investigative Journalism', *Journalism Practice*, 17, 189–208, https://doi.org/10.1080/17512786.2021.1919543, accessed 22 November 2022.

Murray, D., McDermott, Y., and Koenig, K. A. (2022). 'Mapping the Use of Open Source Research in UN Human Rights Investigations', *Journal of Human Rights Practice*, 14 (2), 554–81.

Nast, C. (2022). 'Open Source Intelligence May Be Changing Old-School War', *Wired UK*, https://www.wired.co.uk/article/open-source-intelligence-war-russia-ukraine, accessed 22 November 2022.

NewsGuard. (2022). 'Russia-Ukraine Disinformation Tracking Center', *NewsGuard*, https://www.newsguardtech.com/special-reports/russian-disinformation-tracking-center, accessed 17 November 2022.

Nicholls, T. (2019). 'Detecting Textual Reuse in News Stories, At Scale', *International Journal of Communication*, 13, 1–25.

OECD. (2022). 'Disinformation and Russia's War of Aggression against Ukraine', OECD, https://www.oecd.org/ukraine-hub/policy-responses/disinformation-and-russia-s-war-of-aggression-against-ukraine-37186bde/, accessed 17 November 2022.

Ofcom. (2022). *News Consumption in the UK*, https://www.ofcom.org.uk/research-and-data/tv-radio-and-on-demand/news-media/news-consumption, accessed 24 November 2022.

Pantti, M. (2013). 'Getting Closer?', *Journalism Studies*, 14 (2), 201–18.

Phillips, A. (2010). 'Transparency and the New Ethics of Journalism', *Journalism Practice*, 4 (3), 373–82.

Reese, S. D. (2022). 'The Institution of Journalism: Conceptualizing the Press in a Hybrid Media System', *Digital Journalism*, 10 (2), 253–66.

Ristovska, S. (2022). 'Open-Source Investigation as a Genre of Conflict Reporting', *Journalism*, 23 (3), 632–48.

Sambrook, R., Lewis, C., Alfter, B., Kayser-Bril, N., Koch, A., and Clements, J. (2018). *Global Teamwork: The Rise of Collaboration in Investigative Journalism*, https://ora.ox.ac.uk/objects/uuid:4a2d40ba-c7c3-482d-9f59-cc67b0c7f555, accessed 22 November 2022.

Scott, C. (2018). How BBC Africa Eye used open-source tools to debunk myths around that video of murder in Cameroon, https://www.journalism.co.uk/podcast/how-bbc-africa-eye-used-open-source-tools-to-debunk-that-video-of-murder-in-cameroon/s399/a729190/, accessed 15 December 2022.

Serafin, T. (2022). 'Ukraine's President Zelensky Takes the Russia/Ukraine War Viral', *Orbis*, 66 (4), 460–76.

Siddique, H., Voce, A., McMullan, L., and Hulley-Jones, F. (2020). 'Mark Duggan Shooting: Can Forensic Tech Cast Doubt on Official Report?', *The Guardian*, June 10, http://www.theguardian.com/uk-news/ng-interactive/2020/jun/10/mark-duggan-shooting-can-forensic-tech-cast-doubt-on-official-report, accessed 24 November 2022.

Sienkiewicz, M. (2015). 'Open BUK: Digital Labor, Media Investigation and the Downing of MH17', *Critical Studies in Media Communication*, 32 (3), 208–23.

Sienkiewicz, M. (2016). 'Open Source Warfare: The Role of User-Generated Content in the Ukrainian Conflict Media Strategy'. In M. Pantti (ed.), *Media and the Ukraine Crisis: Hybrid Media Practices and Narratives of Conflict*, pp. 19–34. New York: Peter Lang.

Skovsgaard, M. (2014). 'A Tabloid Mind? Professional Values and Organizational Pressures as Explanations of Tabloid Journalism', *Media, Culture & Society*, 36 (2), 200–18.

Somerville, K. (2017). 'Framing Conflict – the Cold War and after: Reflections from an Old Hack', *Media, War & Conflict*, 10 (1), 48–58.

Trevelyan, M. (2022). 'Russia Shifts Stance on Hospital Bombing That Sparked World Outrage', *Reuters*, March 10, https://www.reuters.com/world/europe/russia-says-claim-that-it-bombed-childrens-hospital-are-fake-news-2022-03-10/, accessed 30 November 2022.

· 5 ·

FAKING SENSE OF WAR: OSINT AS PRO-KREMLIN PROPAGANDA[1]

Marc Tuters and Boris Noordenbos

WarFakes or War on Fakes ('Voina s feikami', hereafter WF) is the name for a cluster of mainly Russian-language channels on the social media platform Telegram, as well as a multilingual website, devoted to debunking fake news on the Russian invasion of Ukraine.[2]

These channels and the website present themselves as reputable fact-checking resources, in the mode of Snopes or Politifact, whose purpose is to verify false news that misleadingly tries to pass itself off as neutral and ideologically unbiased. WF's main channel produces an average of two dozen posts per day that are intended to expose supposed 'fakes' in war coverage by Western and Ukrainian outlets, as well as critical Russian platforms. In the posts, identified 'fakes' are followed by explanations of the 'truth', which consistently echo and reinforce the Kremlin's official narratives about the war. These posts are participatory, allowing visitors to add their own comments and to click on one of nine pre-set 'emoticons', which express a range of attitudes, from support to concern. The core WF Telegram channel appeared on 24 February 2022, the first day of the full-scale Russian military invasion of Ukraine, followed by a suite of localised clone channels in the subsequent days and weeks. These local spin-offs included channels for, among other regions, Rostov, Belgorod, annexed Crimea, and the Republic of Kalmykia. They reposted content from the core Telegram channel, while targeting a more local audience.

The aim of this chapter is twofold. First, an analysis of WF's messaging on the Russian war against Ukraine deepens insight into the role currently played by digital technologies in the Russian propaganda strategy. Emblematic of Russia's twenty-first-century persuasion campaigns has been the state-sponsored channel RT, which has garnered a substantial audience outside Russia via social media platforms like YouTube. Through its clever use of digital communication, RT has obfuscated its origins in the Russian political establishment and reinforced its brand identity as an 'alternative' to a Western-dominated ecosystem of mainstream media (Yablokov and Chatterjee-Doody 2022: 13). Analysing WF's reporting, this chapter considers recent developments in the Kremlin's mobilisation of the anti-establishment potential of social media, demonstrating how online platforms are co-opted to manufacture support for the narratives and policies of the Russian authorities.

Second, and more specifically, the chapter analyses how WF hijacks practices of online verification associated with open-source intelligence (OSINT) to create the illusion of crowdsourced knowledge production. Even though WF's funding and ownership are unknown, the project can be conclusively tied to the Kremlin through a pattern of promoting the site's content via official state channels, as revealed by our earlier research (Tuters and Lazaruk 2022). What necessitates deeper investigation is how WF (mis-)uses fact-checking and OSINT to feed into the fantasy – common amongst contemporary conspiracy theorists, as well as those eager to disprove them – that participatory media empower 'independent thinkers' to become 'arbiters of the truth' (Jane and Fleming 2014: 84). In our analysis, WF channels this impetus to expose the 'lies' of the authorities and the powerful, which the WF moderators locate in Ukraine, and ultimately in 'the West'.

Weaponising OSINT

Analysing the WF platform as representing recent innovations in the Russian propaganda strategy, we zero in on the channel's messaging around the mass killing of Ukrainian civilians by the Russian Armed Forces in the Ukrainian city of Bucha, near Kyiv. While the Bucha massacre of spring 2022 triggered a wave of international outrage, the Russian authorities sought to portray it as a Western-backed Ukrainian false flag operation. Our analysis of WF's reporting on the affair shows that the platform introduces novel dimensions both to the Kremlin's persuasion strategies and to the wider participatory dynamics of contemporary online propaganda. This innovation pivots on a set of investigative and interpretative practices, from which WF derives its grassroots appeal, while building what amounts to a fake crowdsourced verification resource.

A substantial proportion of WF's posts adhere to a particular house style that exploits the rhetorical and aesthetic authority of open-source intelligence to engage in detail-oriented debunking of usually Western news reporting on the Ukraine invasion. An example of this house style is the frequent OSINT-inspired use of red circles to draw attention to alleged manipulation techniques (see Figure 5.1). Such posts promote the idea that media representations of the war cannot be trusted since they are easily subjected to manipulation. The only way to guard against this malleability of mediated representation, then, is to apply critical media literacy and question everything. WF promotes such scepticism by (mis)using OSINT techniques, inviting audiences into lengthy deconstructions of Ukrainian and Western narratives, while the moderators' conclusions more often than not closely align with those of the Kremlin.

Matthew Fuller and Eyal Weizman (2021: 5) describe OSINT as an 'anti-hegemonic' practice whose objective is 'to produce facts that contest statements' out of [s]craps of information [that] are then compiled into systems, including narrative structures'. OSINT has become a prominent genre in conflict reporting in which networks of amateur sleuths collaborate in piecing together evidence – by repurposing publicly available datasets and tools. The first high-profile demonstration of OSINT came in 2014, when a network of researchers affiliated with Bellingcat applied these techniques to the case of the Malaysia Airlines Flight 17 disaster, which was downed over the contested Donbas region of Ukraine killing all 283 passengers and 15 crew on board.[3] Although the Russian government denied involvement in the shooting down of the airplane, the network of Bellingcat investigators used a combination of geolocation and image analysis to provide convincing evidence that the plane was shot down with a surface-to-air missile system that belonged to the Russian Federation. Eight years later, three men were found guilty following a trial in absentia in the Netherlands, which drew on OSINT research (Rankin 2022). In the current war in Ukraine, a decentralised network of researchers – coordinated through the Twitter hashtag #OSINT – consistently apply these methods to all military actions and claims emerging from both sides in the conflict.

Mimicking the work of OSINT collectives like Bellingcat, WF co-opts its tactics to support the channel's central premise: that the truth about the war in Ukraine can only be determined through a collective effort of piecing

Figure 5.1: WF's (mis)use of OSINT.
Source: War on Fakes (2022d)

together data from different sources and registers of information. In general, what WF appropriates from OSINT is its epistemic authority to manufacture intelligence in a grassroots manner, through the reappropriation of various digital devices available to anyone with a computer and adequate expertise. In conceptualising WF as 'weaponizing OSINT', we draw on Fuller and Weizman's conception of OSINT as a form of 'investigative aesthetics', which involves both detailed 'sensing' and a reworking of diverse sensory data into modes of 'collective sense-making' (2021: 4). Thus, they theorise this double practice as pivoting on a component of aesthetics, which they define as the capacity to experience, detect, and register perceptively, that is, 'a state of ... alertness' (ibid.: 37) to matter, whether with a human body, with technology, or through environmental entities. Satellite photography is in this definition an aesthetic practice of sensing, yet a sunflower, too, is a 'sensor' in that it is 'aestheticized to light' (ibid.: 47). The central argument by Fuller and Weizman is that 'investigative aesthetics' take first-order sensing to new levels. As a collective undertaking, it adjudicates relations between different registers of perception, and integrates scraps of sensory data from multiple directions into narrative and interpretive patterns: 'If aesthetics is about sensing and making sense, its pairing with investigation is a demand for a reworking and heightening of the aesthetic sensorium' (ibid.: 108).

As the Bucha massacre case study will demonstrate, this collective and eclectic practice of close-up sensing and sense-making undergirds WF's innovation of participatory propaganda. WF's mimicry of OSINT at once promises its users investigative and interpretive agency and simultaneously limits it to pro-Kremlin consensus and activism as the only viable outcome. The (apparent) role of social media users as participants in a collective truth-finding operation acquires additional weight through a persistent framing of foreign reporting as involved in an aggressive (information) war against Russia. In this context, ideological alignment with the channel, and by extension the Kremlin, appears as the way 'vy uberezhëte sebia i svoikh blizkikh ot strashnogo oruzhiia desinformatsii i propagandy' [you will protect yourself and your loved ones from the terrible weapon of disinformation and propaganda], as the moderators put it (War on Fakes 2022a).[4] By this same process, media literacy, which is generally considered as a common good, is weaponised, too. As such, WF may also be understood as representative of a more general set of concerns in the field of media studies. This has led some scholars to question the promotion of media literacy on its own, without dealing with the broader normalisation of systemic narratives of distrust – a phenomenon which extends well beyond the Russian context (boyd 2018).

Participatory propaganda

WF's attempt to involve the public in a fake grassroots' form of propaganda is not entirely new. In fact, it perpetuates propagandistic strategies developed by the Putin-government ever since the 2010s, while further tailoring them to the affordances of the social media ecosystem. Dina Sharafutdinova's (2020) socio-psychological analysis has recently shown that the Putin administration increasingly focuses its persuasive strategies on the engagement of the apolitical sections of society through the incitement and exploitation of affect. The major political news- and talk shows of Russia's television-dominated offline media sphere pivot on a genre of 'agitainment' (Tolz and Teper 2018), which whips up feelings of fear, anti-Western hatred and post-Soviet national humiliation, while harnessing these emotions for the consolidation of pro-Kremlin unanimity (Sharafutdinova 2020). The media institution that best represents this strategy in the international arena is RT, whose motto is 'Question More'. It has been argued that this RT invitation to 'question more' is 'not about finding answers, but fomenting confusion, chaos, and distrust. They spin up their audience to chase myths, believe in fantasies, and listen to faux [. . .] "experts" until the audience simply tunes out' (Armstrong 2015).

While this participatory approach is taken to a new level on Telegram, the technique of identifying material as fake that is (usually) not misinformation is not unique or especially new in Putin's Russia. Indeed, the labelling of major American and European news outlets as biased is a routine strategy on prime-time political talk shows such as *60 Minutes*, broadcast on the state-owned channel Russia-1 (Noordenbos 2023), as well as the popular Russian state TV programme *Antifake*, which falsely claimed that the Bucha massacre was a hoax (Mackey 2022). Although WF's alignment with the Russian establishment is hard to miss, it distinguishes itself from other Kremlin propaganda broadcast channels by presenting itself as a grassroots initiative, in line with the participatory imperative and alternative identity of the newest social media environments. Not only does WF pretend to be independent of the Kremlin, it also claims to operate outside of politics altogether, motivated by benevolent humanitarian principles. This is stated in the English-language mission statement on WF's website:

> Welcome to the 'War on Fakes' project. We are the owners and administrators of several Russian non-political telegram channels. We don't do politics. But we consider it important to provide unbiased information about what is happening in Ukraine and on the territories of Donbas because we see signs of an information war launched against Russia. Our mission is to make sure that there are only objective publications in the information space. We do not want ordinary people to feel anxious and panicked because of information wars. We are going to look into every fake and give links to the real refutations. Be safe, be at peace, be with us. (War on Fakes 2022b)

In the guise of this ethical call to use fact-checking to cut through the fog of war, WF enrols the public as partisans in the information battlefield. What makes this approach powerful is the degree of agency that it seems to offer the audience, propelled by the specific affordances of social media platforms. By their very definition, affordances cannot be determinative of users' actions, rather they constitute a 'multifaceted relational structure' between a technological object and its intended use, which functions to constrain as well as to enable choice along certain more or less desirable paths of action (Faraj and

Azad 2013). Part of WF's participatory propaganda strategy is its nudging of the audience towards particular uses of social media technologies, meanwhile inculcating a set of behaviours, emotions, and assumptions. All of these pivot on WF's (partly implicit) metaphor of the information sphere as a battlefield, and of the amateur internet user as an enlisted defender of the nation under siege. The moderators not only encourage users to submit potential fake news (which they say they will meticulously vet), they also ask them to disseminate the channel's findings across platforms, and beyond Russia's borders. A brutal irony here is that this crowdsourced information warfare model appears initially to have been developed some years earlier, in Kyiv, as part of an effort to combat Russian misinformation entitled StopFakes (Khaldarova and Pantti 2016: 892).

WF's strategy of enrolling the public as partisans in the Kremlin's information war reflects wider, global shifts in online disinformation campaigns. Recent scholarship on propaganda and disinformation has drawn attention to new forms of persuasion, which co-opt and cultivate grassroots messaging, thus defying traditional top-down models of propaganda. Starbird, Arif and Wilson (2019) suggest the term 'collaborative work' for strategic operations that allot a central role to common users as the (sometimes unwitting) co-creators and disseminators of manipulative information. René DiResta (2021: np) has coined the term 'ampliganda' for such projects, highlighting how they involve the audience as 'an active participant in creating and selectively amplifying narratives that shape reality'. Most useful for our purpose here, however, is the notion of 'participatory propaganda', proposed by Alicia Wanless and Michael Berk (2022: 113), a term that describes 'the deliberate, and systematic attempt to shape perceptions, manipulate cognitions and direct behaviour of a target audience while seeking to co-opt its members to actively engage in the spread of persuasive communications'. Such participatory strategies constitute a more invasive form of propaganda than the one-to-many model, blurring neat distinctions between propaganda's production and consumption, and between organic and coordinated online messaging.

Pro-Kremlin messaging on Telegram and beyond

Efforts to debunk Western reporting on the war in Ukraine are widely present in the pro-war Russian Telegram sphere. Other notable examples include rlz_the_kraken, with about 200K subscribers (Silverman and Kao 2022). Channels like this routinely discredit and ridicule Western and Ukrainian journalists and politicians, but not all of them make fact-checking a central and explicit part of their identity, as does WF. Another, but related, genre of pro-Kremlin Telegram accounts includes channels run by self-proclaimed military bloggers, correspondents and analysts. Most notable among them are Wargonzo (1.3 million subscribers) and Rybar (1.1 million subscribers), which focus on military-strategic matters and report on the combat situation. The latter has been the most high-profile non-governmental channel on the war in Ukraine. Rybar publishes daily OSINT-driven updates on the military situation, especially on the positions of Ukrainian troops and material. These reports are typically accompanied by detailed maps and are based on intelligence provided by (pro-)Russian informants on the ground. Its posts have been frequently cited by major global news media like *CNN* and *Bloomberg* (Pankratova 2022a). While decidedly patriotic in tone, Rybar has occasionally criticised the Kremlin's strategic decisions, especially in the wake of the chaotic partial Russian mobilisation. The government's efforts to tighten control over this and similar channels culminated in late December 2022, when Rybar's founder Mikhail Zvinchuk (a former employee of the press service of the Ministry of Defence) was enlisted in a task force, established by President Putin, to coordinate the government's mobilisation campaign with the social media reporting by military bloggers (Kremlin 2022). At the time of analysis WF, while showing similarities with these other patriotic, war-focused outlets, remained as the largest Telegram channel with anonymous moderators and an explicit fact-checking profile, its core channel having around 800.000 subscribers.

Telegram's user base is larger than that of Twitter and the platform has the reputation of an encrypted platform. Although it does allow for secret chats, the data that we are looking at is not private. Telegram's size makes it hard to generalise, but overall the platform has a softer touch when it comes to censoring content than for instance Twitter. For this reason, it has attracted 'extreme' communities and figures that have been banned from other social media platforms and has been referred to as a 'dark corner' of the internet (Rogers 2020).

As Telegram has now banned Russian state media from the platform, following pressure from Europe (Scott 2022b), WF is arguably a significant outlet for promoting the Kremlin's narrative. Due to Telegram's design, it is difficult to determine who is responsible for creating the content of the WF cluster. An investigation of the source code of the WF website, however, shows that it is maintained by nine user accounts including one labelled as 'administrator' (Romero 2022). Beyond this, we do not definitively know who is responsible for the collection and production of the project's content. We can, however, identify the platform as a channel of state-sponsored propaganda, based on how its content is promoted via social media. In what appears as a clear strategy to weaponise Russian diplomacy (Scott 2022a), the website has been shared thousands of times on the Facebook pages of Russian embassies and official 'houses of culture', the world over (Tuters and Lazaruk 2022).

Using the Facebook research tool Crowdtangle we found in a previous analysis that the main promoters of WF content on Facebook were indeed Russian embassies and Russian houses of culture, both of which are under the jurisdiction of the Russian Ministry of Foreign Affairs. Each of their Facebook pages had on average about 10K subscribers with an average engagement rate of about 700 per post – which is a measure of participation with the content. Additionally, that same research found that Maria Zakharova, the director of the Information and Press Department of the Ministry of Foreign Affairs of the Russian Federation twice reposted WF's content from her own Telegram channel, which has a verified status intended to indicate that the content is authentic and of general public interest (Tuters and Lazaruk 2022).

A qualitative analysis of the sample of the most engaged with content from the first month of the war also revealed a thematic pattern across posts, the single most popular of which was the denial of Russian culpability for war atrocities. Among the most prolific examples of the latter are WF's efforts at debunking reporting on the massacre in Bucha. Indicative of the reach of this new kind of pro-Kremlin messaging, this research also observed that the single most engaged with Facebook reposting of WF content (outnumbering even the repostings by Russian embassies and houses of culture) was a post by the American filmmaker Oliver Stone, pointing to what he calls some 'Sherlock Holmes clues to what's really going on in Bucha'.[5] Yet, as we will see in the case below, WF does not provide real detective work, instead, like RT it foments confusion, chaos, and distrust. Yet unlike RT, rather than making the audience tune out, WF encourages them to participate.

Case study: What's really going on in Bucha, according to WarFakes

The research presented here builds on a previous empirical study of WFs, conducted by one of the authors together with a group of students shortly after the Russian military invasion of Ukraine and developed in collaboration with the Ukrainian data designer Karina Lazaruk, who in previous research has combined qualitative and quantitative methods to map WFs network and analyse a sample of the Telegram channel's content (Tuters and Lazaruk 2022). The present chapter, by contrast, seeks to drill down into a specific case study, applying a close reading method to posts on the WF channel and website pertaining to 'what's really going on in Bucha'. Indeed, a deeper understanding of WF's participatory propaganda requires close-up analysis of its investigative and interpretative work. What are the specific forms of OSINT performed by WF? Or, in Weizman and Fuller's (2021) terms, what are the modes of sensing and sense-making the channel encourages? How, in its relation to the audience, does WF inculcate heightened attention to different registers of data, and what are its methods for inferring interpretive patterns across them? Finally, how does the channel's investigative aesthetics relate to a participatory mode of propaganda?

After the retreat of Russian soldiers from Bucha in late March 2022, photographs and videos began to circulate on social media of killed Ukrainian civilians laying in the streets of this Ukrainian city. Footage recorded by the Ukrainian police and the Territorial Defence Forces, and later by CNN, BBC and AFP, showed dozens of murdered civilians, some of whom had their hands tied behind their backs and were shot in the back of the head. Testimonial evidence by Bucha residents further incriminated Russian soldiers, and Russian responsibility for the crimes was confirmed by an extensive investigation by Human Rights Watch, whose report linked Russian forces to summary executions of civilians in the city (Human Rights Watch 2022). As with practically all the events in the current war, teams of OSINT investigators also participated in 'the hunt for the butchers of Bucha' (Wise 2022).

Bucha is a relevant focal point for analysing WF's 'investigative aesthetics', due to the momentous international attention the event attracted, and the Russian government's high stakes in the case. News about Russian atrocities against civilians threatened the state-sanctioned framing of the war as a 'special military operation' with the goal to liberate the (Russian-speaking) population of Ukraine from the militant neo-Nazis and fascists purportedly ruling them. Previous research has drawn attention to the ubiquity in Russian reporting on Ukraine, ever since the Maidan protests, of a recycled late-Soviet propaganda paradigm regarding the Great Patriotic War. These repurposed the Second World War tropes typically associate Western-European fascism – including its alleged US-sponsored remanifestation in Ukraine – with atrocities against the civilian population (Gaufman 2015; Khaldarova 2021). Unsurprisingly then, the Russian government was quick to deny Russian involvement in the killings of civilians in Bucha. On their Telegram channel, the Ministry of Foreign

Affairs posted a statement in English by the Russian Ministry of Defence, which contended that 'the photos and video footage from Bucha are another hoax, a staged production and provocation by the Kiev regime for the Western media, as was the case in Mariupol with the maternity hospital, as well as in other cities' (Russian Ministry of Foreign Affairs 2022).

The Ministry's argumentation focused on three points. First, during the Russian occupation, Ukrainian troops had allegedly shelled Bucha continuously, which explained the civilian casualties. Second, directly after the Russian withdrawal on 30 and 31 March, Bucha mayor Anatolii Fedoruk had declared the liberation of the city in a video message, but, the Defence Ministry emphasised, 'did not even mention any locals shot in the streets with their hands tied' (ibid.). Evidence had, according to the ministry's statement, only started to emerge days later, which was additional proof that the killings would have been staged. Third, the photographed bodies did not show the 'typical cadaver stains' that were to be expected if they had been in Bucha's streets since March (ibid.). The arguments' incongruity was however left unaddressed: If the dead civilians had been victims of Ukrainian shelling during the Russian occupation, the purported lack of 'cadaver stains' remained unexplained. In the days that followed, more incriminating evidence against Russian soldiers continued to emerge. It is against this context of the Kremlin's official messaging on Bucha that we can observe how WF closed the gap between maintaining its grassroots pose and 'investigative' practice, while at the same time backing up the Kremlin's inconsistent and increasingly unsustainable 'staged provocation' narrative. Indeed, in observing the messaging on Bucha, the central tension in WF's participatory propaganda – between obfuscated pro-state conformism and a pose of unbiased investigative rigour – vividly comes to the fore.

In the first week after the Ministry's statement (between 3 April and 10 April), WF published 30 posts on Bucha on its Russian-language core Telegram channel, as well as three 'long-reads' on their website. While these echoed the Kremlin's conspiracy theory of Bucha as an orchestrated attempt to incriminate Russia, *none* of the posts on the core channel directly referenced the Ministry of Defence. Instead, to refute Ukrainian and Western accounts, WF relied on a diverse assortment of data and interpretations largely taken from non-governmental social media accounts, including selectively picked content from Russian news platforms such as the Latvian-based *Meduza* agency, known for its opposition to the Kremlin. In the one case that WF *did* reference the Ministry's interpretation, in one of their 'long-reads' on Bucha, they did so only by way of conclusion, noticing how their own investigative insights also appeared to align with the Kremlin's account of events (War on Fakes 2022a).

Not all 30 Telegram posts on Bucha focused directly on the massacre itself. Some drew attention to the lack of consensus about Bucha in the UN Security Council. Others situated the Bucha killings in a wider historical context of Western-staged provocations or encouraged the audience to spread WF's conclusions beyond Russia's borders. Nearly a third of the Bucha posts involved investigative aesthetics. Replicating OSINT practices, they juxtaposed digitally available data (press photos, drone images, social media video clips, citizen testimonies, etc.) and subjected them to heightened forms of watching and reading, as well as efforts at sense-making. The interpretive work drew on three, often overlapping, modes of OSINT-style analysis: the dating and geo-positioning of visual material, the identification of incongruities in the explanations of the enemy, and the detection of characteristic patterns in the behaviour of Ukrainian soldiers and their supposed Western sponsors.

Illustrative of the latter is a post of 4 April that commented on a much-discussed video presumably showing the execution of hand-bound Russian POWs by the Georgian Legion, who fight on the Ukrainian side (War on Fakes 2022c). This post drew attention to the material used to tie the Russian captives' wrists and compared it to photographs of Bucha victims in which the same material and wrist-tying technique could allegedly be seen. According to WF, this was a 'kharakternyi priznak deistvii natsionalisticheskikh batal'onov, kotoryi oni «na avtomatizme» primeniaiut vezde' [characteristic sign of the activities of nationalist [Ukrainian] battalions, [a method] they 'automatically' apply anywhere] (ibid.). In other cases, WF's sense-making was even more speculative. A post of the same day, for instance (see Figure 5.1), focused on incongruities in foreign presentations of evidence in Bucha. It showed a grid in which multiple press photos of the Bucha victims were juxtaposed. With red circles, users' attention was directed to the slightly different positions of the bodies in each of them. The same circles were used to spotlight the movement of 'rekvizit' [props], specifically a red bank card and a handbag, apparently personal belongings of the victims: 'Riadom s telom vidna krasnaia bankovskaia kartochka (priamo vozle loktia). Na drugoi fotografii eë tozhe net. Na foto Reuters eta kartochka lezhit s tremia drugimi kartochkami uzhe sil'no dal'she' [Next to the body a red bank card is visible (directly next to the elbow). In the other photograph it is absent. In the photo by Reuters the card lies with three other cards significantly further removed]. The post did not spell out its conclusion, but the close-up 'sensing' across sources, in combination with the repeated word 'props', was clearly meant to suggest that the displacement of bodies and items pointed to the massacre's staging. This interpretative frame was already announced in the post's opening, albeit through a double negative: 'Feik: Trupy na ulitse Buche ne byli "razlozheny" spetsial'no' [Fake: The bodies in the street in Bucha were not 'spread out' [there] deliberately] (War on Fakes 2022d).

Finally, the dating and geolocating of data were the central stake of WF's efforts to debunk incriminating research published by the *New York Times* (NYT) (Browne et al. 2022). The original NYT publication of 4 April had itself used OSINT methods to rebut claims by the Russian Defence Ministry that the killings were 'staged' after Russian soldiers withdrew from Bucha. The newspaper's Visual Investigations team matched satellite imagery from the company Maxar, with photographs and videos taken on the ground. Triangulating individual bodies in Bucha's Yablunska street, they dated their appearance between 9 and 11 March, during the Russian occupation. WF responded with a virulent campaign that effectively sought to *fight OSINT with OSINT*. Between 5 and 10 April, seven posts were devoted to the NYT evidence, as well as one multilingual long-read on their website.

The latter piece, titled 'Are the satellite images from Maxar's to be trusted?' – featured material from the pro-war Telegram channel Rybar, which specialises in OSINT and GEOSINT investigations. Rybar had published screenshots of the freely accessible part of Maxar's satellite logbook, which purportedly showed that there were no satellites crossing over Bucha on the specific dates mentioned by NYT. The Rybar investigators concluded that Maxar's recording had been 'sdelana 31 marta ili pozzhe' [made on or after March 31st] (War on Fakes 2022e). Using SunCalc for an astronomical analysis of shadows in Maxar's recordings, they concluded that the earliest possible satellite imagery of the bodies was from 1 April, 11 am GMT, when Ukrainian troops already controlled Bucha. WF combined this investigation with other data, packaging it in a conspiracy story about the provocation in Bucha, which allegedly fitted a long-standing pattern of Western-orchestrated staging of (visual) evidence.

These and other posts spotlight two characteristic features of WF's investigative aesthetics, the first of which is its self-presentation as 'anti-hegemonic investigation' (Fuller and Weizman 2021: 21). The implicit problem at the centre of WF's reporting on Bucha was not (only) that the truth was (supposedly) unknown, but that powerful enemies (Western organisations and journalists) had purportedly usurped and misrepresented it through trickery. Besides the anti-hegemonic work of sowing doubt, discrediting, and debunking 'mainstream' reports, WFs coverage of Bucha showed a second, related characteristic tactic, which sought to heighten the audience's sensing and sense-making. Apart from presenting the public with ready-made proof and conclusions, the channel inculcated detail-focused OSINT-style practices of reading, viewing and patterning. Thus, the moderators addressed users not as the passive consumers of a conspiracy-based alternative explanation, but as active co-investigators. Even though the fake vs truth format typically conveyed a pre-determined conclusion, the promotion of close-reading across diverse materials suggested that truth-finding was processual and required *work* to be performed by the audience.

In WF's coverage on Bucha, this 'work' pivoted on meticulous attention to visual and textual detail, as well as connections across torrents of heterogeneous data. As the moderators explained in the announcement of one of their long-reads: 'V usloviiakh informatsionnoi voiny kraine vazhno razobrat'sia v mel'chaishikh detaliakh provokatsii, kotorye gotoviat ukrainskie tekhnologi' [In a situation of information warfare it is of the highest importance to figure out the most minute details that the Ukrainian [information] technologists prepare [for us]] (War on Fakes 2022f). Users were further instructed on how to modify the material to enhance the perception of such significant minutiae:

> zdes' na 12 sekunde «trup» sprava dvigaet rukoi. Na 30 sekunde v zerkale zadnego vida «trup» saditsia. Tela na video budto by spetsial'no razlozhili radi sozdaniia bolee dramatichnoi kartinki. Eto khorosho vidno, esli vosproizvodit' video so skorost'iu 0,25 ot normal'noi.
>
> [here in the 12th second [of the clip], the 'corpse' on the right moves its hand. In the 30th second one can see in the rear view mirror a "corpse" sit up. The bodies in the video are apparently spread out [over the area] on purpose to create a more dramatic picture. This is clearly visible when the video is played at 25% of the normal speed]. (War on Fakes 2022g)

Wedding anti-hegemonic, conspiracy-based debunking to practices of investigative aesthetics, WF's coverage of Bucha thus appealed simultaneously to its users' suspicion and gullibility, while framing the audience's meticulous watching and reading 'between the lines' as a crucial contribution to the nation's information war.

Conclusion

WF's coverage of Bucha shows how easily the authority of investigative aesthetics can be turned against itself. Mimicking the NYT investigation, Rybar and WF pretended to (critically) extend the August newspaper's investigative report with a flood of swiftly produced and hard-to-check data that may have confused users, instead of rationally convincing them. In this respect, WF's content on Bucha seemed to purposefully erode rather than solidify the basis for truth-finding. At the same time, the fact-checking format, and the professed war against 'fakes', served to enlist activist publics critical of Western-dominated mainstream 'media bias' – just as RT had once sought to do with programmes like 'How to Watch the News with Slavoj Zizek'.[6] Through this tactic, WF portrays itself akin to the anarchist Indymedia network from the period immediately before the growth of social media platforms (Atton 2004). In its opposition to traditional news organisations, the 'radical media' in the period of Indymedia was generally presumed to be against the state. WF, by contrast, mobilises the critical potential of radical media precisely in the service of the state. While the project presents itself as independent and even apolitical, WF's content is consistently shared by Russian embassies across the world.

At the same time, the Bucha case demonstrates how WF's investigative aesthetics are adapted to the contemporary dynamics of the sharing economy of social media, in ways that are different from an earlier era of 'radical media'. This dynamic reaches beyond the audience's engagement with, and commenting on, WF's posts and includes encouragement to disseminate the platform's research in users' networks, thus giving online crowds a participatory role not only in sensing and sense-making, but also in the circulation of propaganda. Indeed, in the Bucha case, the moderators pointedly appealed to users to forward the channel's investigations to English-speaking acquaintances, friends and relatives. As one of the bilingual posts put it, this might be 'the only way they will be able to see an alternative and objective view of the events and find out what is really happening' (War on Fakes 2022h).

Ultimately, WFs participatory ethos extended to the very sources of the channel's propagandistic content. In the reporting on Bucha, the channel frequently curated, and borrowed from, investigative work published by multiple other (apparently) non-governmental social media accounts. As seen above, WF leaned heavily on the OSINT work presented on Rybar. Even before Rybar's official inclusion in Vladimir Putin's task force on the Russian mobilisation campaign, the independent Russian news platform The Bell published material indicating that Rybar received funding from the oligarch and Putin confidant Yevgenii Progozhin, and that the project may be connected with the Russian Federal Security Service (Pankratova 2022a; 2022b). Nevertheless, throughout 2022, Rybar strove to maintain its pose of objectivity. At the end of that year, the 'support the project' button on the channel still linked users to a text characterising the Rybar project in terms similar to WF's grassroots self-description: 'Rybar is a non-commercial project that exists on the naked enthusiasm of the owners and on the [Russian] population's efforts' (Rybar 2022). Via WF, content from platforms like Rybar entered the official information channels of the Russian state. The Russian embassy in Slovakia, for instance, reposted WF's Maxar long-read (in Slovakian translation) on its Facebook page.[7] This closely aligns with the concept of 'ampliganda' (DiResta 2021) and underlines the multi-directional, cross-platform dynamics through which it tends to operate.

On all these various levels – the encouragement of users' heightened attention to visual minutiae, the speculative suggestion of patterns to be cognitively completed by the users themselves, the channel's mining of non-governmental social media accounts for useful material, and the request to share its content widely – WF's propaganda hinges on the online public's participation. It is hard to find a clearer example of the state's co-optation of the affordances of social media, both their sharing economy and their radical aesthetics – which are today embodied by OSINT – than the WF project. Yet, this combination of state co-optation and the ethos of grassroots participation frequently left WF in an awkward position, as illustrated by the advice that occasionally accompanied the reporting on Bucha:

> Vsegda neobkhodimo vnimatel'no, vzveshenno i vdumchivo sledit' za situatsiei, pereprover'iat' postupaiushchuiu informatsiiu i zhdat' ofitsial'nykh podtverzhdenii ili oproverzhenii. Tak vy uberezhëte sebia i svoikh blizkikh ot strashnogo oruzhiia desinformatsii i propagandy.
>
> [It is always necessary to follow the situation attentively, carefully, and thoughtfully, to double-check the incoming information and wait for official confirmation or denial. That way you will protect yourself and your loved ones from the terrible weapon of disinformation and propaganda]. (War on Fakes 2022a)

Retaining the ethos of a critical fact-checking platform, by and for citizen-investigators, the passage simultaneously advocates patient alignment with 'official confirmations and denials', referring to those coming from the Kremlin. This irreconcilable mix of criticism and conformism goes to the heart of WF's participatory propaganda and its consistent support of the Kremlin's denial of Russian responsibility for the atrocities in Ukraine.

Notes

1 This article is developed from empirical research initially conducted with Karyna Lazaruk, Borka Balogh, Marta Ceccarelli, Emillie de Keulenaar, Kiara Khorram, Devin Mitter, Son Nguyen, Stijn Peeters, Emilie Schwantzer, Cemal Tahir, Alexander Teggin, Yana Mashkova and Anton Mishchuk.
2 https://t.me/s/warfakes and https://waronfakes.com.
3 https://www.bellingcat.com/tag/mh17/.
4 All translations from Russian are our own unless otherwise noted.
5 https://www.facebook.com/100044201750919/posts/537980271018693, accessed 24 January 2023.
6 https://archive.org/details/RT_20190322_113000_How_to_Watch_the_News_with_Slavoj_Zizek.
7 https://www.facebook.com/100068847295360/posts/283622387276002, accessed 24 January 2023.

References

Armstrong, M. (2015). 'RT As a Foreign Agent: Political Propaganda in a Globalized World', *War on the Rocks*, 4 May, https://warontherocks.com/2015/05/rt-as-a-foreign-agent-political-propaganda-in-a-globalized-world/, accessed 30 March 2023.

Atton, C. (2004). *An Alternative Internet: Radical Media, Politics and Creativity*. Edinburgh: Edinburgh University Press.

boyd, d. (2018). 'You Think You Want Media Literacy … Do You?', *Data and Society*, https://points.datasociety.net/you-think-you-want-media-literacy-do-you-7cad6af18ec2, accessed 30 March 2023.

Browne, M., Botti, D., and Willis, H. (2022). 'Satellite Images Show Bodies Lay in Bucha for Weeks, Despite Russian Claims', *The New York Times*, 4 April, https://www.nytimes.com/2022/04/04/world/europe/bucha-ukraine-bodies.html, accessed 30 March 2023.

DiResta, R. (2021). 'It's Not Misinformation. It's Amplified Propaganda', *The Atlantic*, 9 October, https://www.theatlantic.com/ideas/archive/2021/10/disinformation-propaganda-amplification-ampliganda/620334/, accessed 30 March 2023.

Faraj, S., and Azad, B. (2013). 'The Materiality of Technology: An Affordance Perspective'. In Leonardi, P., Nardi, A., and Kallinikos, J. (eds), *Materiality and Organizing: Social Interaction in a Technological World*, pp. 237–58. Oxford: Oxford University Press.

Fuller, M., and Weizman, E. (2021). *Investigative Aesthetics: Conflicts and Commons in the Politics of Truth*. London: Verso Books.

Gaufman, E. (2015). 'Memory, Media, and Securitization: Russian Media Framing of the Ukrainian Crisis', *Journal of Soviet and Post-Soviet Politics and Society*, 1 (1), 141–73.

Human Rights Watch. (2022). 'Ukraine: Russian Forces' Trail of Death in Bucha: Preserving Evidence Critical for War Crimes Prosecutions', 21 April, https://www.hrw.org/news/2022/04/21/ukraine-russian-forces-trail-death-bucha, accessed 14 April 2023.

Jane, E., and Fleming, C. (2014). *Modern Conspiracy: The Importance of Being Paranoid*. London: Bloomsbury.

Khaldarova, I. (2021). 'Brother or "Other"? Transformation of Strategic Narratives in Russian Television News During the Ukrainian Crisis', *Media, War & Conflict*, 14 (1), 3–20.

Khaldarova, I., and Pantti, M. (2016). 'Fake News: The Narrative Battle over the Ukrainian Conflict', *Journalism Practice*, 10 (7), 891–901.

Kremlin. (2022). 'Rasporiazhenie o rabochei gruppe po obespecheniiu vzaimodeistviia organov publichnoi vlasti i organizatsii po voprosam mobilizatsionnoi podgotovki i mobilizatsii, sotsial'noi i pravovoi zashchity uchastnikov spetsial'noi voennoi operatsii', *Kremlin.ru*, 20 December, http://kremlin.ru/acts/news/70155, accessed 30 March 2023.

Mackey, R. (2022). 'Russian TV Is Filled with Images of Bucha's Dead, Stamped with the Word "Fake"', *The Intercept*, 4 April 2022, https://theintercept.com/2022/04/12/bucha-massacre-russia-tv-fake-ukraine-war/, accessed 30 March 2023.

Noordenbos, B. (2023). 'A (Cold) War for Vaccines: Retro-Conspiracism in Kremlin-Aligned Russian Discourse on Sputnik V'. In P. Knight and M. Butter (eds), *Covid Conspiracy Theories in Global Perspective*, chapter 21. London: Routledge.

Pankratova, I. (2022a). 'Kto vedet voennyi telegram-kanal "Rybar": rassledovanie The Bell', *The Bell*, 16 November, https://thebell.io/kto-vedet-voennyy-telegram-kanal-rybar-rassledovanie-the-bell, accessed 30 March 2023.

Pankratova, I. (2022b). 'Sozdatel' "Rybaria." Prodolzhenie rassledovaniia The Bell', *The Bell*, 19 November, https://thebell.io/sozdatel-rybarya-prodolzhenie-rassledovaniya-the-bell

Rankin, J. (2022). 'Three Men Found Guilty of Murdering 298 People in Shooting Down of MH17' *The Guardian*, 17 November, https://www.theguardian.com/world/2022/nov/17/three-men-found-guilty-of-murdering-298-people-in-flight-mh17-bombing, accessed 30 March 2023.

Rogers, R. (2020). 'Deplatforming: Following Extreme Internet Celebrities to Telegram and Alternative Social Media', *European Journal of Communication*, 35 (3), 213–29.

Romero, L. (2022). 'How "War on Fakes" Uses Fact-Checking to Spread Pro-Russia Propaganda', https://www.politifact.com/article/2022/aug/08/how-war-fakes-uses-fact-checking-spread-pro-russia/, accessed 30 March 2023.

Russian Ministry of Foreign Affairs. (2022). 'Statement by the Russian Defence Ministry', Telegram channel *Russian MFA*, 3 April, https://t.me/s/MFARussia/12230, accessed 30 March 2023.

Rybar. (2022). 'Rekvizity dlia pomoshchi komande Rybaria', 3 May 2022, https://telegra.ph/Rekvizity-dlya-pomoshchi-komande-Rybarya-05-03, accessed 30 March 2023.

Scott, M. (2022a). 'Russia Turns Its Diplomats into Disinformation Warriors', *POLITICO*, 7 April, https://www.politico.eu/article/russia-diplomats-disinformation-war-ukraine/, accessed 30 March 2023.

Scott, M. (2022b) 'Telegram Bans Russian State Media After Pressure from Europe', *POLITICO*, 4 March, https://www.politico.eu/article/russia-rt-media-telegram-ukraine/, accessed 30 March 2023.

Sharafutdinova, G. (2020). *The Red Mirror: Putin's Leadership and Russian's Insecure Identity*. Oxford: Oxford University Press.

Silverman, C., and Kao, J. (2022). 'In the Ukraine Conflict, Fake Fact-Checks are Being Used to Spread Disinformation', *Nieman Lab*, 10 March, https://www.niemanlab.org/2022/03/in-the-ukraine-conflict-fake-fact-checks-are-being-used-to-spread-disinformation/, accessed 14 April 2023.

Starbird, K., Arif, A., and Wilson, T. (2019). 'Disinformation as Collaborative Work: Surfacing the Participatory Nature of Strategic Information Operations', *Proceedings of the ACM on Human-Computer Interaction*, 3 (CSCW), 127:1–127:26.

Tolz, V., and Teper, Y. (2018). 'Broadcasting Agitainment: A New Media Strategy of Putin's Third Presidency', *Post-Soviet Affairs*, 34 (4), 213–27.

Tuters, M., and Lazaruk, K. (2022). *Weaponized OSINT: The New Kremlin-Sponsored Participatory Propaganda*, https://networkcultures.org/tactical-media-room/2022/07/22/weaponized-osint-the-new-kremlin-sponsored-participatory-propaganda/, accessed 2 April 2023.

Wanless, A., and Berk, M. (2022). 'Participatory Propaganda: The Engagement of Audiences in the Spread of Persuasive Communications'. In D. Herbert & S. Fisher Høyrem (eds), *Social Media and Social Order*, chapter 8. Berlin: De Gruyter, 111–137.

War on Fakes. (2022a). 'Chto sluchilos' v Buche? Polnyi razbor ukrainskoi provokatsii', Telegram channel *Voina s Feikami*, 5 April 2022, https://войнасфейками.рф/civil/chto-sluchilos-v-buche-polnyj-razbor-ukrainskoj-provokacii/, accessed 14 April 2023.

War on Fakes. (2022b). 'Manifest: Welcome to the "War on Fakes" Project', *War on Fakes*, no date, https://waronfakes.com, accessed 2 April 2023.

War on Fakes. (2022c). 'Feik: Rossiiskie voiska zaviazyvaiut ruki belymi lentami za spinoi i rasstrelivaiut mirnykh zhitelei', Telegram channel *Voina s Feikami*, 4 April 2022, https://t.me/warfakes/1949, accessed 2 April 2023.

War on Fakes. (2022d). 'Feik: Trupy na ulitse v Buche ne byli "razlozheny" spetsial'no', Telegram channel *Voina s Feikami*, 4 April 2022, https://t.me/warfakes/1948, accessed 2 April 2023.

War on Fakes. (2022e). 'Stoit li doveriat' sputnikovym video ot Maxar', Telegram channel *Voina s Feikami*, 5 April 2022, https://войнасфейками.рф/analitika/stoit-li-doverjat-sputnikovym-video-ot-maxar/, accessed 2 April 2023.

War on Fakes. (2022f). 'V usloviakh informatsionnoi voiny kraine vazhno razobrat'sia v mel'chaishikh detaliakh provokatsii, kotorye gotoviat ukrainskie tekhnologi', Telegram channel *Voina s Feikami*, 5 April 2022, https://t.me/warfakes/1965, accessed 2 April 2023.

War on Fakes. (2022g). 'Feik: Rossiiskie voennye pokinuli Buchu, predvaritel'no ostaviv ogromnye zhertvy sredi mirnogo naseleniia', Telegram channel *Voina s Feikami*, 3 April 2022, https://t.me/warfakes/1896, accessed 2 April 2023.

War on Fakes. (2022h). 'Ves' mir pristal'no sledit za tem, chto seichas proiskhodit v gorode Bucha', Telegram channel *Voina s Feikami*, 4 April 2022, https://t.me/warfakes/1940, accessed 2 April 2023.

Wise, J. (2022). 'The Hunt for the Butchers of Bucha', *Intelligencer*, 8 April, https://nymag.com/intelligencer/2022/04/osint-sleuths-hunt-for-russian-war-criminals-in-bucha.html, accessed 2 April 2023.

Yablokov, I., and Chatterje-Doody, P. (2022). *Russia Today and Conspiracy Theories: People, Power and Politics on RT*. London: Routledge.

Part Three:
Everyday Media in War

· 6 ·

TIKTOK(ING) UKRAINE: MEME-BASED EXPRESSIONS OF CULTURAL TRAUMA ON SOCIAL MEDIA

Tom Divon and Moa Eriksson Krutrök

As digital media pervades every aspect of our lives, the ways in which we record, view and respond to wars are being shaped by these technologies. Within our deeply mediatised society (Couldry and Hepp 2017), in times of crisis, individuals turn to social media to tell their stories of trauma and grief (Eriksson 2016; Leaver and Highfield 2018). This allows the specific realities of war, trauma and collective suffering to be witnessed, shared, seen and remixed. This chapter delves into the war in Ukraine as it is depicted and mediated through the lens of one of the most prominent Ukrainian TikTok users of 2022, Valeria Shashenok (@valerisssh). Through this example, we examine how ongoing cultural trauma and its audiovisual representations are presented on digital platforms. In particular, we explore how users leverage TikTok's technological features, such as duets, stitches and the LIVE, to create meme-based templates for communicating the realities of warfare, showing how these templates shape digital expressions of trauma. Expanding previous work on cultural trauma, collective grief, and history in digital spaces (Abidin, 2019; Divon and Ebbrecht-Hartmann 2022; Eriksson 2016; 2018; Eriksson Krutrök 2021; Leaver & Highfield 2018), this chapter places emphasis on the role of audiovisual memes on TikTok as templates for war storytelling in Ukraine in 2022.

War influencers

At the time of writing, @valerisssh is a twenty-one-year-old Ukrainian TikTok user, characterised as a war influencer for her consistent TikTok uploads that highlight the daily challenges of residing in a conflict-ridden region of Ukraine. We define war influencers as users who inhabit a distinctive space on social media, located at the intersection of citizen journalism (Allan and Thorsen 2009), voluntary witnessing (Klausen 2015), microcelebrity activism (Tufekci 2013), and online content creation (Brake 2014). While war influencers produce content to 'get attention and build social capital' (Gómez 2019: 15), they do so with the intention of reporting, commenting on and amplifying audience knowledge and attention regarding the traumatic scenery of a war zone.

War influencers reside in sites of trauma and invite masses of people to consume snippets of their realities of war by using unconventional means of popular internet dialects (i.e. humour, irony and memes). They subvert the conventional standards of evidence required of journalists from war-torn regions, commonly referred to as the *burden of proof* (Lionis 2020). These individuals are often expected to serve as ambassadors, imparting a didactic retelling of their experiences with trauma, marginalisation and political upheaval. However, war influencers are not bound by the same ethical and normative standards as those involved in more professionalised forms of trauma communication, and they lack any institutional affiliations typical of media outlets or social movements.

War influencers can contribute to the commodification of trauma. They seek recognition by leveraging the conventional practices of content crafting on social media (i.e. TikTok's memes and dances); in this way, they are able to create a distinct form of trauma aesthetic. This aesthetic can be considered as a set of audiovisual and textual affective codes that are performed by users who translate trauma into content and transform the profound traumatic gravity of war to others via templates for content creation. This type of communicative aesthetic is 'entangled with the technical structures of the platforms that are used' (Schreiber 2017: 145) and has political and epistemological consequences for how users are informed and educated about wars, atrocities and traumas on TikTok.

@valerisssh has become well known as a war influencer for her quirky and memetic storytelling visuals from inside Ukraine, and she has rapidly accumulated 1.3 million followers (as of April 2023). Her first war-related video ('POV: Living in a Bomb Shelter') achieved viral status, propelling her to become the most recognisable content creator on TikTok who addresses the invasion of Ukraine. Amid tragic events such as losing her brother, the destruction of her friends' houses and taking refuge in a local bomb shelter, she has been able to provide millions of TikTok users around the world with a real-time glimpse into the harsh realities of war. Journalists have compared @valerisssh's public resonance to that of Anne Frank regarding the Holocaust, as both documented their time under occupation and (un)intentionally created rare autobiographies (Vidal Egea 2022). Their different media for documentation – analogue and digital diaries – are embedded in their message, resulting in an intimate portrayal of their mundane lives under war.

@valerisssh, as a witness of existential insecurity, has attempted to galvanise the world into action, using her content as a vehicle for expressing trauma. In a BBC interview in March 2022, she expressed her intent to show international audiences the everyday realities of the war to deflect from the idea that it is a 'Ukrainian problem'; instead, she emphasised that 'this is a world problem' (BBC News 2022), echoing the way in which politicians and media personalities also addressed the war. Most prominently, Ukrainian president Volodymyr Zelensky stated in a public appearance during the same month that 'the world must stop the war' (Thebault and Pannett 2022). In the middle of March 2022, she fled the ongoing war in Ukraine, moving to Italy via Poland. According to the UN refugee agency (UNHCR 2022), 7,405,590 Ukrainians have become refugees since 24 February 2022. Until fleeing Ukraine, @valerisssh had posted around fifty videos on her everyday experiences of war. Through her daily updates as a refugee, @valerisssh enabled her million followers to closely follow and immerse themselves in her journey, with many expressing relief in the comments section upon witnessing her 'get out safe'.

In late June 2022, @valerisssh released a Kindle ebook titled *Things That Just Make Sense in a Bomb Shelter*, featuring some of her most popular TikTok content. The title capitalises on the well-known TikTok meme template of 'things in (...) that just make sense', which has gained significant traction on the platform. Currently, @valerisssh is sharing videos on TikTok that chronicle the process of filming a documentary on her experiences as a Ukrainian refugee, as well as her participation in international events related to cultural diplomacy. In September 2022, she was invited to the European Parliament and met with the president of the European Commission, Ursula von der Leyen, and other high-profile parliamentarians. These events have been continuously documented on her TikTok account.

Cultural trauma memes

Memes are a form of user-generated content, reproduced by imitation and rapidly spread, often with creative variations of their content, form and stance (Shifman 2014). In Dawkins' (1976) original coinage of the term *meme*, the concept specifically focused on how cultural contexts move between individuals. Within internet communities, memes refer to multimodal communicative expressions in digital contexts, reflecting both political and societal issues in playful ways. According to Mortensen and Neumeyer (2021: 2375), memes 'stay within the subversive and create frontiers to political elites and the mainstream, but in their playful appropriation of political contexts, they may challenge and push these very same frontiers'; moreover, 'as their template travels effortlessly, memes continue to playfully appropriate new political contexts and to (re)negotiate frontiers in the political'.

There are various ways in which this can be achieved. Zidani (2021) explored the ways in which Palestinians living in Israel framed political issues using cynical and critical memes to represent the ongoing conflict zone. Cervi and Divon (2023) found that Palestinians used memes as audiovisual templates, utilising the playful affordances of platforms such as TikTok to communicate their suffering and struggle in the Israeli–Palestinian conflict. As highly replicable and mutable digital artefacts, memes were also harnessed as *counterspectacles* (McCrow-Young and Mortensen 2021) as part of a strategy by users to generate meme-based public engagement against the terror organisation ISIS.

As observed by Merrill and Lindgren (2021), in the wake of the bombing of the Manchester Arena in 2017, the city's enduring civic symbol, the Manchester bee, was reinvigorated in public responses to the traumatic event through both digital and non-digital channels, including hashtag usage (#manchesterbee) and social media-shared images. Additionally, specific meme figures, such as kitten memes, have been observed to serve as coping mechanisms in the face of acts of terrorism (Jensen et al. 2020), while some memes are crafted with a grotesque aesthetic, inherently conveying subversiveness (Galip 2021). In this manner, collectives can harness memes to summon the engagement of digital publics within distinct timeframes and various contexts, such as fostering a sense of collective identity within minority communities like the LGBTQ (Gal, Shifman and Kampf 2016) or during periods of conflict to galvanize engagement in national identity activism (Divon 2022).

Through memes and the culture of digital responsiveness, it becomes evident that the understanding and representation of cultural trauma can vary, particularly in relation to historical events, leading to conflicts among individuals over narratives and collective memory. Notable examples include animated e-cards challenging hegemonic memory in the context of the Soviet victory in Russia (Makhortykh and Sydorova 2017), the *edit wars* between Russian users over Wikipedia pages depicting the country's disputed history with Ukraine (Dounaevsky 2013) and the use of Instagram comments and visuals to amplify *dark tourism* at Holocaust-related sites (Commane and Potton 2019).

Users possess the ability to negotiate, challenge and enter into dialogue with narratives of past cultural traumas, leading them to rapidly adapt to digital platforms' affordances (Gibson 1977). Generally used to describe what media technologies allow users to do, affordances are the 'multi-faceted relational structure between an object/technology and the user that enables or constrains potential behavioural outcomes in a particular context' (Evans et al. 2017: 36). By enabling cultural trauma to weave through social media's vernaculars of features, practices and aesthetics, the affordances of digital platforms extend users' invitations to international audiences to witness, cope with, commemorate, learn from and discuss globalised and marginalised cultural traumas of the past and present.

Trauma on TikTok: Features, memes and #Challenge

The importance of studying the relationship between mediatised traumas and users' online grassroots coping mechanisms is evident in the case of @valerisssh's profile. This 'holistic case study' (Van Hout and Bingham 2013: 386) shows how @valerisssh captures TikTok's emerging tendency for users to translate adversities into this platform's playful audiovisual grammar of features, memes and trends. TikTok has emerged as one of the fastest-growing social media platforms worldwide. As a platform built around short-form user-generated videos, it enables users to actively contribute and engage with content by creating short-looping videos on a wide range of topics (Kennedy 2020). Through a small-scale video editing timeline, users can manipulate their content with in-camera speed controls, image composites, collaborative split screens, filters, music, lip-synching templates and various socio-technical affordances. These assemblages of social and technical affordances enabled by the interface design are seen as 'action-taking possibilities and meaning-making opportunities' (Vatrapu 2009: 1), allowing a dynamic interplay between digital environments and users.

The design of TikTok capitalises on its users' short attention span, and the platform's infrastructure matches their scrolling habits. On opening the platform, users face the 'For You' page. This is TikTok's landing page, where users engage with personalised content streams and 'actively seek out, learn, participate in, and engage in what is "going viral" at the moment' (Abidin 2021: 79). Users can communicate on the 'For You' page with the help of digital connectors such as hashtags, keywords, filters and audio memes. TikTok's fast-paced environment stimulates users to become active creators ('TikTokers'), who are urged to produce their own content rather than simply consume it. TikTokers enjoy the creative freedom to play and experiment; however, the platform can simultaneously circumscribe their creativity by nudging them towards certain visibility norms (Zeng and Kaye 2022) and 'penalize' them for lack of discipline in content creation that doesn't align with the platform's vernaculars (Duffy and Meisner 2023).

TikTok provides a venue for users to express and communicate cultural trauma through its distinct vernaculars. Gibbs et al. (2015: 257) described platform vernaculars as the 'genres of communication' that 'emerge from the affordances of particular social media platforms and the ways they are appropriated and performed in practice'. Medina Serrano et al. (2020) underscored how TikTok's technical features allow for interaction in so-called *communication trees* using the platform's *duet* function. This function is shown on the right-hand side of the screen, and it enables users to respond to other users' videos while keeping the original posts intact. In this way, users can react, critique, endorse or comment on the original video in new and creative ways. Ebbrecht-Hartmann and Divon (2022) explored the dialogic structure of the duet in the context of history-related content, examining how the feature allows users to react to Holocaust survivors' testimonies, autobiographies and traumatic memories. The circulation of duet videos on TikTok creates a novel practice of digital co-witnessing resulting in the establishment of a commemorative community (Divon and Ebbrecht-Hartmann 2022).

Other functions, such as the *stitch*, enable communication to be *sewn* with and through other videos on TikTok. By digitally quoting a particular part of another video, the stitch can be used as a tool for criticising problematic statements, such as comparisons between the persecution of Jews during the Holocaust and anti-vaxxers opposing state regulations against the COVID-19 pandemic (Ebbrecht-Hartmann and Divon 2022). Through the stitch feature, users have been able to amplify the visibility of burning social issues and develop innovative ways of self-expression and resilience. For example, the feature has been used to highlight the struggles of immigrant communities (Jaramillo-Dent et al., 2022), and for the GriefTok community, the stitch was used to challenge traditional norms surrounding mourning and created new forms of digital grieving (Eriksson Krutrök, 2021). Another communicative feature is the *response to comments*, which provides interactive possibilities for TikTok creators, viewers and commenters to be in constant dialogue with and amplify one another's voices. This is the case with TransTok, whose community members use this feature to expose, educate and form a safe space for trans people to share their hardships and traumas (Olivares García 2022).

TikTok has emerged as a prominent platform where users feel comfortable sharing their intimate thoughts and experiences. Beyond its features for video production and user interaction, the platform's powerful audiovisual grammar of memes redefines conventional coping mechanisms by allowing trauma to be explored through play, subversion, and performative affect (Cervi and Divon 2023). Blending 'pop culture, politics and participation in unexpected ways' (Shifman 2014: 4), memes are grounded in contextualism, as their interpretations are dependent on the cultural and subcultural understandings of users. With each new remix, memes are reappropriated to produce new iterations and variations of broader ideas, making the 'quintessential participatory artefact: open, collaborative and adaptable' (Milner 2013: 12).

On TikTok, memes' participatory nature is often conveyed through the culture of *challenges*. These are collaborative tasks initiated by random individuals and governed by a set of performative guidelines that inspire users to adopt a competitive, playful and creative mindset. Zulli and Zulli (2020: 11) examined the formation of 'imitation publics', which refers to the 'collection of people whose digital connectivity is constituted through the shared ritual of content imitation and replication' around the culture of TikTok challenges. Extending the typical structure, challenges are complex multimodal memes configured by layers of moving images, text and sound, and they are widely disseminated as part of the continuous algorithmic amplification of viral videos. Participation in challenges necessitates that users have a high degree of attunement to the specific task at hand, as well as proficiency in utilising the templates provided, which, in turn, enhances their mastery of vernacular literacy and increases their chances of achieving algorithmic visibility (Zeng and Abidin 2021).

TikTok's audio-meme challenges have become an internet practice in which users playfully experiment with and subvert cultural discourses and norms, including cultural traumas. While challenges inhabit the platform's driving force of mimesis and serve as many users' preferred idiom, sound, which has already been contextualised as a *memetic text* (Zulli and Zulli 2020), is at the core of their virality. Sound becomes harnessed as audio memes, which have been considered the 'driving template and organising principle' (Abidin 2021: 80) of TikTok videos. Users employ replicable units of viral sound and then remix, repurpose and incorporate them into videos as background music or as lip-syncing material. Users are encouraged to invent new contexts and stories using creative strategies to generate unique storytelling environments that spark feelings of belonging and solidarity (Vizcaíno-Verdú and Abidin 2022). Audio-meme challenges on TikTok can be seen as a playful practice through which users draw algorithmic attention to critical sociopolitical issues and traumatic events, leveraging the viral dissemination and exposure of sounds. For instance, in the context of school shootings in the United States, TikTok's audio-meme challenges have conveyed the tragic dimension of generational trauma, often translated into parody memes that satirize the character of a shooter (Vickery 2020).

Living in a bomb shelter

The first time @valerisssh gained attention on TikTok was on 26 February 2022, when she re-uploaded a video with English text that had initially been posted two days earlier in Ukrainian. In this video, @valerisssh is shown in full in front of the camera, snapping her fingers to the popular Italian song 'Che La Luna', sung by Louis Prima in 1972. This Sicilian song has received worldwide popularity and is performed in a so-called tarantella, a form of Italian folk dance music with an upbeat tempo. As @valerisssh sways, snapping her fingers to the music, the text layered on top of the video reads as follows: 'THINGS IN OUR BOMB SHELTER WHAT MAKE SENSE,' illustrating a 'things in (...) that just make sense' meme template where specific aspects of a person's surroundings serve as evidence of a particular situation or context; these videos often feature niche cultural elements, such as kitchen utilities from specific parts of the world or creative solutions to household problems.
This is a type of meme showing a specific point-of-view (POV). On TikTok, users employ the POV shot differently from its traditional usage. Rather than focusing solely on the user's perspective through their eyes, it presents the user as a whole, turning them into a medium for depicting specific situations. In this context, the POV adopts performative dimensions, effectively turning these videos into political spectacles intended to raise awareness about contentious

issues such as gender, violence, and racism (Cervi and Divon 2023). @valerisssh used this memeified template to show her life in a bomb shelter. Her initial frame, featuring her lightly bouncing and snapping her fingers, transitions to showcase various aspects of her daily life in the shelter. First, she captures her father sitting at a desk with his computer and keyboard, rhythmically snapping his fingers from side to side. The accompanying text overlay on this brief sequence reads, 'Dad made office like a shelter,' indicating that her father has transformed a section of the bomb shelter into his makeshift office. In the following scene, her mother exuberantly joins in, wearing a smile as she leaps and dances to the music, accompanied by the overlaid text, 'Mom wanna go to Poland and pick strawberries.' While continuing to snap her fingers in time with the song, @valerisssh provides glimpses of their surroundings, including their makeshift 'Ukrainian military breakfast' featuring bananas and a package of cookies, their 'Personal gym,' and a 'Shower for cleaning ass,' among other facilities. These scenes collectively emphasize that the cellar has been repurposed into a living space during the war.

As the video ends, @valerisssh shows their refrigerator with a few tin cans, a salad and leftovers wrapped in plastic. The text reads, 'Fridge with out avocado', accompanied by a puking emoji. This underscores TikTok users' inclination to prioritize everyday aesthetics over the depiction of glamorous lifestyles, as illustrated by her depiction of everyday struggles. Through her point-of-view (POV), she encourages viewers to immerse themselves in her world, fostering active participation rather than passive observation. (Raun 2012). As an iconic symbol of youthful aesthetics, avocado toast has gained widespread popularity as the quintessential snack to showcase on social media, even leading to the coining of the term 'avocado-toast millennials' (Mizrahi 2021). Through a clever reference to avocados, @valerisssh taps into the widely recognized trope of avocado consumption as a symbol of indulgence and financial comfort. However, she subverts this notion by drawing attention to the absence of avocados in her bomb shelter fridge, conveyed with a puking emoji. This creative use of symbolism effectively conveys the disruption of everyday life during wartime. In doing so, she offers a glimpse of the sacrifices made by people in war zones to avocado-toast millennials while leveraging the ironic tone that characterizes TikTok's vernacular.

Another iteration of this meme – 'MY TYPICAL DAY IN A BOMB SHELTER' – instantly accumulated more than 750,000 likes. In this version, as in the original one, @valerisssh takes the viewers on a quick walkthrough, providing a glimpse into the surreal reality of life during times of war, as she perceives it. For example, standing in her pyjamas in the middle of the bomb shelter, she creatively employs a heat gun as a makeshift hairdryer, exemplifying how everyday objects can be repurposed to navigate the unconventional challenges of life in such conditions, where adaptability and improvisation are paramount Nevertheless, @valerisssh broadens viewers' understanding of the repercussions of war by transitioning them beyond the shelter's confines and revealing the devastation inflicted by Russian bombs through her POV footage. She implores her followers to 'check out what Putin do' in her city, underscored by a cluster of hugging face emojis.

Once again, TikTok's vernacular of playfulness, irony and cynicism creates an experience infused with dissonance through the use of emojis. Ordinarily, hugging face emojis are linked to expressing emotions of joy, achievement, and optimism. However, in @valerisssh's video, these emojis, among others, do not align with the typical cultural expectations of how to mediate atrocities online. Still, on TikTok, normalised performances of emotions have a place for insurrection, recreation and sophistication due to the platform's technosocial affordances allowing users to 'playfully experiment with and subvert cultural discourses and norms' (Vickery 2020: 2). The intricate blend of audiovisual elements within the video, including text, sceneries of ruins and bombarded structures, emojis, and upbeat sound, is orchestrated through TikTok's memetic labour, and creates an affective resonance that may appeal to younger individuals, allowing for a collective sense-making experience in the face of adversity. This emotional impact is evident through the emergence of a responsive community around the video, where users collectively cope with the traumatic images of war by replying with duets or stitches to @valerisssh's video, expressing gestures of shock and sorrow while filming themselves watching her videos, and adding messages expressing empathy ('my heart goes out to Ukraine').

The participation in this challenge, which involves the use of the 'things in (...) that just make sense' meme to repurpose content into new memeified templates, demonstrates how the continuous creation of memes on the platform allows an extended temporality for spreading awareness in war zones. Spanning 15 to 30 seconds, a challenge's memetic cycle triggers user reactions to each subsequent iteration, generating powerful loops of videos that continuously amplify and disseminate the experience of trauma, resulting in increasing affective exposure to the realities of war. TikTok's 'imitation publics', as described by Zulli and Zulli (2020), reuse sounds and memes in a collective ritual of remixing available templates on the platform to express their critical sociopolitical concerns. As new memes continually surface, these challenges, which entail the reimagining and recreating of content from the perspectives of individual users like @valerisssh, persist over time. Consequently, audio memes on TikTok take on a central role in storytelling, offering a structure for contextualising the ongoing war.

'It's (War) Corn'

As new meme challenges arise on TikTok, their structural elements are seamlessly integrated into the narrative of individual users' content. One such meme challenge encouraged social media users to use a specific sound referencing corn. The original clip was uploaded in August 2022, many months after @valerisssh had fled Ukraine, and it included an interview with a child eating corn. This clip gained virality on TikTok and subsequently on Twitter, Instagram and other platforms. The interview was carried out by the Instagram account @recesstherapy, where interviewers go out into the street to ask children questions. The original post has since been viewed more than 26 million times (Abidin 2022). The instant phenomenon of the corn kid was based on his funny responses to the interviewer's questions. For instance, when asked about his fondness for corn, he enthusiastically exclaims, 'I mean look at this thing. I can't imagine a more beautiful thing! It's CORN!' These interview segments were later transformed into a song[1] that became a part of over 390,000 TikTok videos showcasing users' love for a wide range of topics, from workouts and partners to pets.

By using this popular sound, @valerisssh was able to recreate the traumatic experience of the war in Ukraine. In her video from 30 August 2022, she uses the corn sound with clips from several of her previously posted videos of February and March 2022. In this video, she repurposes older footage, incorporating a mismatched hand gesture borrowed from her previous content to adapt to a new meme format, showcasing how her videos are intentionally designed to fit within existing meme structures. This strategy of recontextualising and reusing her content through trending audio is one way in which her documentation of the war is able to extend linear forms of storytelling about ongoing trauma. In this video, viewers are taken back to Chernihiv's streets, where they witness the aftermath of previous bombings, an abandoned supermarket, and the kitchen of their bomb shelter, where @valerisssh's mother is seen cooking once more. By utilising archived footage from her time in Ukraine, @valerisssh leverages the corn meme challenge to effectively communicate the devastation of her former hometown to TikTok's audience, emphasizing that the conflict in

Ukraine is not a relic of the past but an ongoing reality that continues to shape the lives of those affected by it.

The provocative footage shown in the playful demonstration of warfare, combined with the 'It's Corn' sound, not only captured the attention of users but also gained sustained algorithmic visibility on TikTok, remaining on users' 'For You' pages for an extended period. This video received 3.8 million likes in a matter of days and more than 40,000 comments. It was bookmarked almost 150,000 times and shared within and outside of the platform 11,500 times. As proposed by Zeng and Abidin (2021), the strategy of reusing popular memes is vital for individual users' visibility on the platform. Thus, @valerisssh's repurposing of old footage extends the temporality of her war experiences, effectively revitalizing older content and allowing it to re-enter viral circulation on TikTok. In this way, cultural trauma becomes incorporated into ongoing reformulations of mediated content creation, facilitated by the affordances of digital platforms. By playfully appropriating and co-opting viral sound-based memetic templates, @valerisssh places cultural trauma within empathetic and interactive contexts, making war more relatable, digestible and negotiable in ways that accelerate generational attention (Divon and Ebbrecht-Hartmann 2022).

Discussion

@valerisssh's case provides valuable insights into the viral nature of war-related content on TikTok, as her videos achieved widespread popularity both on the platform and beyond during the invasion of Ukraine. Through her unique perspective as a young TikTok user, and by utilising the distinct audiovisual aesthetics of the platform, her videos resonated with and reached a diverse array of audiences amidst the invasion. In a context where the need for international recognition was and remains immense, @valerisssh has used her TikTok creations to spread awareness of both the war's atrocities and everyday lives in a country under attack.

As user-generated videos stimulate an affective and competitive appeal, their internet existence is highly motivated by video producers who seek virality. Viral videos describe the phenomenon in which 'video clips become highly popular through rapid, user-led distribution via the Internet' (Burgess 2008: 3). In light of their casualness, low production values and tendency to proliferate, viral videos can 'effect deeply polarised reactions, especially from critics who believe they desecrate memory' (Gibson and Hugh-Jones 2012: 126).

Nonetheless, by amassing a substantial viewership and heightened visibility, @Valerisssh has demonstrated the significant impact of TikTok in war-torn regions, solidifying her position as a war correspondent, commemorator, and communicator, all while navigating the complexities of influencer culture. Prior to the war, @valerisssh's videos were solely based on her daily experiences with no particular context. However, since the invasion of Ukraine, her communicative labour has crept into viral influencer practices and strategies on social media (Bishop 2022), assuming the mantle of a war influencer.

The case of @valerisssh contributes to the ongoing discourse on the memeification of cultural trauma. Memes occupy a pivotal role within the TikTok ecosystem, providing a platform for the enactment of narratives centered on trauma, adversity, and conflict through the utilization of meme-based templates (Divon 2022). This, in turn, has led to the emergence of a distinct trauma aesthetic. The platform vernaculars of TikTok, such as memes and sound, have become powerful tools for reaching a wide audience. Specifically, forms of memetic expression such as POV and corn have emerged as significant means of mediating the war in Ukraine, leveraging the diverse functionalities provided by social media platforms to enable individuals to share their personal experiences of trauma within digital frameworks. This enables TikTok users with strong vernacular literacy skills to express and disseminate cultural trauma in deeply mediated and unconventional ways through their videos (Eriksson Krutrök 2021; Hussein and Aljamili 2020).

Memes reside within their own specific cultural, political and societal contexts. Both pro- and anti-Russian memes have the capacity to transition between opposing camps. This transformation between contexts is sometimes difficult to trace, especially for digital audiences, as seen during the Crimean crisis in 2014 (Denisova 2019). These narratives might appear playful in contrast to traumatic ones, particularly when they revolve around avocados instead of death tolls. As noted by Lu and Steele (2019), conveying a sense of exhilaration can serve as a mode of resistance for marginalized groups in response to oppressors. Russia's actions, which encompass events like the suppression of protesters during the Euromaidan revolution, the annexation of Crimea, the ongoing conflict in Donbas, and the protracted war that began in February 2022 (Shmigel 2022), have imposed a collective trauma on Ukraine that has endured for years. In this context, @valerisssh's acts of playfulness and irony can be viewed as embodied forms of resistance through which the Ukrainian people cope with years of Russian oppression.

These deeply mediatised narratives (Couldry and Hepp 2017) of cultural trauma challenge ideas that critical societal conditions are reacted to only in mournful ways. Instead, this chapter illustrates how the intersections of play and joy within the context of memes can provide a unique framework for connecting in times of war. By providing unique and mediated avenues for interaction, these forms of connection have the potential to subvert prevailing dominant narratives. This historical phenomenon is exemplified by humor's sociological role in boosting morale during the occupation of Czechoslovakia in the Second World War (Orbdlik 1942). Moreover, after 9/11, humor eventually emerged as a coping mechanism, strengthening communal resilience following an initial humor-absent period (Ellis 2003).

The story of @valerisssh sheds light on the temporal nature of trauma on social media, as the instantaneity of content creation during the Russian invasion of Ukraine provided a space for users to engage directly with the unfolding situation and with those who were affected. In digital contexts, the temporalities of trauma narratives on TikTok can expand beyond the immediate moment of experience to become more enduring, facilitating personal expressions to function as arenas for collective commemoration (Leaver and Highfield 2018). As videos become recycled and repurposed for new memeified contexts, the temporal boundaries of cultural traumas are reconceptualised in socially mediated spaces like TikTok. While originally designed as trends, these meme-based expressions of short-term memorialization leave lasting imprints, becoming archived as users transform their profiles into living repositories of evidence and extend their online mourning practices (Abidin 2019). TikTok's affordances enable users to constantly reimagine previously posted content through trending memes, resulting, intentionally or not, in platforms taking a stance as it infrastructurally carries cultural trauma narratives into prolonged exposure and heightened visibility. This capability of TikTok's affordances to maintain war and trauma at the forefront of the public consciousness is crucial in an era of ongoing crises, where *old news* is all too easily forgotten and collective amnesia looms.

References

Abidin, C. (2019). 'Young People and Digital Grief Etiquette'. In Z. Papacharissi (ed.), *A Networked Self and Birth, Life, Death* (pp. 160–174). New York: Routledge.

Abidin, C. (2021). 'Mapping Internet Celebrity on TikTok: Exploring Attention Economies and Visibility Labours', *Cultural Science Journal*, 12 (1), 77–103.

Abidin, C. (2022). 'It's Corn! How the Online Viral "Corn Kid" is on a Well-Worn Path to Fame in the Child Influencer Industry', *The Conversation*, 13 September, https://theconversation.com/its-corn-how-the-online-viral-corn-kid-is-on-a-well-worn-path-to-fame-in-the-child-influencer-industry-189974, accessed 14 September 2022.

Allan, S., and Thorsen, E. (eds) (2009). *Citizen Journalism: Global Perspectives*. New York: Peter Lang.

BBC News. (2022). 'Ukraine: Documenting the War on TikTok', 8 March, https://www.bbc.com/news/av/world-europe-60656613, accessed 26 June 2022.

Bishop, S. (2022). 'Influencer Creep', *Real Life Magazine*, 9 June, https://reallifemag.com/influencer-creep/,accessed 11 January 2023.

Brake, D. R. (2014). 'Are We All Online Content Creators Now? Web 2.0 and Digital Divides', *Journal of Computer-Mediated Communication*, 19 (3), 591–609.

Burgess, J. (2008). '"All Your Chocolate Rain are Belong to Us"?: Viral Video, YouTube and the Dynamics of Participatory Culture'. In G. Lovink and S. Niederer (eds), *Video Vortex Reader: Responses to YouTube*, pp. 101–9. Amsterdam: Institute of Network Cultures.

Cervi, L., and Divon, T. (2023). 'Playful Activism: Memetic Performances of Palestinian Resistance in TikTok# Challenges'. *Social Media+ Society*, 9 (1), 20563051231157607.

Commane, G., and Potton, R. (2019). 'Instagram and Auschwitz: A Critical Assessment of the Impact Social Media Has on Holocaust Representation', *Holocaust Studies* 25 (1–2), 158–81.

Couldry, N., and Hepp, A. (2017). *The Mediated Construction of Reality*. Cambridge: Polity Press.

Dawkins, R. (1976). *The Selfish Gene*. Oxford: Oxford University Press.

Denisova, A. (2019). *Internet Memes and Society: Social, Cultural and Political Contexts*. Abingdon, Oxfordshire: Routledge.

Divon, T. (2022). 'Playful Publics on TikTok: The Memetic Israeli–Palestinian War of #CHALLENGE'. In C. Arkenbout & L. Scherz (eds), *Critical Meme Reader: Memetic Tacticality*, pp. 88–105. Institute of Network Cultures, Amsterdam.

Divon, T., and Ebbrecht-Hartmann, T. (2022). '#JewishTikTok: The JewToks' Fight against Antisemitism'. In T. Buffone (ed.), *TikTok Cultures in the United States*, pp. 47–58. Philadelphia: Routledge.

Divon, T., and Ebbrecht-Hartmann, T. (2022). 'Performing Death and Trauma? Participatory Mem (e) ory and the Holocaust in TikTok# POVChallenges'. *AoIR Selected Papers of Internet Research*, https://doi.org/10.5210/spir.v2022i0.12995.

Dounaevsky, H. (2013). 'Building Wiki-History'. In E. Rutten, J. Fedor, and V. Zvereva (eds), *Memory, Conflict and New Media: Web Wars in Post-Socialist States*, pp. 130–42. Philadelphia: Routledge.

Duffy, B. E., and Meisner, C. (2023). 'Platform Governance at the Margins: Social Media Creators' Experiences with Algorithmic (In)isibility'. *Media, Culture & Society*, 45 (2), 285–304.

Ebbrecht-Hartmann, T., and Divon, T. (2022). 'Serious TikTok: Can You Learn About the Holocaust in 60 Seconds?', *MediArXiv*, 4 September 2022, https://doi.org/10.33767/osf.io/nv6t2, accessed 5 September 2022.

Ellis, B. (2003). 'Making a Big Apple Crumble: The Role of Humor in Constructing a Global Response to Disaster'. In P. Narvaez (ed.), *Of Corpse: Death and Humor in Folklore and Popular Culture*, pp. 123–40. Logan: Utah State University Press.

Eriksson, M. (2016). 'Managing Collective Trauma on Social Media: The Role of Twitter After the 2011 Norway Attack', *Media, Culture and Society*, 38 (3), 365–80.

Eriksson, M. (2018). 'Pizza, Beer and Kittens: Negotiating Cultural Trauma Discourses on Twitter in the Wake of the 2017 Stockholm Attack', *New Media and Society*, 20 (11), 3980–96.

Eriksson Krutrök, M. (2021). 'Algorithmic Closeness in Mourning: Vernaculars of the Hashtag #Grief on TikTok', *Social Media+Society*, 7 (3).

Evans, S. K., Pearce, K. E., Vitak, J., and Treem, J. W. (2017). 'Explicating Affordances: A Conceptual Framework for Understanding Affordances in Communication Research', *Journal of Computer-Mediated Communication*, 22 (1), 35–52.

Gal, N., Shifman, L., and Kampf, Z. (2016). '"It Gets Better": Internet Memes and the Construction of Collective Identity', *New Media and Society*, 18 (8), 1698–714

Galip, I. (2021). 'The "Grotesque" in Instagram Memes'. In C. Arkenbout, J. Wilson, and D. de Zeeuw (eds), *Critical Meme Reader: Global Mutations of the Viral Image*, pp. 27–40. Amsterdam: Institute of Network Cultures.

Gibson, J. J. (1977). *The Theory of Affordances*. Boston: Houghton Mifflin.

Gibson, S., and Hugh-Jones, S. (2012). 'Analysing Your Data'. In C. Sullivan, S. Gibson, and S. Riley (eds), *Doing Your Qualitative Psychology Project*, pp. 127–53. Newcastle upon Tyne: Sage Publications.

Gibbs, M., Meese, J., Arnold, M., Nansen, B., and Carter, M. (2015). '#Funeral and Instagram: Death, Social Media and Platform Vernacular', *Information, Communication and Society*, 18 (3), 255–68.

Gómez, A. R. (2019). 'Digital Fame and Fortune in the Age of Social Media: A Classification of Social Media Influencers', *aDResearch: Revista Internacional de Investigación en Comunicación*, 19, 8–29.

Hussein, A. T., and Aljamili, L. N. (2020). 'COVID-19 Humor in Jordanian Social Media: A Socio-Semiotic Approach', *Heliyon*, 6 (12), e05696.

Jaramillo-Dent, D., Contreras-Pulido, P., and Pérez, A. (2022). 'Immigrant Influencers on TikTok: Diverse Microcelebrity Profiles and Algorithmic (In)Visibility', *Media and Communication*, 10 (1), 208–21.

Jensen, M. S., Neumayer, C., and Rossi, L. (2020). '"Brussels Will Land on Its Feet Like a Cat": Motivations for Memefying #Brusselslockdown', *Information, Communication and Society*, 23 (1), 59–75.

Kennedy, M. (2020). '"If the Rise of the TikTok Dance and E-girl Aesthetic has Taught Us Anything, It's that Teenage Girls Rule the Internet Right Now": TikTok Celebrity, Girls and the Coronavirus Crisis', *European Journal of Cultural Studies*, 23 (6), 1069–76.

Klausen, J. (2015). 'Tweeting the Jihad: Social Media Networks of Western Foreign Fighters in Syria and Iraq', *Studies in Conflict and Terrorism*, 38 (1), 1–22.

Leaver, T., and Highfield, T. (2018). 'Visualising the Ends of Identity: Pre-Birth and Post-Death on Instagram', *Information, Communication and Society*, 21 (1), 30–45.

Lionis, C. (2020). 'If a Duck is Drawn in the Desert Does Anybody See It? Humour and Infrastructures of Palestinian Statehood'. In S. Damir-Geilsdorf and S. Milich (eds), *Creative Resistance: Political Humour in the Arab Uprisings*, pp. 223–42. Bielefeld: Transcript-Verlag.

Lu, J. H., and Steele, C. K. (2019). '"Joy is Resistance": Cross-Platform Resilience and (Re)invention of Black Oral Culture Online', *Information, Communication and Society*, 22 (6), 823–37.

Makhortykh, M., and Sydorova, M. (2017). 'Social Media and Visual Framing of the Conflict in Eastern Ukraine', *Media, War and Conflict*, 10 (3), 359–81.

McCrow-Young, A., and Mortensen, M. (2021). 'Countering Spectacles of Fear: Anonymous' Meme "War" Against ISIS', *European Journal of Cultural Studies*, 24 (4), 832–49.

Medina Serrano, J. C., Papakyriakopoulos, O., and Hegelich, S. (2020). 'Dancing to the Partisan Beat: A First Analysis of Political Communication on TikTok', *12th ACM Conference on Web Science (WebSci '20)*, 6–10 July, Southampton, UK.

Merrill, S., and Lindgren, S. (2021). 'Memes, Brands and the Politics of Post-Terror Togetherness: Following the Manchester Bee after the 2017 Manchester Arena Bombing', *Information, Communication and Society*, 24 (16), 2403–21.

Milner, R. M. (2013). 'Pop Polyvocality: Internet Memes, Public Participation and the Occupy Wall Street Movement', *International Journal of Communication*, 7 (34), 2357–90.

Mizrahi, J. (2021). 'The Spending Habits of Avocado-Toast Millennials are More Complex Than You Think', *The Guardian*, 24 October, https://www.theguardian.com/commentisfree/2021/oct/25/the-spending-habits-of-avocado-toast-millennials-are-more-complex-than-you-think, accessed 2 September 2022.

Mortensen, M., and Neumayer, C. (2021). 'The Playful Politics of Memes', *Information, Communication & Society*, 24 (16), 2367–77.

Olivares García, F. J. (2022). 'The Communication of Sexual Diversity in Social Media: TikTok and Trans Community', *IROCAMM: International Review of Communication and Marketing Mix*, 5 (1), 83–97.

Orbdlik, A. (1942). 'Gallows Humor: A Sociological Phenomenon', *American Journal of Sociology*, 47, 709–16.

Raun, T. (2012). 'DIY Therapy: Exploring Affective Self-Representations in Trans Video Blogs on YouTube'. In A. Karatzogiann and A. Kuntsman (eds), *Digital Cultures and the Politics of Emotion*, pp. 165–80. London: Palgrave Macmillan.

Schreiber, M. (2017). 'Audiences, Aesthetics and Affordances Analysing Practices of Visual Communication on Social Media', *Digital Culture & Society*, 3 (2), 143–64.

Shashenok, V. (2022). *Things That Just Make Sense in a Bomb Shelter*. Salzburg: Storylution Gmbh.

Shifman, L. (2014). *Memes in Digital Culture*. Cambridge, MA: MIT Press.

Shmigel, P. (2022). 'Centuries of Russian Oppression Have Forged Ukraine's Remarkable Resilience', *Atlantic Council*, 22 May, https://www.atlanticcouncil.org/blogs/ukrainealert/centuries-of-russian-oppression-have-forged-ukraines-remarkable-resilience/, accessed 14 October 2022.

Thebault, R., and Pannett, R. (2022). 'Ukraine's Zelensky Calls for Global Protest Marking One Month of War', *The Washington Post*, 24 March, https://www.washingtonpost.com/world/2022/03/24/zelensky-message-global-protest-ukraine, accessed 12 December 2022.

Tufekci, Z. (2013). '"Not This One": Social Movements, the Attention Economy, and Microcelebrity Networked Activism', *American Behavioral Scientist*, 57 (7), 848–70.

UNHCR. (2022). *Ukraine Refugee Situation. Operational Data Reportal*, https://data.unhcr.org/en/situations/ukraine, accessed 22 September 2022.

valerisssh. [@valerisssh]. (n.d.). 'Photographer. How to Help Ukraine?', *TikTok*, https://www.tiktok.com/@valerisssh, accessed 7 April 2022.

Van Hout, M. C., and Bingham, T. (2013). '"Silk Road", The Virtual Drug Marketplace: A Single Case Study of User Experiences', *International Journal of Drug Policy*, 24 (5), 385–91.

Vatrapu, R. K. (2009). 'Towards a Theory of Socio-technical Interactions'. In U. Cress, V. Dimitrova, and M. Specht (eds), *European Conference on Technology Enhanced Learning*, pp. 694–9. Berlin: Springer.

Vickery, J. R. (2020). 'The Memeification of #Schoolshootings in the U.S.: Youth, TikTok and Playful Mediated Bodies', paper presented at *AoIR 2020: The 21st Annual Conference of the Association of Internet Researchers*, http://spir.aoir.org, accessed 5 February 2023.

Vidal Egea, A. (2022). 'From Anne Frank's Diary to TikTok: The Ukraine War (Almost) Live', *El País*, 19 March, https://english.elpais.com/international/2022-03-19/from-anne-franks-diary-to-tiktok-the-ukraine-war-almost-live.html, accessed 26 June 2022.

Vizcaíno-Verdú, A., and Abidin, C. (2022). 'Music Challenge Memes on TikTok: Understanding In-Group Storytelling Videos', *International Journal of Communication*, 16, 883–908.

Zeng, J., and Abidin, C. (2021). '"#OkBoomer, Time to Meet the Zoomers": Studying the Memefication of Intergenerational Politics on TikTok', *Information, Communication and Society*, 24 (16), 2459–81.

Zeng, J., and Kaye, D. B. V. (2022). 'From Content Moderation to Visibility Moderation: A Case Study of Platform Governance on TikTok', *Policy & Internet*, 14 (1), 79–95.

Zidani, S. (2021). 'Messy on the Inside: Internet Memes as Mapping Tools of Everyday Life', *Information, Communication and Society*, 24 (16), 2378–402.

Zulli, D., and Zulli D. J. (2020). 'Extending the Internet Meme: Conceptualizing Technological Mimesis and Imitation Publics on the TikTok Platform', *New Media and Society*, 24 (8), 1872–90.

· 7 ·

'GRANDMA WARRIORS' ON YOUTUBE: NEGOTIATING INTERSECTIONAL DISTINCTIONS AND DE/LEGITIMISATIONS OF THE WAR IN UKRAINE

Marja Lönnroth-Olin, Satu Venäläinen, Rusten Menard, Teemu Pauha and Inga Jasinskaja-Lahti

From the outset, the war in Ukraine has commonly been described as a 'media war' or 'information war' as invested parties wrestle for control of the mediascape. Within Russia's closed media space, the narrative of 'the special operation' is strictly controlled by the government. Ukraine also monitors its media space to secure the cohesion of the national and international community in wartime. Along with traditional media, social media has played a key role in circulating information about and imagery of contemporary conflicts, and it has been instrumentalised as a weapon of war. In Ukraine, the use of social media for political mobilisation started long before Russia entered Ukraine on 24 February 2022. The Latvian media company LETA analysed Twitter posts from the first six months of 2014 (Lange-Ionatamishvili, Svetoka and Geers 2015), identifying an increasing polarisation between pro-Russian and pro-Ukrainian social media users as the conflict escalated: approximately 12 per cent of all tweets related to the conflict in Eastern Ukraine were interpreted as aggressive, with the most aggressive being related to human casualties and including epithets such as 'fascist' and 'Ruscist'. Tweets were also heavily dominated by pro-Russian stances. Additionally, since the annexation of Crimea, pro-Russian voices have systematically cultivated fear, anxiety and hate among ethnically Russian (and other non-Ukrainian) populations of Ukraine in both traditional and social media (Lange-Ionatamishvili et al. 2015).

Official media producers as well as ordinary Russians and Ukrainians turned to the Internet to voice their views, hopes and fears. According to Mejias and Vokuev (2017), the Russia–Ukraine conflict demonstrates that social media can give both the political elite and ordinary citizens the power to generate both accurate and inaccurate information. The Internet therefore became the proving ground for a flourishing participatory digital culture to express pro-Russian and pro-Ukrainian stances, including through the use of memes (Wiggins 2016). Due to its ability to regenerate information at high speed and at little cost, social media is a highly dynamic, user-driven, constantly changing environment in which it is relatively easy for a message to 'go viral'. It is also an environment in which it is difficult to track the initial source of information, verify its authenticity and separate fact from fiction (Lange-Ionatamishvili et al. 2015). In the current war, which is characterised by rampant disinformation, eyewitness accounts have become crucial in communicating lived experiences of war. Social media and the use of smartphones have made it possible for ordinary citizens to share their accounts with international audiences and to give a human face to a war that is otherwise controlled by the state and official media. Social media also enables international audiences to communicate their stance and their understanding of the war.

In wartime, taking a stance and disseminating propaganda have often relied on maternal imagery (de Volo 2004). In addition, wars are often justified in the name of protecting women and children (Yuval-Davis 2004). Yet older women have seldom been the focus of research on how gender is deployed in justifications of war. As we demonstrate below, this is despite the fact that intersecting meanings linked to 'grandmotherhood' play an important role in legitimising the violent defence of nations. In this chapter, we discuss how grandmotherhood is weaponised in the context of the war in Ukraine and how the intersections of age, generational distinctions and nationality inform this weaponisation. We do this by examining online discussions of videos depicting two persons labelled 'grandmothers' in the war in Ukraine. One of these videos portrays a Ukrainian grandmother from the so-called 'Babushka battalion' during her military training. The other video shows an encounter between an older woman and Ukrainian soldiers whom the older woman first mistakes for Russian military troops and welcomes with a Soviet flag.

Grandmotherhood in the Ukrainian context

Russian and Eastern European (including Ukrainian) grandmothers have a special role in social life. They are active participants in the traditional gendered division of labour and make a significant contribution to childcare (Zdravomyslova 2010). The construction of 'the grandmother' (*babushka* in Russian and *babusja* in Ukrainian) also consists of attributing to her several powerful and praiseworthy qualities – such as wisdom, love, care, 'all-seeing' and 'all-knowing' – all of which contribute to an understanding of the grandmother as a symbol of endurance and strength (Tiyainen 2013). This characterisation of grandmotherhood partly arises from social ordering and demographics. In Russia, for instance, women not only retire earlier but also live longer than men (Shadrina 2022). This way of giving grandmotherhood meaning can also at least partially be attributed to the (post)Soviet gender contract – that is, how social reproduction in society is organised and who is responsible for the organisation of everyday life – in which work and motherhood are central to women's societal roles (Rothkirch, Temkina and Zdravomyslova 2007). In her analysis of labour and welfare policy discussions in Ukraine from 1990 to 2015, Trakhanova (2018) demonstrated the existence of an ideology of 'compulsory motherhood'. Reproduction as an obligation to the state and nation was shown to be central to the meaning of womanhood.

The role of grandmothers becomes emphasised especially in times of turmoil (e.g. the perestroika and the collapse of the Soviet Union) as women take up a 'stoic carer' role, taking care of and providing for the family (Shadrina 2022; Tiyainen 2013). The powerful role given to grandmothers in wartime is also evident in the Ukrainian war, evidenced in part by the popularity of the videos we focus on in this chapter. Even though not all participants in the online discussions of the videos take up a clear position on the war and its legitimacy, we nevertheless argue that for many social media users, commenting on the videos constitutes a way of articulating and justifying a stance. We also argue that doing so is enabled by the intersectional meanings and distinctions that are mobilised and constructed in these online discussions.

Social media representations of two 'babushkas' in the Russian war against Ukraine

The materials we draw upon to illustrate different portrayals of grandmotherhood in the war were gathered from YouTube in May 2022. Our focus on grandmothers was motivated by an observation we made while exploring social media content soon after the outbreak of the war. We noticed that women in general, and older women in particular, were prominent in images and textual accounts of the Ukraine war. We observed that depictions of older women, for instance, as vulnerable victims or as active supporters or resisters of the war, were disseminated and often went viral on different social media platforms. The image of the 'babushka' has been used in diverse ways and has become a symbol of the plight and strength of the Ukrainian people. She has been pictured as mourning and grieving, cursing the war, seeking refuge and staying to protect the country from invaders. These images have also been used to symbolise the immorality of the attacker. In promoting a Russian perspective, babushka imagery has been utilised to justify the actions of the military.

The two videos that we chose for our analysis each feature an older woman. The older woman in one of the videos acts in defence of Ukraine, while the older woman in the other video shows a commitment to Russia. We chose these two videos (from among dozens on YouTube featuring older women in the Ukraine war) on the following grounds: they were both widely circulated, they depict both Russian and Ukrainian perspectives on the war and they were the first to show up in Google searches. The ways in which the older women and other participants are depicted in the videos guide and trigger the meaning-making we analyse. The interactional dynamics between those commenting on the videos also play a significant role in the online construction of meaning. Instead of tracing these interactional dynamics, our analysis focuses on how those commenting on the videos build meanings through intersecting categorisations and by drawing upon discursive resources that the videos make available (cf. Venäläinen and Menard 2022). Our analysis illustrates how discursive resources enable them to build meaning in flexible ways, to 'pick a side', and to formulate positions on the legitimacy of violent conflict more generally.

To provide some context for the comments we analyse, we begin by describing the videos. The first video, 'Ukrainian grandma trained to shoot as Russia accuses the West of "hysterically" hyping up invasion' (henceforth referred to as the 'Battalion video'), was uploaded to YouTube on 14 February

2022 – 10 days before the Russian invasion of Ukraine. The video was published on a YouTube channel funded by Chinese state-owned media company Shanghai Media Group. By October 2022, it had attracted approximately 10,800 views and 60 likes. A short caption accompanying the video read, 'Members of Ukraine's Special Forces unit held military training for residents on Sunday to teach them self-defence. Among many young faces, a 79-year-old grandmother aroused attention.' The video is 2 minutes 19 seconds long and was produced as a news clip that focuses on the feelings and thoughts of Ukrainian civilians during the days leading up to the war.

Mariupol resident Valentyna Konstantynovska is one of the people interviewed in the video. Although she is shown for less than 20 seconds, the title and caption of the video make her the centre of attention. Konstantynovska is shown in a lying-down position, practising how to aim and fire an assault rifle (see image 1). She looks at the interviewer behind the camera and declares her preparedness to defend her home, country, city and children. The interview with Konstantynovska is conducted in Ukrainian, and the video has English subtitles. The video also has English captions explaining the situation in Ukraine, which suggests that it is intended for an international audience. Social media users commented on this video in English.

On the following day, 15 February, a slightly longer version (3 minutes 45 seconds) of this video was uploaded to the YouTube channel *Radio Free Europe/Radio Liberty*, a US-funded organisation that broadcasts in Eastern Europe, Central Asia, the Caucasus and the Middle East. Here, the video is entitled 'Far-Right Ukrainian Military Unit Teaches Children and Pensioners to Defend Their Country'. This title frames the video rather differently from the one given to the shorter version of the video. Associations with the far right are further highlighted in the description accompanying the video:

> A 79-year-old resident of Mariupol in Ukraine's south, Valentyna Konstantynovska [...] was among a group of civilians, including children, who were shown weapons and instructed on how to use them. The training was run by a Ukrainian National Guard unit connected to the far-right Azov Battalion, which the FBI linked in 2018 with neo-Nazi ideology and white supremacist organizations.

By October 2022, the video had logged approximately 32,000 views and 270 likes.

The second video, entitled 'WTF? Old lady with Soviet flag mistakes Ukrainian soldiers for Russians, soldier makes fun of her?' (henceforth referred to as the 'Flag video'), was uploaded to YouTube on 8 April 2022. The 2 minutes

Image 1: A screenshot from the Battalion video depicting an older woman training to shoot with an assault rifle.

13 seconds video shows an older man being asked by the person recording the mobile phone video to praise Putin and Russian forces. The man refuses to do so. Then an older woman (presumably his partner) holding a Soviet flag appears (image 2). When asked, the woman acknowledges that she has been waiting for Putin, to which the person behind the camera reacts by offering food. A person dressed in a Ukrainian uniform appears, hands the woman a plastic bag, takes the flag from her, lays the flag on the ground and steps on it. The woman then gives the plastic bag back and accuses the uniformed person of stepping on a flag for which her parents gave their lives. The exchange is in Russian, but the video has English subtitles. In October 2022, the video had approximately 327,000 views and 9,900 likes.

Our material consists of the comments on these two videos. There were 7,889 comments on the Flag video at the time of writing, while the two slightly different published versions of the Battalion video had 75 and 310 comments, respectively. We find the difference in the number of comments interesting, yet we can only speculate on the reasons for this. It could be that the Battalion video stimulated less discussion because it was published before the outbreak of the war. The fewer number of comments on the Battalion video could also be because it arguably has less controversial content, in the sense that the older woman is portrayed as defending her nation against an aggressor. The Flag video was posted a few months into the war,

Image 2: A screenshot from the Flag video depicting an older woman holding a Soviet flag.

and the older woman is portrayed as supporting Putin but also as being exposed to danger and disrespect. This video seemed to prompt more affective responses.

The comments on both videos were mostly in English, although the Flag video prompted some Russian comments as well as some isolated comments in various other languages. The comments in Russian were translated by the fifth author. The length of the comments varied from a few words to a few sentences. In the following sections, we place our reading of the material in dialogue with previous research on womanhood, motherhood and nationhood in violent conflicts. We specifically illustrate how intersecting categories of age, gender and national belonging are produced and negotiated in these discussions.

Intersections of age, womanhood and motherhood in military conflicts

Previous research on how intersecting categorisations around age, womanhood and motherhood are produced and symbolically deployed in conflict zones is scarce. Our focus is on the role of grandmotherhood in the construction of nation and in the justification of war. We do this by locating our observations in the landscape of previous research on gender and intersectional identity constructions in military conflicts.

Maternal objects of protection

In the so-called 'grand narrative', the history of the Global North is constructed as 'his story' of bravery in battle and violent conflict, while women's roles are to do with reconstruction and reproduction (Yuval-Davis 1997). Social roles in times of military conflict and war are thus 'appropriately' gendered. Men are given the role of protector, and they are portrayed as soldiers carrying weapons, prepared to fight. Women, on the other hand, are depicted as victims and vulnerable civilians who must flee their homes and seek refuge with their children (Williams 2016).

Nationalist projects are entangled with these gendered grand narratives, with womanhood often equated with motherhood and given meaning through the intersection and use of ethnonationalist and sociocultural discourses (Beukian 2014). Shared ancestry and origin are stressed in the ethnonationalist discourse, with women constructed as biological (re)producers of the nation. In this sociocultural discourse, women are seen as vessels of cultural transmission and as reproducers of national ideologies (Yuval-Davis 2004). Linked to tradition and heritage, the 'motherhood construct' is therefore crucial in building national narratives. From generation to generation, mothers transmit and reproduce life, customs and values (Yuval-Davis 2004). Moreover, women are seen as symbols of ethnic and national boundaries and mark the 'us' (see Cockburn 1998; Yuval-Davis 1997; Anthias and Yuval-Davis 1989). This is reflected in, for example, the language of 'motherland' and 'mother tongue', through which not only womanhood, but also culture and ethnic authenticity, is idealised (Beukian 2014).

We argue that social media users rely on these traditional gendered meanings – which position women as both agents of socialisation and as targets of men's protection – when commenting on the two YouTube videos and the older women featured in them. The extracts demonstrate how social media users build representations in which older women are to be protected, while also making salient links to common history and ancestry. In comments triggered by the Battalion video, for example, older women are understood as vulnerable. Placing them in combat is constructed as a sign of immorality and as disrupting the gendered norms of war:

> Yes. Help them fight rather than flee. Like a child or grandma can do much. The Ukrainian government is shameless, fucking hell. This is just sad. Just tell them 'You will be of no use, spare your life' and let them be on their way to safety. (Battalion video)

Virtues commonly associated with masculinity – such as honour, courage, and heroism – are central to norms that are used to construct soldierly conduct (Mankayi 2008). In the following excerpt, we can see how social media users also draw upon and negotiate these traditional gendered meanings when commenting on the Flag video:

> Я плачу каждый раз, когда вижу это видео! Но я радуюсь отчасти, что оно есть и все могут видеть истинное лицо "украинской армии"! Позор. Позор. Это не солдат и не мужчина. Россия пришла спасать от таких как они Украину и себя, свою землю!! Столько лжи вокруг России, но в нас дух этой бабушки, мы одна большая семья и выстоим! Нацизм должен быть уничтожен.
>
> [I cry each time I watch this video! But I am happy that it exists and everyone can see the true face of the 'Ukrainian army'! Shame. Shame. This is not a soldier and not a man. Russia came to save Ukraine and itself, its own land from people like this!!! So many lies about Russia, but we have the spirit of this granny, we are all one big family and we will survive! Nazism should be eliminated.] (Flag video[1])

The older woman holding a flag is a symbol of the Soviet past, shared motherland and peace, whereas wars are fought by (real) men in professional armies, their task being to protect the vulnerable. In the comments triggered by the Flag video, the Ukrainian soldier as an aggressor and the older woman as the target are frequently mobilised in building stances on Ukrainian immorality and disrespect, and on breaking the rules of 'proper' masculinity. The older woman (and all women like her) are thus constructed as both weak and deserving of respect – a construction that is used to build narratives in justification of the war. This aligns with Grigor and Pantti's (2021) analysis of the Russian media's use of visuals in war reporting, where constructions of good versus evil participants rely on imagery of women, children and older people as helpless victims. They identified a recurring trope of the mourning babushka, which reinforces the narrative of Russia as the protector and the evilness of the enemy. The following extracts further illustrate the intersectional mobilisation of similar meanings around gendered and aged vulnerability, and the construction of the unsoldierly conduct of the Ukrainian army:

> [...] real proof that the Ukrainian army has no respect at all, take the old lady's flag, throw it on the ground and step on it, dare the old and weak, poor thing .... (Flag video)
>
> Burly Ukrainian soldier versus diminutive elderly lady. This seems highly representative of the Ukrainian military. (Flag video)

In the Ukrainian context, Onuch and Martsenuyk (2014) analysed how the Euromaidan protests were discussed by activists in terms of a gendered division of labour, while Strelnyk (2019) examined how motherhood was mobilised in women's activism during the protests. These studies show that the ways in which the protests were militarised aligned with the traditional gendered division of labour. Men were given active and agentic roles in the protest zone and on the front line. In contrast, women were tasked with coordinating actions in the background, supporting and nurturing 'those who fight'. Women were also positioned as objects of protection and admiration, and as providing feminine beauty. Moreover, women's roles in Maidan were negotiated through motherhood, as women were described by men as mothers and daughters whose bravery and contribution to the protests were evidenced by their sacrifice of letting their husbands and sons – the 'real fighters' – go to Maidan (Banner 2008; Dowler 1998). In turn, women were given identities of 'real mothers' who needed to combine protesting and staying at home with the children, and 'pseudo mothers' who 'mothered' male activists by taking care of them. Thus, the arguably least likely candidates, women activists, were used to reproduce traditional gender roles prevailing in Ukrainian society.

Older women as a symbol of national heritage

Portrayals of women in war that highlight motherhood have been prominent (Banner 2008), with motherhood being intimately woven into antimilitaristic movements and mobilisations of resistance (Yuval-Davis 2004). As noted earlier, women whose resistance is given meaning through motherhood are generally not considered to be active combatants. Rather, women are given the role of supporters, nurturers and reproducers. Highlighting the role of motherhood in wartime confines women to the domestic sphere, positioning them as protectors of the home who fight for 'the sanctity of the heart' (Dowler 1998).

Motherhood has been deployed particularly in the national identity construction of nations that are considered young and vulnerable, or nations with a 'problematic' neighbour and traumatic history of genocide as in the case of Armenia (Beukian 2014) and Israel (Berkovitch 1997). In the Israeli context, motherhood is seen as a 'national mission' and thus as a public role. Women have a duty to the nation that has significance for the future of the state (Berkovitch 1997). Beukian's (2014) analysis of Armenian identity similarly highlights that the construction of Armenian 'femininity as motherhood' is central. This conception of motherhood is shaped by a specific history of genocide, survival (during the early years of independence and the diaspora), war (in Karabakh) and the struggle to preserve Armenian identity after a forcible eviction from the country. In the Chechen–Russian conflict, motherhood has been mobilised as anti-Russian resistance, since after mass deportations, the high birth rate of Chechens has been seen as an expression of communal solidarity and as a way of recovering losses (Banner 2008). Chechen women have therefore been viewed as key actors in the preservation of generations and culture.

Constructing the continuity of nations and national identities through motherhood is particularly relevant when looking at the complex Ukraine–Russia relations, which are characterised by the history of Holodomor and painful independence from the Soviet Union, the prolonged military conflict in Eastern Ukraine, the Russian annexation of Crimea in 2014 and the current struggle to preserve Ukrainian identity after the occupation and following forced displacement. In the roles given to Ukrainian women, mothers and grandmothers on the home front, front line and in places of asylum, the importance of preserving culture and generations is emphasised. A consideration of these roles also helps in unpacking the Ukrainian discourse of saving mothers and children first, as the vitality of the nation is seen as being dependent on them.

It is evident that when commenting on the videos, social media users rely on these ethnonationalist gendered meanings that equate womanhood with motherhood and nationhood. In addition to portraying women as objects of protection, as demonstrated in the previous section, users' comments also construct celebratory portrayals of feminised strength. Here, older women in the videos are depicted as mothers of the nation, symbolising the history and future of the nation and its values, thus embodying a continuity of identities:

Бабулечка, милая, живи ещё долго и счастливо. Ты наша гордость и пример для всех. Этим "воякам" стоит у тебя многому научиться. Они слабы, а ты сильна духом.

[Dear granny, live a long and happy life. You are our pride and an example for all of us. These 'soldiers' have a lot to learn from you. They are weak, but you are strong in your spirit.] (Flag video)

A strong nation or a strong civilization is not created by men, it's created by mothers like her who groom their sons. (Flag video)

A sweet woman so faithful to the memory and Motherland that her parents defended. They won with the red banner, which she kept all her life. She didn't trade the flag for food. The vileness of the military, who took away the flag, threw it on the ground and trampled it into the mud with their boots, is striking. The military stepped on the memory, on the life of this woman. They trampled into the mud her soul and the memory of her ancestors who gave peace to the whole world!!! (Flag video)

Nationhood and its (gendered) strength is constructed in these extracts through the intersections of womanhood, motherhood and age. The older woman represents strong women of the nation who have endured hardship yet fulfilled their task as reproducers of culture by being mothers and bringing up new generations. Power is thus constructed within the accepted norms of femininity in violent conflict. Moreover, the 'grandmother' is used as a symbol of loyalty to a shared Soviet history and as part of the narrative of the great patriotic war – this is a mobilisation of grandmotherhood that serves to construct a sense of a collective pursuit to maintain and protect the nation. This again aligns with the expectations of acceptable femininity during war, where women are expected to wait, remain loyal to the nation and encourage remembrance and endurance (Grayzel 2014). Similarly to the constructions of vulnerability in the previous section, this portrayal works to render the soldier as an illegitimate and immoral actor who disrespects the shared heritage that the older woman stands for:

Верно! Наши предки, старики и дети – это святое!!! И в этом знамени частичка каждого живого русского!!!!!! Это мир, достоинство и честь русских солдат!

[Correct! Our ancestors, the elderly and children – it is sacred!!! And there is a part of every living Russian in this flag!!!!! It is about peace, honour and the kindness of Russian soldiers!] (Flag video)

Not acknowledging the sacrifice of older generations and their importance as transmitters of values and traditions marks the Ukrainian soldiers in the video as lacking honour and dignity. Portrayals such as these work to delegitimise Ukrainian action during the war, thereby encouraging its condemnation.

The construction of masculinised agency

As shown in the previous section, the agency ascribed to women in nation-building projects has traditionally been confined to the domestic sphere to ensure the continuity of the gendered social order and nation. However, women are not always simply portrayed as passive symbols or reproducers of the nation in times of conflict. Women are occasionally granted at least some agency as participants in resistance, gaining access, to a greater or lesser extent, to the public sphere (Beukian 2014; Williams 2016). In previous research, women's agency in violent conflict has been evidenced by highlighting their active participation in nationalist and independence movements through, for example, adopting a traditional or cultural dress code (Beukian 2014). Women's agentic roles in joining combat or seeking asylum, or by engaging in non-violent resistance movements in which motherhood becomes the foundation of their claims, have also been discussed (Kaufman and Williams 2010). The mother can come to symbolise silent, non-violent resistance to oppression, thus turning perceived weakness into strength (Fagan 1999). As Dowler (1998) argues, the mother can become a powerful symbol of resistance, turning women's participation into a weapon of solidarity, one that signifies the 'triumph of the weak'.

Yet in some of the comments that we analyse, social media users ascribe *masculinised* agency to women. Bravery and strength are attributed to women as they put 'morally weak' men in their place, such as when the woman with the flag greets the soldiers. The soldiers in turn are emasculated and viewed as lacking soldierly virtues:

> Bad ass soldier. Taking on the old lady. But grandmother has nuts of steel. And pride. I do not want your shitty food you are stepping on my flag. This is being brave!!!! (Flag video)

> К стальной Бабушке пришли подлые, пластиковые солдатики. они не знали что в Этой миленькой Бабуле столько Бронированной Стали. СЛАВА БАБУЛЕ!!!! СЛАВА РОССИИ!!!
> [Corrupt toy soldiers came to this grandmother made of steel. They didn't know that there is so much Bulletproof Steel in This dear Granny. GLORY TO THE GRANNY!!!! GLORY TO RUSSIA!!!] (Flag video)

> I don't know why people are criticising the old lady. I respect her courage and willingness to try. Regardless of age, if she's armed and trained on that automatic

weapon, put the target in front of her. It's not a joke, she will do damage. (Battalion video)

The woman in the Battalion video is represented as actively and violently protecting her country with a gun, despite her age and gender. This disrupts the gendered norms of war, as taking a clear role in combat is not typically associated with women in military conflicts. Additionally, women's traditional role in activism is peacebuilding, not the taking up of arms (Yuval-Davis 2004). Social media users make sense of the older women's actions in a somewhat gender-subversive way. They do this by reversing the positions of the woman and the soldiers, so that bravery in war is associated with the older woman rather than with the soldiers.

Thus, on the one hand, militarised women disrupt the gendered norms of war. On the other hand, such women are masculinised in order to make sense of their courage, fighting and taking up of arms. Banner (2008) argues that the Russo–Chechen conflict gave women the opportunity to take on tasks traditionally considered masculine, such as combat and tactical operations. However, it has been noted that the granting of agentic positions to women during wartime depends on the intensity and duration of the conflict. Beukian (2014), in the context of Armenia, and Dowler (1998), in the context of Northern Ireland, demonstrate that although women fought alongside men in these conflicts, this was seen as a necessary deviation from the traditional gender order to secure the survival of the nation and protect the domestic sphere. After the imminent danger was over, women were expected to return to their traditional roles in the nationalist project as mothers, caretakers, wives and agents of socialisation.

Discussion

We have explored how conceptions of womanhood, motherhood and grandmotherhood intersect with age and nationality in the construction of meanings around and stances on violent conflict. We placed previous literature on these themes in dialogue with our readings of comments on two YouTube videos that represent older women as participants in the war in Ukraine. Our chapter demonstrates that social media users, irrespective of which side they are on, comment on the two videos to construct meanings that both align with and depart from traditional gendered portrayals of women in war. Aligning women with traditional roles is done through associating women with nationhood and considering them as objects of protection. Stressing the women's capacity to act bravely in defence of their nation represents a departure from traditional gendered portrayals of women. This subverts common ways of viewing women, particularly ageing women, as passive objects in need of protection. Our readings and observations resonate with previous studies on gender and conflict that highlight the role of womanhood and motherhood in the construction of national identity (Berkovitch 1997; Strelnyk 2019). We provide more evidence that women's bodies and the protection of them continue to symbolise defence of the nation and its borders. Women's bodies occupy a key position in discourses that legitimise war and discourses that are used to construct threats as coming 'from the outside' (Yuval-Davis 1997). The comments we discussed in this chapter appeal to the righteousness of defending the vulnerable and mistreated – a discursive strategy that aligns with conventional gendered positionings that intersect with age.

However, the women in the videos are also portrayed in the comments as active, brave and proud defenders of their nation. In 'warrior societies' (Berkovitch 1997), the masculine 'warrior' notion can thus be extended to women during military conflict and war. Womanhood and motherhood are here positioned as being 'a national mission', where women are given a public role, with duties to the nation and significance for the future of the state. Yet grandmothers and older women in general have been little discussed in relation to war. We have demonstrated in this chapter how intersections of older age and gender may be used in constructions of nationhood and legitimisations of war. Our analysis of YouTube discussions contributes to understanding why and how grandmotherhood becomes a powerful symbol of fighting and resistance that is used for maintaining 'the warrior spirit' of conflicting parties.

Engaging with social media – publishing, commenting, liking and sharing posts – can have varying functions in a collective pursuit to make sense of war. Social media can be used as a shared space to consider and evaluate stances on war. However, it can also be used to express and justify political opinions and to challenge opposing perspectives. We have shown that the processes of making sense of war in this way have an international scope. At the same time, meanings are negotiated from particular positions of national belonging. By conducting our analysis of users' comments in dialogue with previous research, we also demonstrate that the way in which intersections of womanhood and motherhood in violent conflict are mobilised share similarities across different spatial and temporal contexts.

However, there are some specificities in this material on the Ukraine war that call for closer examination. These specificities are primarily to do with the perception of morality and legitimacy of military action that relies on the intersections of age and gender. In the videos and users' comments on them, the babushka figure comes to symbolise the context-specific boundaries, history, values and spirit of the national collectives in this particular military conflict. We argue that the meanings associated with grandmotherhood and womanhood in the context of the war in Ukraine enable constructions that can be mobilised for legitimising both sides of the war. The constructions and mobilisations that we highlight in this chapter function to both reproduce and challenge gendered positionings, particularly in terms of agency. These dynamics – where both locally specific and more general meanings interact – can be fruitfully analysed with an eye on the intersectional categorisations at play.

Note

1 All translations from Russian to English are done by the fifth author unless otherwise noted.

References

Anthias, F., and Yuval-Davis, N. (eds) (1989). *Woman-Nation-State*. Basingstoke: Macmillan.

Banner, F. (2008). 'Mothers, Bombers, Beauty Queens: Chechen Women's Roles in the Russo-Chechen Conflict', *Georgetown Journal of International Affairs*, 9 (2), 77–88.

Berkovitch, N. (1997). 'Motherhood as a National Mission: The Construction of Womanhood in the Legal Discourse in Israel', *Women's Studies International Forum*, 20 (5–6), 605–19.

Beukian, S. (2014). 'Motherhood as Armenianness: Expressions of Femininity in the Making of Armenian National Identity', *Studies in Ethnicity and Nationalism*, 14 (2), 247–69.

Cockburn, C. (1998). *The Space Between Us: Negotiating Gender and National Identities in Conflict*. London: Zed Books.

Dowler, L. (1998). '"And They Think I'm Just a Nice Old Lady": Women and War in Belfast, Northern Ireland', *Gender, Place and Culture: A Journal of Feminist Geography*, 5 (2), 159–76.

Fagan, H. (1999). 'Women, War and Peace: Engendering Conflict in Poststructuralist Perspective'. In R. Munck and P. De Silva (eds), *Postmodern Insurgency: Political Identity, Conflict and Conflict Resolution*, pp. 201–16. London: Macmillan.

Grayzel, S. (2014). *Women's Identities at War: Gender, Motherhood, and Politics in Britain and France during the First World War*. London: UNC Press Books.

Grigor, I., and Pantti, M. (2021). 'Visual Images as Affective Anchors: Strategic Narratives in Russia's Channel One Coverage of the Syrian and Ukrainian Conflicts', *Russian Journal of Communication*, 13 (2), 140–62.

Kaufman, J., and Williams, K. (2010). *Women and War: Gender Identity and Activism in Times of Conflict*. Sterling, VA: Kumarian Press.

Lange-Ionatamishvili, E., Svetoka, S., and Geers, K. (2015). 'Strategic Communications and Social Media in the Russia–Ukraine Conflict'. In K. Geers (ed.), *Cyber War in Perspective: Russian Aggression against Ukraine*, pp. 103–11. Tallinn: CDCCOE.

Mankayi, N. (2008). 'Masculinity, Sexuality and the Body of Male Soldiers', *Psychology in Society*, 36, 24–44.

Mejias, U. A., and Vokuev, N. E. (2017). 'Disinformation and the Media: The Case of Russia and Ukraine'. *Media, Culture & Society*, 39 (7), 1027–42.

Onuch, O., and Martsenyuk, T. (2014). 'Mothers and Daughters of the Maidan: Gender, Repertoires of Violence, and the Division of Labour in Ukrainian Protests', *Social, Health, and Communication Studies Journal*, 1 (1), 105–26.

Rotkirch, A., Temkina, A., and Zdravomyslova, E. (2007). 'Who Helps the Degraded Housewife? Comments on Vladimir Putin's Demographic Speech', *European Journal of Women's Studies*, 14 (4), 349–57.

Shadrina, A. (2022). 'Enacting the Babushka: Older Russian Women "Doing" Age, Gender and Class by Accepting the Role of a Stoic Carer', *Ageing & Society*, 1–18, https://www.cambridge.org/core/journals/ageing-and-society/article/enacting-the-babushka-older-russian-women-doing-age-gender-and-class-by-accepting-the-role-of-a-stoic-carer/ABDC38C4A770ECC936AE14163B933C45, accessed 4 October 2023.

Strelnyk, O. (2019). 'Gendered Protests: Mothers' Civic Activism and the War in Ukraine', *Laboratorium: Журнал социальных исследований [Russian Review of Social Research]*, 11 (2), 103–24.

Tarkhanova, O. (2018). 'Essentializing Motherhood: The Ukrainian Woman in Policy Debates', *InterDisciplines*, 9 (1), 37–71.

Tiaynen, T. (2013). *Babushka in Flux: Grandmothers and Family-Making between Russian Karelia and Finland*. Tampere: Tampere University Press.

Venäläinen, S., and Menard, R. (2022). 'Mobilising Gender Equality and Protectionism in Finnish Parliamentary Sessions and Online Discussions Around Immigration: An Intersectional and Critical Discursive Psychological Analysis'. In K. Petterson and E. Nortio (eds), *The Far-Right Discourse of Multiculturalism in Intergroup Interactions*, pp. 25–49. Cham: Palgrave Macmillan.

de Volo, L. B. (2004). 'Mobilizing Mothers for War: Cross-National Framing Strategies in Nicaragua's Contra War', *Gender & Society*, 18 (6), 715–34.

Wiggins, B. (2016). 'Crimea River: Directionality in Memes from the Russia-Ukraine Conflict', *International Journal of Communication*, 10, 451–85.

Williams, K. (2016). 'Women and War'. In K. Ericsson (ed.), *Women in War: Examples from Norway and Beyond*, pp. 17–35. New York: Routledge.

Yuval-Davis, N. (1997). *Gender and Nation*. London: Sage.

Yuval-Davis, N. (2004). 'Gender, the Nationalist Imagination, War, and Peace'. In W. Giles and J. Hyndman (eds), *Sites of Violence*, pp. 170–90. Berkeley, CA: University of California Press.

Zdravomyslova, E. (2010). 'Working Mothers and Nannies: Commercialization of Childcare and Modifications in the Gender Contract (a Sociological Essay)', *Anthropology of East Europe Review*, 28 (2), 200–25.

Part Four:
News and Geopolitics

· 8 ·

THE EMOTIONAL GAP? FOREIGN REPORTERS, LOCAL FIXERS AND THE OUTSOURCING OF EMPATHY[1]

Johana Kotišová

News companies increasingly outsource newswork to freelancers and local collaborators – 'fixers' and producers. The trend has gained new topicality with the advent of the current Russo–Ukrainian war, where the work of media professionals on the ground – local and foreign journalists, producers, fixers, photographers, fact-checkers – and their digital media activities in the online space are crucial factors shaping the dynamics of the war (Hoskins and O'Loughlin 2015).

While there is a growing body of research on the collaboration between local and foreign media professionals and the underlying inequalities in safety, editorial authority, and remuneration (e.g. Baloch and Andresen 2019; Seo 2016), there are several blind spots. Namely, the research too readily accepts as a starting point the division between West and non-West, which assumes that local media workers are fundamentally different from and unequal to Western correspondents, thus inadequately stressing the locals' otherness. These studies sparsely touch upon the liminality, in-between-ness, hybridity and complexity of local media professionals' identities (see Kotišová and Deuze 2022). Furthermore, despite the emotional turn in journalism and media studies (Wahl-Jorgensen 2019) that has made

---

[1] This project has received funding from the European Union's Horizon 2020 research and innovation programme under the Marie Skłodowska-Curie grant agreement No. 887406.

emotionality an important perspective in journalism research, including studies on conflict reporting (e.g. Stupart 2021), cultural journalism (e.g. Kristensen 2021) and local journalism (e.g. Waschková Císařová 2021), the research on fixers has not considered the role of emotions in transnational journalistic collaboration. Moreover, the research has focused on reporting from the Middle East or Pakistan (Khan 2019; Murrell 2010; Palmer 2018). The case of the Russo–Ukrainian war, waged since 2014 and escalated by the Russian full-scale invasion of Ukraine in 2022, has not been addressed from this perspective. The English-language research on Ukrainian media professionals sometimes does mention collaboration with foreign media but focuses rather on the tension between professionalism and activism among post-Maidan Ukrainian journalists (Budivska and Orlova 2017) or journalists' internal displacement (Voronova 2020).

This chapter, based on twenty-two interviews with journalistic actors covering the Russo–Ukrainian war, Ukrainian producers, fixers, journalists, foreign reporters and photographers (both temporarily and permanently based in Ukraine), seeks to shed light on two of these blind spots: the emotions involved in transnational collaboration, and the complexity of the identities of individual actors in the news media. I address the following question: How does the diversity of local and foreign media practitioners' emotional experiences of the war – their emotional distance/proximity – manifest itself in newsmaking processes?

While reporting amidst war is with no doubt shaped by 'hard' circumstances such as security and financial conditions, I argue that many producers, fixers and journalists perceive an 'emotional gap' between the foreigners' detachment and the locals' affective proximity. On the one hand, the locals' emotional closeness to the context they cover can supposedly increase their susceptibility to trauma and post-traumatic stress. On the other hand, foreign reporters' (on short visits) relative distance can result in unethical reporting and behaviour towards sources. Thus, the locals' emotions and empathy are also seen as a 'shield' for the local sources, and hence beneficial to the ethics of the reporting. Moreover, the different levels of closeness are valued because they can lead to complex, higher-quality journalism where local fixers provide their contextual expertise, embodied and in-depth knowledge of the war and its history, while foreign reporters provide perspective and transnational experience. However, I also show that in line with the current postcolonial understanding of transnational journalism (Shome and Hegde 2002) stressing the complexity of local fixers' and journalists' identities (Kotišová and Deuze 2022; Plaut and Klein 2019), the size of this gap depends on the context and can shrink or stretch based on varying proximities to the war (Ahva and Pantti 2014).

Three concepts are central to the argument of this chapter: affective proximity, emotional labour, and empathy. First, affective proximity describes the imagined space between journalists and events which they represent/cover and in which they participate at the same time (Al-Ghazzi 2023; Ahva and Pantti 2014), as is the case for Ukrainian local producers and fixers. The high level of affective proximity of these media professionals covering traumatic events in their community challenges the boundaries between the professional and the personal (Backholm and Idås 2015; Rosen 2011; Kotišová 2017) and adds another layer to the emotional toll of first-hand witnessing of violence. As I will show below, affective proximity does not necessarily follow from geographical proximity (Ahva and Pantti 2014), which makes the uneven distribution of emotions among local and foreign newsworkers more complicated. Second, I use the concept of emotional labour, that is, 'the management of emotion required of employees based on the demands of their job' (Hopper and Huxford 2015: 25), to describe how Ukrainian local producers and fixers 'compartmentalize' different components of emotions and use their emotional experiences as embodied knowledge that benefits journalistic accuracy and ethics. Third, some of my interviewees link the latter, journalistic ethics, to empathy, that is, the ability to recognise others' feeling states and thoughts and to participate in or respond to these states. Antje Glück (2016) describes empathy and emotional capital as indispensable parts of journalistic work, which is corroborated by the importance given to empathy by my interviewees.

Fixers and emotions in conflict reporting: Two recent discoveries

News fixers – local collaborators of foreign reporters covering conflict areas and transnational affairs more generally – are a historical phenomenon deeply entangled with (Western) foreign correspondence (Murrell 2019; Palmer 2018). These local fixers or producers perform a varied mix of logistical and editorial tasks (e.g. Murrell 2019): they drive, arrange permits and press credentials, share their network with the reporters, book hotels, translate during interviews, arrange interviews, suggest stories, angles, sources, and sometimes do parts of the reporting. Nevertheless, they started being systematically discussed in journalism studies only after September 11 in the ensuing 'war on terror' (Palmer 2018; Palmer and Fontan 2007). Research shows that in a world where a part of conflict journalism 'shifts from *creating* to *verifying* content for news organizations' (Hoskins and O'Loughlin 2015: 1327), local and locally based media professionals, typically freelancers, are increasingly important actors in transnational newsgathering (Hamilton and Jenner 2004; Khan 2019; Murrell 2010; 2013; Palmer and Fontan 2007; Pendry 2015; Plaut and Klein 2019; Seo 2016). The trend, facilitated by digital means of content production and distribution, is believed to be driven by decreasing news budgets and, importantly, the degradation of the security situation for journalists in some places. The outsourcing of newswork thus goes hand in hand with the outsourcing of risks (Creech 2018), which forms one of the crucial inequalities in foreign newsgathering.

Among other topics, the research on fixers has focused on 'cultural translation' and 'mediation' of the social, political, and ethnic differences between the locals' and foreigners' cultures of origin (Palmer 2018; Murrell 2013). Linguistic translation (see Amich 2013; Murrell 2015; 2019; Palmer 2018) is only a small part of this cultural translation. Fixers also mediate between reporters and the local way of life (Hoxha and Andresen 2019), thus acting 'as an interface between the correspondent, the sources, and the site' (Palmer 2018: 321). Cultural translation includes providing the reporter with updates and context about political developments and educating them on the local way of organising social life (Bishara 2006, Amich 2013). Bridging the cultural divide also entails making people relaxed and at ease in the unknown context, that is, reducing their anxiety and fear.

Thus, much of the local media workers' mediation involves emotional labour (Hochschild 1983). Their affective proximity to the war (Al-Ghazzi 2023), involvement in local communities and personal interests shape the reporting and, within the conflict reporting industry, raise questions about their professionalism and the validity of the professional value of objectivity, often defined as detachment and impartiality (Tuchman 1972; Ward 2010). The neglect of emotion is understandable, given the still relatively scarce research on local producers and fixers. On the other hand, it is surprising, given, first, the many and severe potential risks for local conflict newsworkers' emotional well-being and mental health (see Al-Ghazzi 2023; IMI 2019), and second, journalism scholars' growing interest in emotion that has been sparked in recent years and has been dubbed the 'emotional', 'subjective' or 'affective' turn in media and journalism studies (Richards and Rees 2011; Pantti and Wahl-Jorgensen 2021). This turn has brought emotions into the spotlight and contributed to the increasing de-tabooisation of emotions and their acknowledgement as an inherent and legitimate part of journalistic practice. Given how important emotional labour is to the collaboration within the transnational teams involved in war reporting, we need to use the emotional lens to look at local producers'/fixers' practices, too.

A part of the body of recent research on emotions in conflict journalism has moved away from understanding journalists' emotions as a professional taboo carrying the danger of bias and misrepresentation, spoiling 'objectivity' or potentially resulting in psychopathologies such as post-traumatic stress disorder (e.g. Feinstein et al. 2002; Kotišová 2019; Wahl-Jorgensen 2013). Instead, contemporary research approaches journalists' emotional capital and emotional experiences as inherent and beneficial to journalism practice. To name just a few examples, Glück's (2016) interviewees – news journalists from two different contexts – see no conflict between the ideal of a detached journalist and feelings of empathy but consider the latter a central quality for good journalistic storytelling and career development. In the same vein, Richard Stupart (2022) argues that journalists' emotions can be understood in terms of aptness and prudence: as potentially justified and useful. Elsewhere, Stupart (2021) illustrates that emotion is vital to practical ethical reasoning. He challenges the classical binary vision of emotionality vs rationality that has manifested itself in journalism studies as the persistent yet practically untenable discursive contrast between objectivity and subjectivity (Van Zoonen 1998).

Methodological note

This chapter is based on semi-structured to in-depth interviews with twelve Ukrainian and ten foreign (mostly European) reporters, journalists, stringers, fixers, producers and photographers covering the Russian–Ukrainian conflict and Ukraine more generally. Six of the local and none of the foreign media professionals identified as female, while the remaining sixteen interviewees identified as male.

The interviews, revolving around the questions of risks and emotional labour in conflict reporting, were conducted between May and November 2021, on location (offline) in Kyiv and Lviv and online from Amsterdam or Brussels. They lasted between 40 minutes and 4 hours. After an informed consent procedure, they were recorded, transcribed, pseudonymised, and thematically analysed (Braun and Clarke 2006) using Atlas.ti. The codes that this chapter builds on include 'emotional gap', 'detachment', 'trauma', 'emotional engagement', and 'emotional labour'. The analysis draws partly on a paper in which I focus on 'neutrality, objectivity', 'self-reflexivity', 'bias', and the like (Kotišová 2023).

The timing of the interviews means that they do not capture the latest developments of the war, but they do address the Maidan revolution and the first phase of the conflict starting in 2014/2015 with the Russian illegal annexation of Crimea (based on a 'referendum' that was not internationally recognised) and the armed conflict in the Donbas between the Ukrainian Armed Forces and a complex tangle of groups and people including Russian military officers, 'volunteers', mercenaries, and local separatists (e.g. Plokhy 2015). This war is distinguished by its 'arrested' character (Hoskins and O'Loughlin 2015). The dynamics of the war are co-shaped by media content and media professionals on the ground, connectivity, and the warring parties working with its digitally mediated ubiquity. Traditional warfare is accompanied by a great amount of dis- and misinformation. One consequence of this intimate link between media logic and the logic of the warfare is that media professionals, being deliberately intimidated and attacked by Russia (RSF 2022), face severe psychological and physical risks when covering areas around the frontline (see CPJ 2022; IMI 2019).

While the pre- and post-February 2022 situations are different (Kotišová 2023), my ongoing informal contact with connections in Ukraine suggests that the Russian invasion created a context where some of the findings presented here have only become more relevant. The scope and brutality of the war have increased, yet Ukraine is still relatively easy to reach. On the one hand, this attracts a substantial number of inexperienced reporters with poor knowledge of the context who are driven by sensationalism (Sardarian 2022). The (battle)field is now full of diverse newcomers: international reporters, some of whom tend to repeat the patterns of insensitive exploitation of the local traumatised sources, and new fixers, many of whom are in precarious positions. On the other hand, we can observe in real time how the general awareness of Ukraine's existence and journalists' knowledge of the context is increasing – which goes hand in hand with greater emotional involvement – and how fixers are becoming more and more resistant and self-organised (Dovzhyk 2022). This means that the 'emotional gap' described in the next section may now be potentially wider and more obvious, or, on the contrary, almost completely obscured.

The Emotional Gap: Locals' engagement, foreigners' detachment

> There is the emotional gap between an international journalist who comes for one week to a country which . . . [he or she] little cares about, and understandably so. . . . this is the toughest, one of the toughest things in fixing. This emotional connection that you feel with people around you and much less emotional connection of people you work with. . . . there was cleavage, a whole cleavage between people who come from outside with very little degree of compassion and us, who were, you know, inside the story. (Albert, Ukrainian journalist and ex-fixer)

Most media professionals I talked to perceive a similar cleavage. On the one hand, there are local or locally based media professionals – fixers, producers, photographers, permanent correspondents and stringers – who are emotionally and/or intellectually engaged in the context. On the other hand, there are foreign reporters with their relative distance. Some locals feel they 'can relate more than a foreigner coming from the USA or London' (Vira, Ukrainian stringer and producer), intellectually and emotionally. By contrast, based on the interviews and also my previous research (Kotišová 2019; see also Jukes 2017), many foreign reporters on short stays cherish their ability to keep their distance. In what follows, I will thus look into the gap and then address the narrated consequences of this gap for the newsmaking process and its ethics.

Local media professionals often feel emotionally close to the violence in their community (Al-Ghazzi 2023). Their affective proximity to the suffering of their fellow citizens and sometimes families makes it difficult, almost impossible, to stay unemotional and disinvolved (see also Budivska and Orlova 2017): 'I have feelings. . . . You know, with the personal stories with the people here, with this situation, I don't think it's possible to be neutral' (Valentin, Ukrainian fixer).

Thus, the Ukrainian interviewees' narratives are often infused with compassion and pity for victims and survivors of the war violence, anger towards the occupying forces and their proxies, and overall sadness about the complex situation in their country. I have also witnessed locals' anger with foreign reporters and sense of 'shame . . . [of participating in] some news report that I can feel, you know, that's not really good' (Olena, Ukrainian photographer and ex-fixer).

All these emotions are particularly insistent and difficult to filter out because of the character of production or fixing jobs that, like other media jobs, require the practitioner 'to be committed well beyond what any profession could ask for' (Deuze and Witschge 2018: 176). Emma, Ukrainian fixer and producer, explained: 'it's more personal maybe, because fixer job it's a little bit more than just a job. It's more things involved, it's part of life. Your life.'

The war zone in the east of Ukraine, the job *inherent* to the war, and also the then contrasting relative peace in the rest of the country completely absorbs some of my interviewees:

> I live through the war and peace, I live through this conflict, as I'm a part of it, and it's a part of me . . . . And when you travel between the territory in war and the territory in peace, especially in the beginning, I felt such a big difference, one second you are in the trenches, and you are being shot at and everything, and then a few hours later, you sit on the terrace in a nice city, and people are wearing white trousers . . . When you travel through the territory in war and the territory in peace, then you have this difference, you feel this difference, you feel the reality, and – what is my reality? Is it war? Or is it peace? And I feel that every time I'm in the peace territory, I know I have to go back. Sometimes when I'm there, and the situation is dangerous, sometimes I think, what the hell am I doing here? Why can't I get another job or something? . . . But the conflict is actually, it's holding me. (Aleks, Ukrainian producer, fixer and filmmaker)

For some, one reason for this absorption and the need to always go back to Donbas is a 'testosterone addiction' (Artem, producer). In the calmer Kyiv, Artem keeps sneezing and is depressed. By comparison, Inna and Vira said they simply like and are lured back by the warmth of the Donbas people.

In some cases, this immersion in the context on several different levels and the need to get the job done can lead the locals to suppress their emotions (see below) or result in self-reported trauma. Vera says that 'Most of us, we have PTSD or trauma' and Inna, Ukrainian stringer and fixer, explains: 'We have been talking with lots of people who had been tortured . . . it's something that really influences you.' Frans, a permanent foreign reporter, explains that processing graphic scenes is probably more difficult for fixers than for other media professionals who 'externalise' the witnessed scenes into a discourse: 'When there is the MH17, and when you see pieces of bodies of children, . . . for a fixer, it's . . . difficult because they don't have the capacity to externalize these feelings that they have. Because they don't write.'

Moreover, producers and fixers most often work either as freelancers or informally, without any contract, protection, or insurance; the precarious conditions force them to hide the potential trauma, which, in turn, easily turns taboo or simply is not discussed and remains unresolved:

> We do not talk about it because – would you hire me if you ... let's say you work for the BBC, you are an editor of the BBC, would you take a piece from a traumatized journalist? (Vira)
>
> Reporters without newsrooms, they have no place to talk. ... in covering conflict and covering trauma, talking and sharing your experience ... is super critical, is the probably ... the only, the most important thing. (Inna)

The combination of the war, the media professionals' emotional immersion, and the lack of support for local freelance collaborators creates a fertile ground for trauma and other mental-health issues indeed. In 2018, a survey (IMI 2019) revealed that 97 per cent of Ukrainian freelance journalists had symptoms which could indicate depression, despite 86 per cent of the respondents stating that they were looking after their psychological and emotional condition.

By contrast, the foreign reporters, especially those on a short-stay, who have either experienced many conflicts and are emotionally blunted or who spend very little time in the country, invest relatively less emotional energy:

> If you are attached to their stories, you can't really move on, you know, to the next thing. ... as time went on and I got more experience doing it, I just approached it more like a job. (Roman, UK-based filmmaker)
>
> One of the things that I'm good at is distancing myself from the story ... I'm always there as a reporter and almost never there as a person. ... of course, you have feelings and stuff, but it comes after you come home. (Mate, European crisis reporter)

As the quotes suggest, foreign reporters see their relative distance as being both shaped and required by their professional motivation, as a necessary professional circumstance or even a professional quality. To successfully perform their job, they suspend or suppress their immediate emotional reactions to otherwise emotionally disturbing experiences – which is a typical form of emotional labour among reporters covering (distant) crises and trauma (Jukes 2017; Kotišová 2019).

Ukrainian media professionals understand that a journalist 'doesn't always have the capacity to personally, deeply, profoundly live through each story' (Olena) and that foreign journalists and media companies stay 'very distant to the conflict' (Pavlo, Ukrainian producer and photographer) as a survival mechanism beneficial to productivity. They acknowledge that foreign journalists 'did a fantastic job, by the way, mainly because of their detachment from the context' (Albert). However, Albert also criticises the cynical detachment of those who come to Ukraine to boost their career and who instrumentalise their sources: 'that, you can feel it very easily ... from a kind of this easy-going attachment' and lack of genuine interest in and respect for sources. Similar criticism of foreign reporters' 'fast food journalism' – stories produced quickly with artificial ingredients (Hoxha and Andresen 2019) – and their lack of empathy also appears in previous research on local producers and fixers (Bishara 2006; Khan 2019).

Shielding the local sources, filtering the message

As the dominant discourse on professionalism and objectivity in journalism involves the contrasts of objectivity and subjectivity, rationality and emotionality (e.g. Stupart 2021; Van Zoonen 1998), this emotional gap and the greater affective proximity among Ukrainians is sometimes interpreted by foreign reporters as potentially leading to bias and prejudice: 'You, like, feel right away that they will think, you are just Ukrainians, so you can't really . . . Your opinion is like biased or whatever' (Olena). Such mistrust and unfavourable interpretation of the locals' affective proximity can be seen as epistemic injustice (Fricker 2007). Epistemic injustice occurs when a person is not trusted based on their group identity (Ukrainians; fixers) without distinguishing and knowing more about the approach of the individual person.

In reality, my interviewees who are successful in the field very consciously compartmentalise different components of their emotions: they separate their affective dimension (what they immediately feel) from their cognition, opinions (what they know and think about the war) and behaviour (i.e. which sources they suggest to interview). This strict emotional labour distinguishes local media fixers from other local content-creating eyewitnesses, such as citizens, activists, or soldiers, who often communicate their immediate emotional reactions (Mortensen 2015). It also points directly to the paradox between the normative constructions of journalism and the moral implications of witnessing (Pantti 2019), since the compartmentalisation of one's emotions is an attempt to overcome this paradox. My Ukrainian interviewees often know how to deal with it: their affect, opinion/knowledge, and behaviour do not necessarily correspond. Pavlo explains: 'When I translate, I don't care about my own thoughts. I'm just translating word by word what people say. That's the most important. That's the job I'm hired for.' Thus, the suspicion that local media professionals hold prejudices that undesirably affect their work often stays only theoretical. Sam, having been based in Ukraine for some years, says: 'I'm not sure if I've ever needed to like have a conversation with anyone about it in Ukrainian context.' Even reporters who did meet fixers trying to push their agenda, were confident that they were able to recognise the potential ideological pressure: '. . . some ideological things or things like that, I am actually quite sensitive to that' (Joseph, European reporter).

Quite the opposite: the emotional gap is often valued by both the locals and the foreigners. It is seen as an opportunity for the locals and foreigners to learn from each other and eventually reach a collaborative form of objectivity where local fixers provide their detailed, embodied knowledge of the war and its history, while foreign reporters provide greater perspective and transnational experience (Kotišová 2023). Moreover, most interviewees who find the capacity to get emotionally involved also recognise some benefits of such involvement for their work. 'If you want to make real stuff, you need to find the emotional capacity to, to internalize it somehow. And become part of the story,' Albert thinks.

Even Mate, who praises his ability to stay detached, sees emotionality as a driving force and a part of the reality on the ground. Thus, the emotional gap usually becomes a starting point for the outsourcing of empathy to the local newsworkers. These fixers and producers spend their emotional energy on persuading people to let the foreign journalists visit or film them, only to explain to the same sources later why the journalists lost interest and are not going to come (Albert). They filter the journalists' exploitative and disrespectful behaviour towards the local sources (Olena) by showing genuine gratitude for their time and stories. They rephrase pushy questions into more cautious ones (Valentin) and soften the communication:

> There is a big difference in terms of, in the way how you speak to people. The journalist is bad, and you are good, you come to a person, and the journalist kind of fooled himself into asking a bad question, and you are the one who softens things. (Inna)

Vira explains the 'softening' – and thus 'shielding' – process in detail while also hinting at its consequences for herself:

VIRA: I also learned by doing how to interview people without traumatizing them. . . . When you work often with people who live on the front line, you filter questions the journalist asks. So you become that shield that separates. . . and take all the harm on yourself. I remember in 2014/15 how it affected me. People just lost their home or their kin, and I have to get all this heat, and then I filter it and translate it to a journalist.

JOHANA: And, like, while you are applying this filter, do you somehow moderate the tone, do you somehow change the message or?

VIRA: ... quite often, the question was very traumatic. Not political, but quite often just traumatic. You've just lost somebody, and I would say: how did you lose your husband? (Smiles) You maybe still didn't realize that you lost somebody close to you, so there is always a way to transform the question in order to not...

JOHANA: How do you ask?

VIRA: Depends on the situation, I mean, what did happen, or where have you been, like you never pronounce actually ... It depends on the situation. It's a very emotional thing that you learn by doing.

The retraumatisation of sources is nothing rare in media reporting on crises and tragedies (Haravuori et al. 2017; Thoresen et al. 2014), and empathy coming either from the local or the foreign journalists seemed to help avoid it throughout the data.

Locals' detachment, foreigners' engagement?

So far, I have retained the terms 'local' and 'foreign' in order to analytically distinguish between actors who originate in Ukraine, thus having more social, political, and ethnic ties to the country, and actors who were originally 'outsiders' and needed to acquire and/or outsource local knowledge (Palmer 2018; 2019). However, the duality of emotional locals and detached, cynical foreigners by no means works perfectly. The very 'local' and 'foreign' distinction is rough and does not reflect the media professionals' complex identities and personal histories. The affective proximity/distance to the conflict is co-shaped by this complexity: some of my interviewees have lived or worked in several different countries, some have partners from Russia or Ukraine, all of which make the war more distant or closer. In other words, the complexity of identities brings into play additional forms of proximity to those based on one's direct involvement in the affected community: physical/spatial, geographical, or social-ideological proximity (Ahva and Pantti 2014).

Thus, some reporters who were not born and raised in Ukraine but had many personal ties on the ground or who were physically very close to the war – threatened, detained, and interrogated in Donbas – could 'lose' their distance:

A friend went to fight, and I watched him fighting and hoped he would survive. ... Listening to what happens there was sometimes painful. (Michael, European reporter)

When I entered Sloviansk, I had chills because it was the first time that I was afraid, that I was fearing violence ... I had the impression that they were ready to cut my head, there was something totally cold in the air, cool violence, which I had never seen on Maidan. (Frans)

Their closeness sometimes stirs up criticism for 'going native' (Hamilton and Tworek 2019), being too close, too moved by the Maidan revolution – exactly as with the epistemic injustice (Fricker 2007) surrounding fixers' emotional involvement.

Vice versa, local media professionals with experience from other conflicts (Halyna, Ukrainian journalist and fixer), having worked a long time in the conflict zone (Pavlo, Valentin), being based far from the east (in Kyiv), having too many assignments (Olena) or focusing on getting the job done (Emma) can be less emotionally connected to the conflict. For example, Pavlo claims: 'The story that I'm the person of this region is not triggering me anymore. ... you still need to keep this distance, you know. Because otherwise, the war will eat you.'

To stay emotionally stable, some local producers even have thought-through strategies of reducing the proximity: for example, Pavlo deliberately distances himself from the conflict by being careful not to make friends in the war zone. His detachment and focus on professionalism, like that of Valentin or Andriy, is thus a result of a very similar type of emotional labour performed by the foreign reporters. Furthermore, one person can experience the same situation in diverse ways depending on whether they are covering it as a fixer, as a reporter, or as an editor. As Halyna puts it, 'Emotional involvement is very different depending on what I represent.'

All these specific experiences reduce the universality of the emotional gap. This shows how being 'local' vs 'foreign' to Ukraine (at a certain moment) is in many cases an inadequately strict division and forms only one of the many identity markers that determine affective proximity.

Conclusion

This chapter explores an essential dimension of the complex transnational conflict reporting ecosystem in Ukraine. I argue that the collaboration between foreign and local media professionals covering the Russian–Ukrainian war is characterised by a perceived 'emotional gap' that varies according to higher and lower levels of affective proximity. This gap is often understood as beneficial to reporting practices and ethics. However, it is far from universal, as the very categories of 'local' and 'foreign' become blurred and as affective proximity depends on a variety of identity markers and their corresponding proximities.

I describe how news fixing and production are permeated by the performance of emotional labour and work, which sheds new light on the importance of local newsworkers. This distribution of emotional work, including the responsibility for the ethical treatment of locals, reflects the still powerful discursive construction of objectivity, detachment, and rationality as opposed to subjectivity and emotionality (e.g. Stupart 2021; Van Zoonen 1998), and the privilege of the former. In this logic, the rational foreign subject subjugates the local (emotionally informed) knowledge by dismissing or exploiting it. The first option, dismissal, corresponds to epistemic injustice, that is, not trusting Ukrainians to be professional enough (Fricker 2007). The second option, exploitation, corresponds to the outsourcing of empathy as an aspect of fixers' immaterial labour (Creech 2018; Khan 2019). Empathy, an indispensable part of good journalism (Glück 2016), is an ability linked to proximity (Ahva and Pantti 2014); therefore, the locals may be seen as better predisposed to 'supply' this element of good journalism.

Thus, while this chapter follows the trend of seeing emotion as potentially beneficial to reporting and journalistic ethics (e.g. Stupart 2022), the reproduction of this power dynamic makes a positive outlook on emotional involvement problematic. First, the practice of 'shielding' local sources has its counterpart in the exploitation and potential traumatisation of the fixers and producers. Second, their emotional work can be easily abused for the opposite effect. Vira told me about a famous photographer who asked her to coerce a man who had just lost his house into tears: 'he wanted me to push on him. So that the man would be crying for the camera.' Although Vira did not follow the request, this example shows that the emotional gap does not necessarily have a beneficial effect on reporting ethics. At worst, it can turn fixers into components of an exploitation chain consisting of foreign editors, staff reporters, freelance collaborators, local fixers, producers, and sources.

References

Ahva, L., and Pantti, M. (2014). 'Proximity As a Journalistic Keyword in the Digital Era', *Digital Journalism*, 2 (3), 322–33.
Al-Ghazzi, O. (2023). '"Forced to Report": Affective Proximity and the Perils of Local Reporting on Syria', *Journalism* 24 (2), 280–94.
Amich, N. G. (2013). 'The Vital Role of Conflict Interpreters', *NAWA Journal of Language & Communication*, 7 (2), 15–29.
Backholm, K., and Idås, T. (2015). 'Ethical Dilemmas, Work-Related Guilt, and Posttraumatic Stress Reactions of News Journalists Covering the Terror Attack in Norway in 2011', *Journal of Traumatic Stress*, 28 (2), 142–8.
Baloch, K., and Andresen, K. (2019). 'Reporting in Conflict Zones in Pakistan: Risks and Challenges for Fixers', *Media and Communication*, 8 (1), 37–46.
Bishara, A. (2006). 'Local Hands, International News: Palestinian Journalists and the International Media', *Ethnography*, 7 (1), 19–46.
Braun, V., and Clarke, V. (2006). 'Using Thematic Analysis in Psychology', *Qualitative Research in Psychology*, 3 (2), 77–101.
Budivska, H., and Orlova, D. (2017). 'Between Professionalism and Activism: Ukrainian Journalism after the Euromaidan', *Kyiv-Mohyla Law and Politics Journal*, 3, 137–56.
CPJ. (2022). '25 Journalists and Media Workers Killed in Ukraine', *Committee to Protect Journalists*, https://cpj.org/data/killed/2022/?status=Killed&motiveConfirmed%5B%5D=Confirmed&motiveUnconfirmed%5B%5D=Unconfirmed&type%5B%5D=Journalist&type%5B%5D=Media%20Worker&cc_fips%5B%5D=UP&start_year=2014&end_year=2023&group_by=location, accessed 18 January 2023.
Creech, B. (2018). 'Bearing the Cost to Witness: The Political Economy of Risk in Contemporary Conflict and War Reporting', *Media, Culture & Society*, 40 (4), 567–83.
Deuze, M., and Witschge, T. (2018). 'Beyond Journalism: Theorizing the Transformation of Journalism', *Journalism*, 19 (2), 165–81.
Dovzhyk, S. (2022). 'Opinion: Secret Diary of a Ukrainian "Fixer"', CNN, https://edition.cnn.com/2022/07/20/opinions/ukraine-fixer-war-foreign-journalists-dovzhyk/index.html?fbclid=IwAR0DzAJIcAQ7CXqZq_lWrdcerMoY1pxIq2cVZZVEDji57u2iOIBstEz2u-k, accessed 20 July 2022.
Feinstein, A., et al. (2002). 'A Hazardous Profession: War, Journalists, and Psychopathology', *American Journal of Psychiatry*, 159 (9), 1570–75.
Fricker, M. (2007). *Epistemic Injustice: Power & the Ethics of Knowing*. Oxford: Oxford University Press.
Glück, A. (2016). 'What Makes a Good Journalist?', *Journalism Studies*, 17 (7), 893–903.
Hamilton, J. M., and Jenner, E. (2004). 'Redefining Foreign Correspondence', *Journalism: Theory, Practice & Criticism*, 5 (3), 301–21.
Hamilton, J. M., and Tworek, H. (2019). 'Scoop: The Challenge of Foreign Correspondence'. In J. E. Katz and K. K. Mays (eds), *Journalism and Truth in an Age of Social Media*, pp. 133–50. Oxford: Oxford University Press.

Haravuori, H., et al. (2017). 'The Impact of Journalism on Grieving Communities'. In L. C. Wilson (ed.), *The Wiley Handbook of the Psychology of Mass Shootings*, pp. 170–87. Chichester: John Wiley & Sons.

Hochschild, A. R. (1983). *The Managed Heart*. Berkeley: University of California Press.

Hopper, K. M., and Huxford, J. (2015). 'Gathering Emotion: Examining Newspaper Journalists' Engagement in Emotional Labor', *Journal of Media Practice*, 16 (1), 25–41.

Hoskins, A., and O'Loughlin, B. (2015). 'Arrested War: The Third Phase of Mediatization', *Information, Communication & Society*, 18 (11), 1320–38.

Hoxha, A., and Andresen, K. (2019). 'The Development of Roles in Kosovo: From Fixers to Journalists', *Journalism Studies*, 20 (12), 1732–46.

IMI. (2019). 'Ukraine Freelance Journalists Survey: Factsheet', *Institute of Mass Information*, https://imi.org.ua/en/infographics/ukraine-freelance-journalists-survey-i1621, accessed 20 September 2022.

Jukes, S. (2017). *Affective Journalism – Uncovering the Affective Dimension of Practice in the Coverage of Traumatic News*. PhD Thesis, Goldsmiths University, London.

Khan, A. (2019). 'Fixers in Corporate Media: Pashtun Journalists under Threat in North Western Pakistan', *Conflict & Communication Online*, 18 (1), 1–9.

Kotišová, J. (2019). *Crisis Reporters, Emotions, and Technology: An Ethnography*. Cham: Palgrave Macmillan.

Kotišová, J. (2017). 'When the Crisis Comes Home: Emotions, Professionalism, and Reporting on March 22 in Belgian Journalists' Narratives', *Journalism*, 21 (11), 1710–26.

Kotišová, J., and Deuze, M. (2022). 'Decolonizing Conflict Journalism Studies: A Critical Review of Research on Fixers', *Journalism Studies*, 23 (10), 1160–77.

Kotišová, J. (2023). 'The Epistemic Injustice in Conflict Reporting: Reporters and "Fixers" Covering Ukraine, Israel, and Palestine', *Journalism* (online first), https://doi.org/10.1177/14648849231171019, accessed 20 April 2023.

Kristensen, N. N. (2021). 'Critical Emotions: Cultural Criticism as an Intrinsically Emotional Type of Journalism', *Journalism Studies*, 22 (12), 1590–607.

Mortensen, M. (2015). *Journalism and Eyewitness Images: Digital Media, Participation, and Conflict*. New York: Routledge.

Murrell, C. (2010). 'Baghdad Bureaux: An Exploration of the Interconnected World of Fixers and Correspondents at the BBC and CNN', *Media, War & Conflict*, 3 (2), 125–37.

Murrell, C. (2019). 'Fixers as Entrepreneurs', *Journalism Studies*, 20 (12), 1679–95.

Murrell, C. (2015). *Foreign Correspondents and International News Gathering: The Role of Fixers*. New York: Routledge.

Murrell, C. (2013). 'International Fixers: Cultural Interpreters or "People like Us?"', *Ethical Space*, 10 (2/3), 72–9.

Palmer, L. (2018). '"Being the Bridge": News Fixers' Perspectives on Cultural Difference in Reporting the "War on Terror"', *Journalism*, 19 (3), 314–32.

Palmer, L. (2019). *The Fixers: Local News Workers' Perspectives on International Reporting*. New York: Oxford University Press.

Palmer, J., and Fontan., V. (2007). '"Our Ears and Our Eyes": Journalists and Fixers in Iraq', *Journalism*, 8 (1), 5–24.

Pantti, M., and Wahl-Jorgensen, K. (2021). 'Journalism and Emotional Work', *Journalism Studies*, 22 (12), 1567–73.

Pantti, M. (2019). 'Journalism and Witnessing'. In K. Wahl-Jorgensen and T. Hanitzsch (eds), *The Handbook of Journalism Studies*, pp. 151–64. London: Routledge.

Pendry, R. (2015). 'Reporter Power: News Organisations, Duty of Care and the Use of Locally Hired News Gatherers in Syria', *Ethical Space*, 12 (2), 4–13.

Plaut, S., and Klein, P. (2019). '"Fixing" the Journalist-Fixer Relationship: A Critical Look Towards Developing Best Practices in Global Reporting', *Journalism Studies*, 20 (12), 1696–713.

Plokhy, S. (2015). *The Gates of Europe: A History of Ukraine*. New York: Basic Books.

Richards, B., and Rees, G. (2011). 'The Management of Emotion in British Journalism', *Media, Culture and Society*, 33 (6), 851–67.

Rosen, J. (2011). '11 September in the Mind of American Journalism'. In B. Zelizer and S. Allan (eds), *Journalism After 11 September*, pp. 35–43. London: Routledge.

RSF. (2022). 'Russian Troops in Ukraine are Compiling Lists of Journalists for Questioning', *Reporters Without Borders*, https://rsf.org/en/russian-troops-ukraine-are-compiling-lists-journalists-questioning, accessed 18 January 2023.

Sardarian, S. (2022). 'International Media are Abusing the Heroism of Ukraine's Journalists', *Open Democracy*, https://www.opendemocracy.net/en/odr/international-media-ukraine-war-fixers-journalists-producers/?fbclid=IwAR2aypVQdMMLAQfqs6-WCiw6lgPKD-zlnBxQWK8Pecn2QqwerRHkb1VgKK7E, accessed 30 March 2022.

Seo, S. (2016). 'Marginal Majority at the Postcolonial News Agency: Foreign Journalistic Hires at the Associated Press', *Journalism Studies*, 17 (1), 39–56.

Shome, R., and Hegde, R. S. (2002). 'Postcolonial Approaches to Communication: Charting the Terrain, Engaging the Intersections', *Communication Theory*, 12 (3), 249–70.

Stupart, R. (2022). 'Anger and the Investigative Journalist', *Journalism*: online first, https://journals.sagepub.com/doi/10.1177/14648849221125980, accessed 20 September 2022.

Stupart, R. (2021). 'Feeling Responsible: Emotion and Practical Ethics in Conflict Journalism', *Media, War & Conflict*, 14 (3), 268–81.

Thoresen, S., Jensen, T. K., and Dyb, G. (2014). 'Media Participation and Mental Health in Terrorist Attack Survivors', *Journal of Traumatic Stress*, 27 (6), 639–46.

Tuchman, G. (1972). 'Objectivity as Strategic Ritual: An Examination of Newsmen's Notions of Objectivity', *American Journal of Sociology*, 77 (4), 660–79.

Van Zoonen, L. (1998). 'A Professional, Unreliable, Heroic Marionette (M/F): Structure, Agency and Subjectivity in Contemporary Journalisms', *European Journal of Cultural Studies*, 1 (1), 123–43.

Voronova, L. (2020). 'Conflict as a Point of No Return: Immigrant and Internally Displaced Journalists in Ukraine', *European Journal of Cultural Studies*, 23 (5), 817–35.

Wahl-Jorgensen, K. (2019). 'An Emotional Turn in Journalism Studies?', *Digital Journalism*, 8 (2), 175–94.

Wahl-Jorgensen, K. (2013). 'The Strategic Ritual of Emotionality: A Case Study of Pulitzer Prize-Winning Articles', *Journalism*, 14 (1), 129–45.

Ward, S. J. A. (2010). 'Inventing Objectivity: New Philosophical Foundations'. In C. Meyers (ed.), *Journalism Ethics: A Philosophical Approach*, pp. 137–52. Oxford: Oxford University Press.

Waschková Císařová, L. (2021). 'The Aftertaste you Cannot Erase: Career Histories, Emotions and Emotional Management in Local Newsrooms', *Journalism Studies*, 22 (12), 1665–81.

· 9 ·

INDIAN PRESS COVERAGE OF RUSSIA'S INVASION OF UKRAINE

Antal Wozniak and Zixiu Liu

While the Russian invasion of Ukraine in February 2022 has been widely condemned and met with severe economic sanctions, especially by Western countries, other governments have been much more restrained in their responses because of their geopolitical and economic interests. India, the world's largest democratic country, has been maintaining historically close ties with the Russian Federation (and the Soviet Union before 1991). Along with Russia, China, Brazil and South Africa, India is a member of the intergovernmental organisation BRICS; it has a 'Special and Privileged Strategic Partnership' with Russia; and its agriculture sector is heavily dependent on fertiliser imports from Russia. These factors have been identified as reasons for India's cautious response to Russia's invasion of Ukraine (Lieberherr 2022). India has abstained from voting for a UN Security Council resolution condemning the Russian attack and in the General Assembly on removing Russia from the UN Human Rights Council. Despite moving away from its traditional foreign policy of non-alignment under the government of Prime Minister Narendra Modi (Pant and Super 2015), India's geopolitical strategy still strives for the highest level of autonomy in international affairs (Hall 2022), and its approach to the war in Ukraine can be seen as a continuation of this strategy.

Research about media coverage of violent conflicts has repeatedly shown that independent news media tend to align with their respective country's geopolitical outlook (Bennett 1990; Entman 2003). However, a research gap exists about the relationship between foreign policy decision-making and news coverage with respect to non-Western and non-European countries. This chapter thus addresses the research question: *How closely does news coverage in independent media outlets in India follow national political elites' interpretations of the situation in Ukraine?* We aim to answer this question by comparing government announcements, parliamentary debate contributions and mainstream news coverage about the Russian invasion of Ukraine in India during the first four weeks of the war. We analyse how the Indian federal government and members of the parliament's lower house have framed the issue and compare this with the issue framing of the war in two widely circulated English-language newspapers with extensive foreign affairs coverage, *The Times of India* and *The Telegraph*.

The sociopolitical and economic contexts of war coverage

Media coverage of international conflicts and wars is often characterised by tension between the journalistic values of neutrality and fairness and an expectation for national news media to be supportive of their 'own side' (Robinson 2004; see also Carruthers 2011; Cottle 2006). War reporting often contains dichotomous framings of us vs them, good and bad, and perpetrators and victims (Hoskins and O'Loughlin 2010; Robinson et al. 2010), providing domestic audiences with interpretations that help to naturalise ideologically driven narratives about friends and foes, right and wrong. There is ample evidence that this also applies to news coverage in the United States and Europe about the Russia–Ukraine conflict since 2014.[1]

Conceptualisations of the relationships between mass media, the state and economic interests provide explanations for independent media outlets' tendency to fall in line with government policies and/or national ideology in times of international conflict. Pertinent to our research question are the political economy critique of foreign affairs coverage, the indexing hypothesis, the hierarchy of influences model and framing theory.

Studies of war coverage from a critical political economy perspective highlight the relationship between journalism, capitalist economics and the exercise of political power (Hamelink 2015). In this school of thought, the mass media are seen as shaping public opinion and naturalising dominant ideologies by reflecting hegemonic ideas about social relations, economic trends, and cultural values within the parameters of a pro-capitalist worldview (Bagdikian 2004; Hodkinson 2017). Some scholars have pointed out how conflict propaganda has prevailed in Western mainstream news coverage with the mass media serving as agents of ideological conformity (Boyd-Barrett 2017; Jowett and O'Donnell 2019). Knightley (2002) concludes that the media have become, especially after the Vietnam War, a complicit and important tool for the reproduction and re-presentation of (Western) governments' 'truth' with almost no interest in probing sceptical cases.

Bennett (1990: 106) argues that reporters 'tend to "index" the range of voices and viewpoints in both news and editorials according to the range of views expressed in mainstream government debate about a single topic'. In other words, dissent among domestic political elites is a precondition for divergent viewpoints to emerge in mainstream media discourse, an observation shared by Hallin (1986) in his study of US news coverage of the Vietnam War. If the cues provided by political elites point towards consensus, mainstream news coverage is likely to remain within these boundaries instead of offering counter-narratives. Bennett et al. (2008) later updated the indexing hypothesis and put forward several notable conditions (such as events, technology, and major breakthroughs by investigative journalists) under which more independent media performance becomes more likely. The 2003 Iraq War provided one of those notable conditions, when the news media shifted its focus towards an anti-war agenda after alleged stashes of weapons of mass destruction in Iraq could not be found (ibid.). However, Baum and Groeling (2010: 4), in their study of news coverage of the Iraq War between 2003 and 2007, contended that '. . . it is difficult to precisely define and measure [notable conditions], and even more difficult to determine ex ante which events are likely to give rise to them'.

We also find explanations for journalism's deference to dominant political-ideological views in more general-purpose models of journalistic practice. Shoemaker and Reese's (1996) hierarchy of influences model identifies *social systems* (e.g. hegemonic ideologies or economic interests) and *social institutions* (e.g. the state) as external factors that shape media content. These extra-medial forces subsume 'lower' levels of influence on journalistic practice: *organisational* pressures, journalistic *routines*, and journalists' *individual* characteristics. This perspective focuses our attention on the conditions under which war coverage is produced. Dominant ideologies determine the parameters of what can and cannot be said; powerful social actors try to influence news coverage by using tactics from political PR to censorship and intimidation; organisational constraints and journalistic work routines further limit the possible scope of media content. For instance, there is often editorial pressure on war correspondents to offer definite answers in a timely manner (Harris and Williams 2018) and journalistic work conditions in general have deteriorated in shrinking newsrooms (Walker 2021). Against the background of these challenges, war reporting has become a litmus test for independent journalism.

The manufactured set of media re-presentations of conflicts are the result of 'the active work of selecting and presenting, of structuring and shaping' (Hall 1982: 64). This journalistic work, conceptualised as media framing, promotes 'a particular problem definition, causal interpretation, moral evaluation, and treatment recommendation' (Entman 1993: 52) about a given issue. Systematically analysing these selective choices 'offers a way to describe the power of a communicating text' (Ibid. 51). Framing theory also describes how *frame repositories* for journalistic framing practice are being provided by (amongst others) political actors as well as national and transnational issue cultures (Brüggemann 2014). Accordingly, Reese et al. (1994: 94) argue that 'no analysis of news media content is complete without a close look at the sources of that content'. In Hallin's (1986) study on news coverage of the Vietnam War in the United States, news media were found to privilege government sources whilst marginalising oppositional ones in the construction of Americans as the 'good guys'. During the 2003 invasion of Iraq, the British media promoted official perspectives through their sourcing (Robinson et al. 2010), allowing the government to both set the news agenda and frame news content. Similarly, Hickerson et al.'s (2011) examination of journalists' sourcing and framing patterns in the case of Abu Ghraib revealed that journalists relied heavily on routine sources and became increasingly dependent on Congressional sources over time.

These theoretical concepts are relevant for understanding today's global public sphere, especially when considering journalistic practices around geopolitical conflicts and associated propaganda efforts (Boyd-Barret 2017). But the models and theories discussed above have been designed with Western journalistic cultures and systems in mind, so additional research is required. When moving beyond Western journalism cultures, journalism's role is often understood as a tool for a country's development (Chattopadhyay 2019). This, arguably, can create even more pressure on journalists to conform with their respective government's political approach to international crises and wars.

Media and the geopolitics of the Russia–Ukraine war since 2014

Our study builds on and extends existing research on media coverage of the ongoing conflict in Ukraine since 2014. In his critical assessment of Western media coverage of events in Ukraine in 2014, Boyd-Barret (2017: 1030) identifies a 'Manichean discourse' in line with commercial considerations and the interests of Western powers. His findings are in accordance with other studies that have focused on the 'propaganda war' between Western nations, Russia, and Ukraine. Roman et al. (2017) – who analysed coverage from Russia, Ukraine and the United States – and Fengler et al. (2020) – who analysed coverage from thirteen countries, including post-Soviet countries in East and Central Europe – conclude that media coverage largely mirrored their respective countries' policies regarding the conflict in Ukraine. Nygren et al. (2018) analysed news about the 2014 Ukrainian crisis in Ukraine, Russia, Sweden and Poland and concluded that coverage was closely tied to each country's political-historic context. Norström's (2019) analysis of Polish coverage in 2014–15 similarly revealed the strong influence of cultural and historical factors and notions of national security. Springer et al. (2022) analysed Swedish and Ukrainian coverage of seven conflictive events in Ukraine in 2017–18 and found Swedish news coverage to be more opinionated in favour of Ukraine and against Russia than even Ukrainian coverage. Ojala and Pantti – analysing news framing of four conflict events in Ukraine in 2014–15 in UK, German, Danish and Finnish newspapers – concluded that newspapers' framing legitimised EU policies of supporting Ukraine, helping to naturalise a geopolitical logic of a 'new cold war' (2017: 41). However, we know relatively little about the structures of reporting the Russia–Ukraine war in countries of the Global South. Our study therefore aims to test the generalizability of previous findings by examining the coverage of Russia's invasion of Ukraine in leading media outlets from a democratic country of the Global South that has particularly close ties to Russia.

India–Russia relations

India's close relationship with Russia is a continuation of its historic ties with the Soviet Union. Since the 1950s, the Soviet Union had vetoed UN Security Council resolutions adverse to India numerous times, especially with respect to the dispute about Kashmir (Sen 2022). Throughout the 1950s, the Soviet

Union also assisted India with its industrialisation efforts and the construction of power plants (Alipov 2022). Russia inherited the close connection with India and a 'Strategic Partnership' was agreed during Vladimir Putin's visit to India in October 2000 (Patney 2017), which was upgraded to a 'Special and Privileged Strategic Partnership' in December 2010 (Pandey and Yadav 2018). India is currently the biggest market for the Russian defence industry (Ghoshal and Ahmed 2022) and the two countries are running a number of joint military programmes (e.g. BrahMos Aerospace[2]). Russia has been supporting India's aim to attain a permanent seat in the UN Security Council (Menon and Rumer 2022). In 2014, Russia and India agreed to set a target of $30 billion dollars in bilateral trade by 2025 (*Financial Express* 2014) and establish a joint study group to look into the feasibility of a free trade agreement (Lal 2014).

Based on the literature, we assume that the domestic media's framing of the conflict will reflect India's special relationship with Russia and the federal government's foreign policy approach over the war. We anticipate critical viewpoints beyond the parameters set by the executive and parliament to be marginal in mainstream news discourse. In particular, we expect limited use of words such as 'war', 'invasion' or 'aggression' to describe the conflict. We also expect Russian government officials to be used in similar frequency to Ukrainian and Western sources in news reports, and Indian officials' statements as well as media coverage to highlight all conflict parties' responsibilities in working towards a peaceful solution.

Research design

We collected official announcements from the Indian Prime Minister's Office (www.pmindia.gov.in), the Ministry of External Affairs (MEA) (https://www.mea.gov.in/index.htm) and plenary speeches from members of the 17th Lok Sabha (http://loksabhaph.nic.in/Debates/Debatetextsearch16.aspx), the lower house of India's federal parliament, during the first four weeks (February 24 – March 23, 2022) of the invasion to establish baseline evidence for the scope of elite political debate against which news coverage in India might have been 'indexed'. We identified relevant communication by searching for 'Ukraine' (and the Hindi word 'यूक्रेन' in the bilingual debate transcripts) in the collected documents. Each press release, ministerial announcement, or plenary speech by a Member of Parliament (MP) was treated as an individual case. For each case, we recorded the date and the speaker (i.e. the Prime Minister, the MEA, or the name of the MP); for MPs, we also coded whether they belonged to a party of the government coalition or an oppositional party (using the *Lok Sabha*'s member search at https://loksabhaph.nic.in/Members/MemberSearch.aspx).

As proxies for mainstream news coverage in India, we selected the English-language broadsheet newspapers *The Times of India* and *The Telegraph*. *The Times of India* was first published in 1838, is owned by *The Times Media Group* and remains the widest-circulated English-language newspaper in India (Audit Bureau of Circulations 2022). In an analysis of election coverage in English-language Indian newspapers, Barclay et al. (2014) found the political orientation of *The Times of India* to be biased towards the Hindu nationalist Bharatiya Janata Party (BJP). To be able to account for political bias in our analysis, we decided to also examine coverage of the war in Ukraine in an English-language newspaper considered to be more critical of the BJP, that is, *The Hindu* or *The Telegraph* (Barclay et al. 2014). We chose *The Telegraph*, for which full texts were accessible via Gale OneFile: News during our period of study. *The Telegraph* is a daily broadsheet newspaper, published in Kolkata since 1982 and owned by the media conglomerate ABP Group. It is currently the fifth most-widely circulated English-language newspaper in India (Audit Bureau of Circulations 2019).

To collect all articles between 24 February and 23 March 2022 that referred to the war in Ukraine in *The Times of India* and *The Telegraph* we used the Gale OneFile: News database and searched for 'Ukraine' in the entire documents. All search results, including full texts of all articles and their respective metadata (i.e. publication date, newspaper, word count, byline), were put into an SPSS dataset. Both authors read all news items to identify and remove duplicates and false positives (e.g. articles mentioning Ukraine but not referring to the conflict). Ultimately, we had 827 relevant news items from *The Times of India* and 178 from *The Telegraph*. We then measured and compared the relative frequencies of interpretive frame elements (Entman 1993) between elite politician's statements and news coverage. The manual coding was divided between the authors and four student research assistants. For each manually coded variable, we established intercoder reliability by having a subset of cases coded by two coders independently (see applicable scores below). The variables for analysis included:

- **Main topic**: Political statements and news items were manually coded by the lead author (Krippendorff's $\alpha = 0.77$) for their main topical focus – the *overall geopolitical situation* (e.g. Russia-NATO relations, international sanctions, military developments), *India's position in the conflict* (e.g. bilateral talks between President Putin and Prime Minister Modi, India's UN votes), the *humanitarian situation in Ukraine* (e.g. people fleeing their homes, life under Russian bombardment), *consequences for Indian citizens* (e.g. the situation of Indians studying in Ukraine), *effects on the global economy* (e.g. international supply chain disruptions, energy crisis in Europe) or *effects on the Indian economy* (e.g. fuel prices in India, developments on the Indian stock exchange).

- **Issue wording**: For each statement and news item, we assessed how the situation in Ukraine was labelled – as *war, conflict, military operation, crisis/ tensions, invasion/aggression/assault, atrocities/terror/horror* or as a *humanitarian crisis*. This analysis was done semi-automatically using search strings to parse full texts. We recorded whether our search terms were present in an article or not, irrespective of how often a term appeared.
- **Blame/responsibility**: A research assistant manually coded the attribution (or repudiation) of responsibility for the escalation of the war to Russia, Ukraine and/or the West in each article. We differentiated between explicit and implicit attributions/repudiations ($\alpha = 0.87$).
- **Solutions**: A research assistant manually coded endorsements or rejections of potential resolutions for the conflict – *ceasefire/immediate end of violence, peace talks/diplomatic dialogue, territorial concessions by Ukraine* or *Russian defeat* ($\alpha = 0.90$).

These variables operationalise elements of issue framing: *problem definition, causal attribution, and treatment recommendation* (Entman 1993). The fourth framing function, *moral evaluation*, is hard to measure reliably with a standardised quantitative coding scheme. It also overlaps with other framing elements, for example, defining the issue as an 'unprovoked attack' carries strong moral connotations. For news articles only, we also analysed *sourcing patterns* by having two research assistants record the number of quoted and paraphrased actors of various types (e.g. Indian government official, NATO official, Ukrainian citizen, etc.) per article ($\alpha = 0.78$).

Results

Media attention

We measured the level of attention given to the issue by *The Times of India* and *The Telegraph* by calculating the share of articles referring to the war as

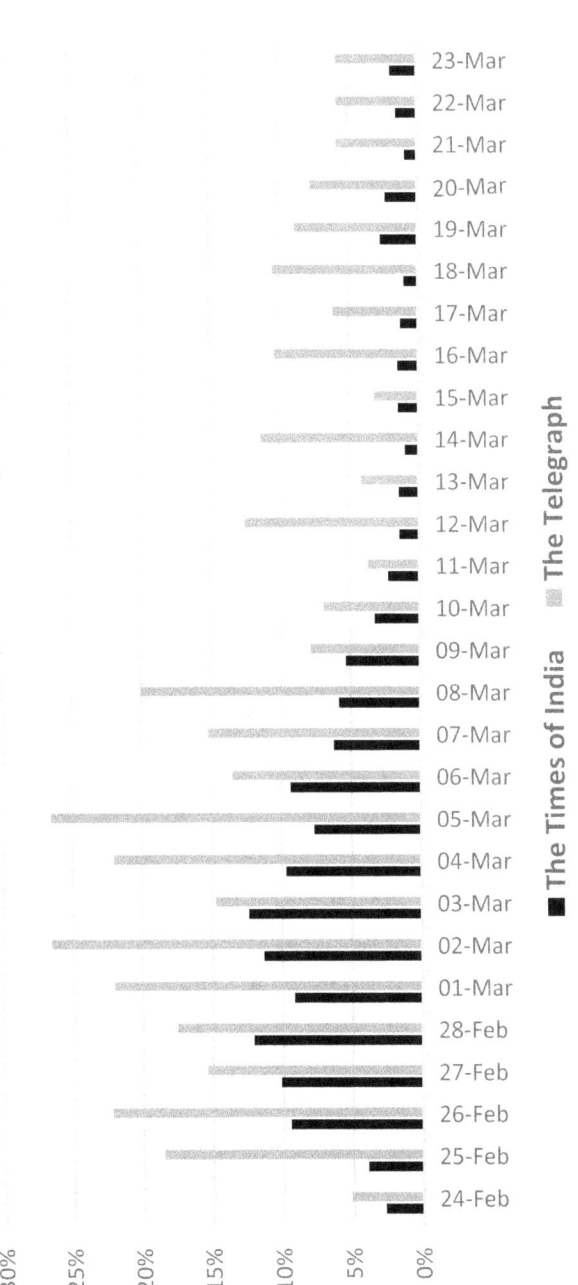

Figure 9.1: Media attention to the war in Ukraine

a percentage of all published articles per newspaper and day (see Figure 9.1). Across all four weeks, 5 per cent of *The Times of India*'s coverage dealt with the Russia–Ukraine war, whereas *The Telegraph* dedicated 12 per cent of its coverage to it. *The Telegraph*'s level of attention to the war is closer to Western news media's regard for the issue; for example, *The Times* (of London) dedicated about 15 per cent of its coverage to the war in Ukraine over the first four weeks. The difference became bigger over time with an attention level of 2 per cent in *The Times of India* compared to an average of 7 per cent in *The Telegraph* during week four of the invasion (17–23 March 2022), a clear indicator of *The Times of India*'s much stronger focus on domestic Indian affairs.

Topical focus

We compared the distribution of main topics in both political statements and news items and conducted Chi-squared tests to determine whether the observed frequencies are independent of the respective sources or not. We find several substantial differences (see Table 9.1) across all four data sources (χ^2 (18, N = 1,085) = 126.70, $p < .001$), and also when we compare government announcements to *Lok Sabha* speeches by members of the opposition (χ^2 (3, N = 86) = 22.37, $p < .001$) and coverage between the two newspapers (χ^2 (6, N = 1,005) = 66.49, $p < .001$).

All official communications by the PM's office and the MEA focused on either the situation of Indian students in Ukraine and *Operation Ganga*, the Indian government's evacuation effort, or India's position in the conflict. Speeches by members of the opposition in the *Lok Sabha* almost always referred to the plight of Indians studying in Ukraine with a handful of contributions also addressing the effects of the war on India's economy.

Patterns in news coverage are somewhat different, but also show a strong tendency for domestication of the issue, especially in the pages of *The Times of India*. Two-thirds of articles during the first four weeks of the invasion focused on the situation of Indian students in Ukraine and the government's evacuation efforts. Combined with the share of articles that mainly dealt with either India's political stance or consequences for India's economy, a total of 85 per cent of coverage in *The Times of India* was devoted to domestic issues and perspectives. This finding appears to be in line with the newspaper's political proximity to the Hindu nationalist government of Narendra Modi and its 'India first' policy. The Modi government has been found to use foreign policy as a means to reproduce its populist claim of representing the people of India

Table 9.1: Relative Frequencies of Main Topics (absolute numbers in brackets)

	PM &MEA (N = 40)	Lok Sabha (opposition) (N = 40)	The Times of India (N = 827)	The Telegraph (N = 178)
Global geopolitics	0% (0)	0% (0)	6.2% (51)	16.3% (29)
India's position	37.5% (15)	0% (0)	8.1% (67)	11.2% (20)
Humanitarian situation in Ukraine	0% (0)	0% (0)	1.5% (12)	3.9% (7)
Consequences for Indian citizens	62.5% (25)	85.0% (34)	67.4% (557)	36.5% (65)
Effects on global economy	0% (0)	0% (0)	1.9% (16)	3.4% (6)
Effects on Indian economy	0% (0)	10.0% (4)	9.3% (77)	20.2% (36)
Other	0% (0)	5.0% (2)	5.7% (47)	8.4% (15)

(Wojczewski 2020), and a media discourse that highlights the government's efforts to save its citizens from the dangers of a foreign war can be seen as supporting such a claim. The Telegraph's coverage, as expected, was somewhat less domesticated (about 68 per cent) and instead provided significantly more reporting about the geopolitics and on-the-ground developments of the war, that is, it gave more room to aspects of the issue not directly related to India's national interests.

Sourcing

On average, *The Telegraph* used more sources (3.7 per article) than *The Times of India* (2.5). We ran ANOVA (analysis of variance) F-Tests and found statistically significant differences in how the two newspapers were sourcing their coverage. *The Telegraph*, in accordance with its more critical stance towards the Modi government and less nationalistic type of coverage, gave more space to oppositional politicians from India, official Ukrainian and Russian sources, as well as domestic and international experts (e.g. scholars or think tanks). *The Times of India*, on the other hand, gave substantially more space to the voices of Indian citizens, driven by its extensive coverage of the plight of Indian students in Ukraine. While the mean differences (1.09 Indian citizens per article in *The Times of India* vs 0.83 in *The Telegraph*) are statistically insignificant, their shares of the overall number of sources differ greatly (Figure 9.2). 44 per cent of news sources in *The Times of India* were Indian citizens, compared to 22 per cent in *The Telegraph*. These findings underline the much stronger

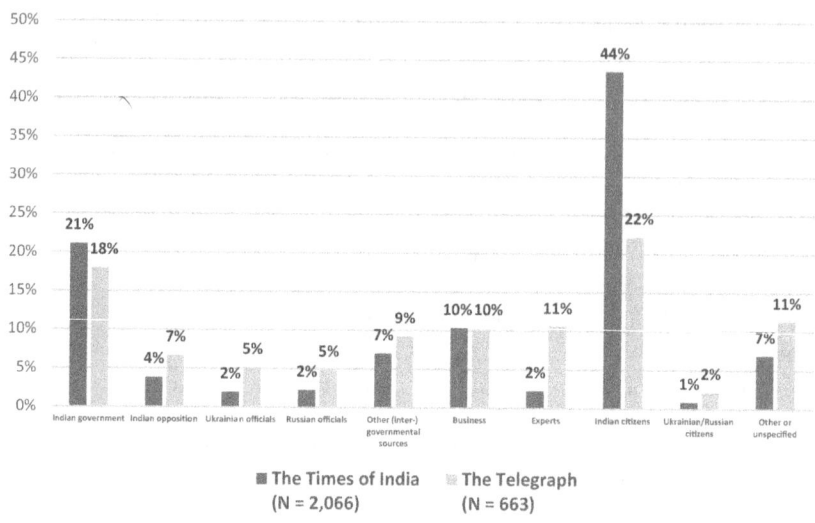

Figure 9.2: Distribution of news sources by actor type

domestication, if not nationalistic fervour, of coverage of the Russian invasion of Ukraine in *The Times of India* compared to *The Telegraph*.

Descriptors

Our analysis of the use of descriptors for the conflict also revealed significant differences in how the issue was framed by government sources, members of parliament, and news media. As expected because of the geopolitical considerations described above, the PM's office and the MEA completely avoided calling Russia's offensive an 'invasion' or 'aggression'. They also preferred to talk about a 'conflict' (in 58 per cent of statements) rather than labelling it a 'war' (15 per cent). Of note is also the focus on a 'humanitarian crisis' in Ukraine in government statements (50 per cent). MPs and both newspapers were much more prone to speak of 'war' or a 'war-like situation' in Ukraine; such wording appeared in three-fourths of *Lok Sabha* speeches and *Times of India* articles and in about two-thirds of *Telegraph* articles. And while only one MP – A. M. Ariff of the Communist Party of India (Marxist) – called Russia's conduct an 'attack on Ukraine', both newspapers featured such wording (Russian invasion, attack, or aggression) extensively; it appeared in one-third of articles in *The Times of India* and almost half of the articles in *The Telegraph*. References to a humanitarian crisis, in stark contrast to government communications, were rather rare in Lok Sabha speeches and media coverage. Chi-squared tests reveal that the observed differences in wording were statistically significant for 'war' (χ^2 (3, N = 953) = 74.11, $p < .001$), 'conflict' (χ^2 (3, N = 953) = 67.16, $p < .001$), 'crisis/tensions' (χ^2 (3, N = 953) = 17.76, $p < .001$), 'invasion/aggression' (χ^2 (3, N = 953) = 43.43, $p < .001$) and 'humanitarian crisis' (χ^2 (3, N = 953) = 78.16, $p < .001$). These findings seem to refute the indexing hypothesis, based on which we expected to find much smaller differences in the choice of words between government announcements and, at least, the more pro-BJP *The Times of India*. We discuss the implications of this result below.

Responsibility

We limited the analysis of attribution (or repudiation) of blame for the war to those news reports that focused on the geopolitical situation, India's position or the humanitarian situation in Ukraine, respectively. We found only marginal and statistically insignificant differences between the two newspapers. Both were much more likely to give room to voices who pointed out Russia's responsibility for the war (either implicitly or explicitly). *The Telegraph*, however, did feature more explicit condemnations of Russia's actions (in 41 per cent of articles) than *The Times of India* (28 per cent), another indicator of its coverage being less beholden of the Modi government's policies. The share of articles containing statements that blamed Ukraine was higher in *The Telegraph* (12 per cent) than in *The Times of India* (3 per cent). Similarly, *The Telegraph* also featured slightly more discussions of the West's responsibility (21 per cent) than *The Times of India* (13 per cent). Overall, however, a narrative that portrayed Russia as the aggressor in the war dominated both newspapers' coverage.

Resolutions

Lastly, we analysed whether news articles contained endorsements or rejections of resolutions to the conflict. Not surprisingly, calls for an immediate ceasefire (in 22 per cent of *Times of India* articles and 21 per cent of *Telegraph* articles, respectively) and a return to diplomatic dialogue (27 per cent and 16 per cent) – positions also repeatedly stressed by the Prime Minister during diplomatic calls and meetings – featured more prominently than assertions that the war could only end with one of the sides emerging victorious (3 per cent in *The Times of India* and less than 2 per cent in *The Telegraph*). We did not find any rejections of these options. While *The Times of India* gave marginally more prominence to the idea of peace talks than *The Telegraph*, both newspapers largely provided the same solution framing, in line with the Indian government's insistence on an end to violence and a return to the negotiating table.

Discussion

The findings presented in this chapter only begin to unravel the complex characteristics of political and media debates about the Russia–Ukraine war in India. More research that investigates discursive patterns over longer periods of time, in additional forums of public debate, in languages other than English and using alternative theoretical tools and analytical strategies is required. Our quantitative measurements of framing elements in government communications, parliament speeches and news reports cannot account for semantic and argumentative intricacies in Indian discourse about the war. They do, however, reveal larger discursive patterns across various sources of information.

Our analysis yields strong evidence for a domesticated discourse during the first four weeks of the war. The government as well as MPs exclusively focused on aspects relating to Indian interests – the safety of Indian students in Ukraine, consequences for India's economy and India's positioning in diplomatic relations. We found that news coverage in two leading English-language newspapers largely followed this domestic focus. *The Times of India* in particular provided extensive coverage of the situation of Indian students and the government's attempts to evacuate them, which we regard as being discursively aligned with the Modi government's populist 'India first' foreign policy approach.

The fact that government sources very rarely spoke of war and completely eschewed labelling the events unfolding in Ukraine as an invasion, attack or aggression, is indicative of the Indian government's efforts to not antagonise its close partner Russia. Curiously, both opposition and government party members were much less reluctant to speak of 'war' or 'war-like' conditions during parliamentary debates. These, of course, happen outside the realm of international diplomacy, which likely explains the relative lack of caution in wording. Both newspapers, however, gave lots of room to statements speaking of 'war' and an 'invasion'. In this regard, news coverage was clearly deviating from elite political cues. While seemingly contradicting the original indexing hypothesis (Bennett 1990), we argue that the war in Ukraine features some 'notable conditions' (Bennett et al. 2008), which might attenuate the indexing effect. First, India is a non-combatant in the war, making notions of patriotic *us* vs *them* thinking much less salient. Second, the newspapers' focus on the human-interest topic of Indian students in Ukraine made dramatic, if not sensationalist, references to war more likely. Indeed, 67 per cent of articles in *The Times of India* dealing with the student issue featured war-related wording. Third, in their reporting about the geopolitics and military-strategic aspects of the invasion, both newspapers relied on foreign sources or used the material provided by wire services (e.g. *Deutsche Welle* in *The Telegraph*), which were obviously not restricted in their word choices by the same considerations driving the Indian government's diplomacy. As regards causal attribution, media coverage – especially in *The Telegraph* – tended to be substantially more critical than the government of Russia's 'special military operation', an endeavour that is believed (by Western analysts) to assert 'Russia's divine right to rule Ukraine, to wipe out the country's national identity, and to integrate its people into a Greater Russia' (Hill and Stent 2022: 108). But *The Telegraph* also gave room to voices who highlight the issue of NATO expansion as a precursor to the current war.

Conclusion

In international affairs, it matters whose story wins (Arquilla and Ronfeldt 2001). Our ambiguous results – strong issue domestication in news reporting but also clear deviation from the government's diplomatic language when describing the conflict – bring to mind the question of what role the media should play during wartime: observers, participants, or catalysts (Gilboa 2002)? Rodrigues (2015) argues that Indian news media at large has changed its role from an observer to that of a partaker since the early 1990s. Ranganathan (2015) has noted Indian news media's impact on the construction of the nation state via 'mediated nationalism' and its effects on foreign policy decision-making. Our analysis reveals patterns in *The Times of India*'s reporting of the war in Ukraine that, while not perfectly 'indexed' to the government's diplomatic wording, correspond with the notion of a mediated nationalist discourse; a discursive approach that aligns with the Modi government's own populist-nationalist style of politics. We also found evidence of more counter-hegemonic patterns of coverage in *The Telegraph*, a newspaper with a fraction of the readership of the *Times of India*.

Overall, our results confirm the news media's tendency to largely concur with their home country's geopolitical positioning and national interests in reporting about international conflicts. Arguably, news coverage at the service of a government's particular national approach to foreign affairs can impede public understanding of complex international security issues and the ability of an electorate to envision alternative approaches to a country's conduct in international relations. From this perspective, the strong domestication of the Ukraine war in Indian news, especially in the influential *Times of India*, can be seen as detrimental to a more open-ended public discourse about India's place in the world.

Notes

1 Contrarily, mass media coverage of foreign policy issues can also influence policymaking by shaping public opinion to which policy-makers have to react (Briggs, Soderlund and Najem 2017). Research, mainly about US foreign interventions, has established that this causal link appears mainly during humanitarian crises and when vital national interests are not prominent (Western 2005; Soderlund et al. 2008). Due to Russia's political and economic power and its strong ties with India, we consider this condition as not being met within the remit of our study.
2 See https://brahmos.com/content.php?id=1, accessed on 15 November 2022.

References

Alipov, D. (2022). 'India-Russia Ties are Time-Tested, Honest and Without Any Hidden Agenda: Russia's Deputy Chief of Mission', *The Times of India*, 12 June, https://timesofindia.indiatimes.com/india/india-russia-ties-are-time-tested-honest-and-without-any-hidden-agenda-russias-deputy-chief-of-mission/articleshow/92164937.cms, accessed 15 November 2022.

Arquilla, J., and Ronfeldt, D. (2001). *Networks and Netwars: The Future of Terror, Crime, and Militancy*. Santa Monica, CA: RAND Corporation.

Audit Bureau of Circulations. (2022). *Highest Circulated Dailies, Weeklies & Magazines Amongst Member Publications (Across Languages)*, http://www.auditbureau.org/files/JJ%202022%20Highest%20Circulated%20(across%20languages).pdf, accessed 19 December 2022.

Audit Bureau of Circulations. (2019). *Highest Circulated Daily Newspapers (Languages Wise)*, http://www.auditbureau.org/files/JD%202019%20Highest%20Circulated%20(language%20wise).pdf, accessed 19 December 2022.

Bagdikian, B. (2004). *The New Media Monopoly*. Boston, MA: Beacon Press.

Barclay, F. P., Pichandy, C., and Venkat, A. (2014). 'Indian Elections, 2014: Political Orientation of English Newspapers', *Asia Pacific Media Educator*, 24 (1), 7–22.

Baum, M., and Groeling, T. (2010). *War Stories: The Cause and Consequences of Public Views of War*. Princeton, NJ: Princeton University Press.

Bennett, W. L. (1990). 'Toward a Theory of Press-State Relations in the United States', *Journal of Communication*, 40 (2), 103–27.

Bennett, W. L., Lawrence, R. G., and Livingston, S. (2008). *When the Press Fails: Political Power and the News Media from Iraq to Katrina.* Chicago, IL: University of Chicago Press.

Boyd-Barrett, O. (2017). 'Ukraine, Mainstream Media and Conflict Propaganda', *Journalism Studies*, 18 (8), 1016–34.

Briggs, D., Soderlund, W. C., and Najem, T. P. (2017). *Syria, Press Framing, and the Responsibility to Protect.* Waterloo, ON: Wilfrid Laurier University Press.

Brüggemann, M. (2014). 'Between Frame Setting and Frame Sending: How Journalists Contribute to News Frames', *Communication Theory*, 24 (1), 61–82.

Carruthers, S. (2011). *The Media at War* (2nd ed.). Basingstoke: Palgrave Macmillan.

Chattopadhyay, S. (2019). 'Development Journalism'. In T. P. Vos and F. Hanusch (eds), *The International Encyclopedia of Journalism Studies.* New York: Wiley, https://onlinelibrary.wiley.com/doi/abs/10.1002/9781118841570.iejs0122, accessed 12 November 2022.

Cottle, S. (2006). *Mediatized Conflict.* Maidenhead: Open University Press.

Entman, R. M. (2003). 'Cascading Activation: Contesting the White House's Frame After 9/11', *Political Communication*, 20 (4), 415–32.

Entman, R. M. (1993). 'Framing: Towards Clarification of a Fractured Paradigm', *Journal of Communication*, 43 (4), 51–8.

Fengler, S., Kreutler, M., Alku, M., Barlovac, B., Bastian, M., Bodrunova, S. S., ... Zguri, R. (2020). 'The Ukraine Conflict and the European Media: A Comparative Study of Newspapers in 13 European Countries', *Journalism*, 21 (3), 399–422.

Financial Express. (2014). 'Narendra Modi-Vladimir Putin Meet: India, Russia to Explore Oil and Gas; Aim for $30 bn Trade', *Financial Express*, 12 December, http://www.financialexpress.com/economy/russian-indian-funds-to-invest-1-billion-in-infrastructure/18126/, accessed 15 November 2022.

Gilboa, E. (2002). 'Global Communication and Foreign Policy', *Journal of Communication*, 52 (4), 731–48.

Ghoshal, D., and Ahmed, A. (2022). 'India, World's Biggest Buyer of Russian Arms, Looks to Diversify Suppliers', *Reuters*, 18 May, https://www.reuters.com/world/india/india-worlds-biggest-buyer-russian-arms-looks-diversify-suppliers-2022-05-18/, accessed 15 November 2022.

Hall, I. (2022). 'India's Foreign Policy: Nationalist Aspirations and Enduring Constraints', *The Round Table*, 111 (3), 321–32.

Hall, S. (1982). 'The Rediscovery of "Ideology": Return of the Repressed in Media Studies'. In M. Gurevitch, T. Bennett, J. Curran, and J. Woollacott (eds), *Culture, Society and the Media*, pp. 61–95. London: Routledge.

Hallin, D. (1986). *The Uncensored War: The Media and Vietnam.* Berkeley, CA: University of California Press.

Hamelink, C. J. (2015). *Global Communication.* Thousand Oaks, CA: Sage.

Harris, J., and Williams, K. (2018). *Reporting War and Conflict.* London: Routledge.

Hickerson, A. A., Moy, P., and Dunsmore, K. (2011). 'Revisiting Abu Ghraib: Journalists' Sourcing and Framing Patterns', *Journalism and Mass Communication Quarterly*, 88 (4), 789–806.

Hill, F., and Stent, A. (2022). 'The World Putin Wants: How Distortions About the Past Feed Delusions About the Future', *Foreign Affairs*, 101 (5), 108–22, https://www.foreignaffairs.com/russian-federation/world-putin-wants-fiona-hill-angela-stent, accessed 13 November 2022.

Hodkinson, P. (2017). *Media, Culture and Society* (2nd ed.). Thousand Oaks, CA: Sage.

Hoskins, A., and O'Loughlin, B. (2010). *War and Media: The Emergence of Diffused War*. Cambridge, UK: Polity.

Jowett, G. S., and O'Donnell, V. (2019). *Propaganda & Persuasion* (7th ed.). Thousand Oaks, CA: Sage.

Knightley, P. (2002). *The First Casualty: The War Correspondent as Hero and Myth-Maker from the Crimea to Kosovo*. Baltimore, MD: John Hopkins University Press.

Lal, N. (2014). 'Rogozin Sets Ball Rolling for Bilateral Trade and Investment', *Russia Beyond*. 28 February, https://www.rbth.com/economics/2014/02/28/rogozin_sets_ball_rolling_for_bilateral_trade_and_investment_33399, accessed 15 November 2022.

Lieberherr, B. (2022). 'Why India Remains Neutral over Ukraine', *Center for Security Studies or the Swiss Federal Institute of Technology Zurich (ETH)*. 12 April, https://isnblog.ethz.ch/international-relations/why-india-remains-neutral-over-ukraine, accessed 28 October 2022.

Menon, R., and Rumer, E. (2022). 'Russian and India: A New Chapter', *Carnegie Endowment for International Peace*. 20 September, https://carnegieendowment.org/2022/09/20/russia-and-india-new-chapter-pub-87958, accessed 12 November 2022.

Norström, R. (2019). *The Coverage of the Russian-Ukrainian Conflict by the Polish Media (2014–2015)*. Berlin: Peter Lang.

Nygren, G., Glowacki, M., Hök, J., Kiria, I., Orlova, D. and Taradai, D. (2018). Journalism in the Crossfire: Media Coverage of the War in Ukraine in 2014. *Journalism Studies*, 19 (7), 1059–78.

Ojala, M., and Pantti, M. (2017). 'Naturalising the New Cold War: The Geopolitics of Framing the Ukrainian Conflict in Four European Newspapers', *Global Media and Communication*, 13 (1), 41–56.

Pant, H. V., and Super, J. M. (2015). 'India's "Non-alignment" Conundrum: A Twentieth-Century Policy in a Changing World', *International Affairs*, 91 (4), 747–64.

Pandey, S. K., and Yadav, A. (2018). 'Contextualising India-Russia Relations', *International Studies*, 53 (3–4), 227–57.

Patney, V. (2017). Introduction. In C. Rekha (ed.), *India-Russia Post-Cold War Relations: A New Epoch of Cooperation*, pp. xiii–xvi. London: Routledge.

Ranganathan, M. (2015). 'The Mediated Nation in the Age of Globalisation'. In U. M. Rodrigues, and M. Ranganathan (eds), *Indian News Media: From Observer to Participant*, pp. 175–202. New Delhi: Sage.

Reese, S. D., Grant, A., and Danielian, L. H. (1994). 'The Structure of News Sources on Television: A Network Analysis of "CBS News", "Nightline", "MacNeil/Lehrer", and "This Week with David Brinkley"', *Journal of Communication*, 44 (2), 84–107.

Robinson, P. (2004). 'Researching US Media-State Relations and Twenty-First Century Wars'. In S. Allan, and B. Zelizer (eds), *Reporting War: Journalism in Wartime*, pp. 96–112. London: Routledge.

Robinson, P., Goddard, P., Parry, K., Murray, C., and Taylor, P. (2010). *Pockets of Resistance: British News Media, War and Theory in the 2003 Invasion of Iraq*. Manchester: Manchester University Press.

Rodrigues, U. M. (2015). 'Introduction: Indian News Media in a Globalised Era'. In U. M. Rodrigues, and M. Ranganathan (eds), *Indian News Media: From Observer to Participant*, pp. 1–33. New Delhi: Sage.

Roman, N., Wanta, W., and Buniak, I. (2017). 'Information Wars: Eastern Ukraine Military Conflict Coverage in the Russian, Ukrainian and US Newscasts', *International Communication Gazette*, 79 (4), 357–78.

Sen, S. (2022). 'Why Is India Standing with Putin's Russia?', *Al Jazeera*, 14 March, https://www.aljazeera.com/opinions/2022/3/14/why-is-istandwithputin-trending-in, accessed 23 December 2022.

Shoemaker, P. J., and Reese, S. D. (1996). *Mediating the Message. Theories of Influences on Mass Media Content* (2nd ed.). New York: Longman.

Soderlund, W. C., Briggs, E. D., Hildebrandt, K., and Sidahmed, A. S. (2008). *Humanitarian Crises and Intervention: Reassessing the Impact of Mass Media*. Sterling, VA: Kumarian Press.

Springer, N., Nygren, G., Widholm, A., Orlova, D., and Taradai, D. (2022). 'Narrating "Their War" and "Our War": The Patriotic Journalism Paradigm in the Context of Swedish and Ukrainian Conflict Coverage', *Central European Journal of Communication*, 15 (2), 178–201.

Walker, M. (2021). 'U.S. Newsroom Employment Has Fallen 26% Since 2008', *Pew Research Center*, 13 July, https://www.pewresearch.org/fact-tank/2021/07/13/u-s-newsroom-employment-has-fallen-26-since-2008/, accessed 13 November 2022.

Western, J. (2005). *Selling Intervention and War: The Presidency, the Media, and the American Public*. Baltimore, MD: John Hopkins University Press.

Wojczewski, T. (2020). 'Populism, Hindu Nationalism, and Foreign Policy in India: The Politics of Representing "the People"', *International Studies Review*, 22 (3), 396–422.

· 10 ·

REPORTING THE WAR IN UKRAINE: ECOLOGICAL DISSIMULATION IN A DYING WORLD

Simon Cottle

The Russian invasion of Ukraine is a deadly reminder that barbarism still stalks the Earth, that warfare is deemed by power holders to be an acceptable means of pursuing geopolitical interests and that human lives are expendable. This latest war also demonstrates once again how the full array of modern means of communication are put to work in the service of information war. Whether on the home front, in the conflict zone, or around the world in attempts to legitimise or de-legitimise warring positions and mobilise or demoralise support. This terrain, rightly, has received considerable academic study across the history of modern warfare and in the context of new and evolving communication technologies (Allan and Zelizer 2004; Cottle 2006; 2009a; Matheson and Allan 2009; Pantti 2016). This chapter deliberately adopts a different vantage point on contemporary war reporting. One that is compelled by the world-in-crisis in which we find ourselves, a world that increasingly unfolds through the deepening catastrophism of multiple, interacting global crises.

The Russian invasion of Ukraine began on 24 February 2022 just over two months after the end of COP26, the UN Conference on Climate Change (13.11.2021). This was the latest UN Climate Change Conference of the Parties warning of catastrophic consequences if the world does not wake up to the reality of climate change, a reality that is now having devastating impact on ecosystems and millions of lives around the planet (IPCC 2022). A conference in which the celebrated British naturalist, David Attenborough, opined, 'Is this how it is doomed to end?'. Not only is war a collective moral failure of humanity it is also an ecological outrage perpetrated on the planet, which, in the context of documented trajectories of civilisational and ecosystem collapse exacerbates and accelerates those same global forces now converging in today's planetary emergency. To what extent does contemporary war reporting give expression to today's growing ecological sensibility and concerns for the well-being of all life on planet Earth? Or, to what extent and how is this ecological sensibility distanced and dissimulated in contemporary war reporting, and at what cost?

This chapter explores these fundamental concerns based on an analysis of BBC news reports of the Russian invasion of Ukraine. Here general patterns and preoccupations of BBC reporting are first documented and how, with rare exceptions, this generally fails to situate the war in Ukraine and its broader ecological ramifications in today's world-in-crisis (Cottle 2009b; 2012). How this ecological dissimulation is enacted is then further explored in respect of how reporting variously *displaces*, *disregards* and *diminishes* ecological concerns and relays *duplicitous* messages charged with environmental claims. In such ways, it is argued, news reporting contributes to the prevailing normative outlook of today's *dominating worldview* – an outlook that underpins anthropogenic threats to the planet's ecology and life on Earth and which is fundamentally antithetical to an ecological sensibility and consciousness. The chapter concludes by returning to those very few BBC news reports that have sought to bring some attention to the ecological consequences of war as well as the multiple world crises both converging in, and exacerbated by, the war in Ukraine. In this handful of rare reports perhaps a glimmer of hope can be found concerning how news journalism could yet better express and deepen ecological awareness in the future – a consciousness that is vitally important if we are to better apprehend and attend to the drivers of climate change and ecological degradation now unfolding at speed and at planetary scale. But first a few words on today's world-in-crisis, conceptualised in relation to theoretical ideas of the Anthropocene, Capitalocene and Symbiocene, and the diverse ways in which warfare and ecology have become historically infused within each other.

A world-in-crisis: 'Modernity in nature'

The world today is in planetary crisis. Multiple existential threats now converge and bear down on the planet's biosphere and all life on earth

(Cottle 2022; 2023). They can be traced for the most part to the predominant economic system premised on unsustainable growth and a corresponding worldview of human exceptionalism and materialist ideas of progress. Human society is confronting the possibility, some will say distinct probability, that human civilisation in now in its endgame (Read and Alexander 2019; Berners-Lee 2021; Wallace-Wells 2019; Servigne and Stevens 2020; Haque 2021; Bendell and Read 2021; Kelly and Macy 2021). Today's existential threats – climate change, biodiversity loss, the sixth mass extinction, zoonotic pandemics, ecological degradations, food, water and energy insecurity and soil erosion, for example, are all deeply entwined in today's cascading crises (Kolbert 2014; Goulson 2021; Lawler et al. 2021; Cowie et al. 2022; IPCC 2022; Millman 2022; OCHA 2022; WFP 2023). Forced migrations, faltering supply chains and financial crises further express and exacerbate these and prove fertile grounds for the rise in polarised politics and authoritarianism and can give rise to new propensities for conflict and war.

Today's 'world civilizational community of fate' (Beck 2009), evidently, is not only confronting the widely known existential threats of climate change and nuclear weapons (Toon 2018; FAS 2022), but a host of further systemic threats that unfold in cascading and compounding interaction, many of them registering in the world's biosphere and ecosystems. No wonder, perhaps, that earth scientists have labelled this epoch as the Anthropocene. Following the Holocene that saw the first settled human communities and emergent agriculture, the Anthropocene is characterised by accelerating growth and unprecedented human impacts on nature and Earth systems (Lewis and Maslin 2018). The 'great acceleration' of human society's footprint on planet earth since the industrial revolution has been clearly documented (Steffen et al. 2015), even if the exact periodisation and degree to which Earth systems and nature are not simply reactive (but in some ways adaptive or constitutive) continue to be explored (Clarke 2014; Tsing 2015; Haraway 2016; Ghosh 2022).

When approached through a lens of political economy and conceived in such terms as the Capitalocene, the changes described under the mantle of the Anthropocene are granted more historical specificity and theoretical explanation (Moore 2015; Patel and Moore 2018). Here colonisation, capitalism and the successive waves of commodification of nature are said to have profoundly shaped both human societies and nature. 'The crisis today,' argues Moore, is 'not multiple but singular and manifold. It is not a crisis of capitalism *and* nature but of modernity-*in*-nature. That modernity is a capitalist world-ecology' (2015: 4). This capitalist world-ecology is now in terminal trouble.

The planet is overshooting most of its ecological boundaries (Raworth 2017; IPCC 2022), including those thresholds of sustainability first signalled fifty years ago as the 'limits to growth' (Meadows et al. 1972), but largely politically ignored since.

The world is now in a race to ecological consciousness, to an appreciation of how human existence is profoundly dependent on and interconnected *inside* the web of life, and how rapacious economic growth as well as ideas of human exceptionalism and materialist progress, have brought human civilisation and the planet's ecosystems to the edge of destruction. Looking into the abyss whilst recognising the complex interdependencies of all life on earth, has given rise to ideas of the Symbiocene, an imagined ecological civilisation premised on a more socially just, ecologically sustainable and therefore symbiotic way of life and living. This sensibility and emergent consciousness (Lent 2021; Korton 2021) is founded on disparate intellectual traditions and practices, including traditional indigenous wisdom (Kimmerer 2013; Yunkaporta 2020), Eastern spiritual traditions such as Buddhism and Taoism (Macy 2021; Hanh 2021), Western Romanticism (Sayre and Löwy 2022), deep ecology (Naess 2021) and, importantly, the new philosophy of science and systems view of life (Capra and Luisi 2014; McGilchrist 2022: 379–778). These ideational and affective currents flow and form as part of today's growing ecological awareness, an ecological 'structure of feeling' (Williams 1985) that is also propelled forward by the 'anthropogenic shocks' (Beck 2016) or latest cataclysms of a world-in-crisis as they crash into daily lives.

Warfare and ecology: Beyond scorched earth

Warfare historically has often involved scorched earth policies or the weaponisation of environments. It has done so by destroying habitats and sources of human sustenance. Burning villages and crops was widely used in Europe in the Thirty Years' War, for example, a tactic that later accompanied Dutch colonial violence against the Bandanese islanders and that of English settlers against Native American tribes (Ghosh 2022). Later, the deliberate policies of exterminating millions of buffaloes in the Great Plains and the flooding of fertile agricultural areas by federal authorities in the United States was pursued with genocidal intent (Ghosh 2022: 68–9). The defoliant Agent Orange was used in Vietnam by the Americans, with devastating impacts on environments, wildlife and human beings. And the deliberate spilling and setting fire to 630-plus oil wells in Kuwait and the draining of the Shi'a Marsh Arabs' marshlands in southern Iraq ordered by Saddam Hussein, are further examples of the weaponisation of nature in times of war. The very air we breathe has also become weaponised, when deliberately deoxygenated in firestorms caused by mass incendiary bombing or when polluted with pathogens or radioactive fallout, or threats of the same.

The UN Environment Programme calculates that at least 40 per cent of all internal conflicts have been linked to the exploitation of natural resources over the last sixty years (UNEP 2015). Impacts of war on environments and ecology can also be less direct, though no less consequential. For example, 90 per cent of animals in the Gorongosa National Park were lost across the fifteen-year Mozambique civil war. This included a population decline of elephants from 2,000 to 200, with their meat used to feed soldiers and their ivory sold to finance weapons and supplies (IRC 2019: 5.6). In Afghanistan, warlords felled trees for funds and war refugees stripped forests for shelter and heating. Together they depleted more than one-third of Afghanistan's entire forests between 1990 and 2007, leading in turn to increased drought, desertification and loss of biodiversity.

All wars can impact environments and ecology. In the first Gulf War, the United States used depleted uranium in its armaments that is known to harmfully leach into landscapes, watercourses and bio-organisms – including human beings. The use of explosive weapons causes massive damage to civilian and industrial infrastructure, but it also often results in the contamination of air, soil and water resources. The war in Ukraine, is no exception, with researchers soon noting 'the heavy toll on the environment, and the risk of significant environmental harm' (Cottrell and Derbyshire 2022).

The waging of war can also generate a significant military carbon bootprint, though this remains mostly out of sight. The US government insisted as self-declared 'world's policeman', that its military carbon footprint be exempt from the Kyoto Protocol. And, following the 2015 Paris Agreement, all governments have a voluntary obligation only to record and publish their military carbon footprints. This represents a major deficit in current world carbon accounting (Weir et al. 2021). Scientists for Global Responsibility estimate that the world's militaries combined, and the industries that provide their equipment, are likely to generate up to 6 per cent of global emissions (Parkinson 2020).

War reconstruction is also, of course, hugely carbon intensive and environmentally consequential. This too contributes to climate change with all its manifold impacts on life forms, different ecosystems and weather patterns converging in today's world-in-crisis. 'If the cement industry were a country, it would be the third largest emitter in the world' (Timperley 2018) and is thought to contribute between 6 and 8 per cent of global manmade carbon emissions. Millions of metric tonnes of cement will be used in civil reconstruction and the building of new homes and societal infrastructure following the destruction of war.

Finally, the cost of war is also a huge ecology opportunity cost. In 2008, it was estimated that the total projected US spending on the Iraq war could have covered all the global investments in renewable power generation that were needed to halt current warming trends, and that 'the war is responsible for at least 141 million metric tons of carbon dioxide equivalent (MMTCO2e) since March 2003', which would be equivalent to the emissions from 25 million additional cars (Bast 2008). The current cost of reconstruction and recovery in Ukraine has been estimated by the World Bank to be $349 billion (World Bank 2022).

As described above, we live in a world of interrelated world crises. War, including the war in Ukraine, is no less deeply and damagingly implicated within these, including climate change, biodiversity loss, environmental degradation as well as forced migrations, economic recession, food, water and energy shortages, military insecurity and the existential threat of nuclear weapons. The Russian invasion and war in Ukraine is 'fuelled, funded and facilitated by fossil fuels' (EJF 2022). And yet, the deeply entwined relationship between war and ecology rarely features in contemporary news reporting, where priorities and preoccupations are routinely disaggregated and oriented elsewhere.

War in Ukraine reporting: Patterns of preoccupation

To establish an overview of the general patterns and preoccupations of the reporting in the UK news media, and to see to what extent and how preceding world ecological concerns inform this, BBC 'War in Ukraine' reporting, compiled and available on its website (https://www.bbc.co.uk/news), was reviewed across a period of almost five months (30 July – 23 November 2022). This produced a sample of 860 news items. BBC News Online includes news items broadcast on the main BBC television news bulletins as well as news items occasionally published elsewhere on BBC platforms, as well as news items only available online. All are produced by BBC journalists working for the UK's leading public broadcaster committed by latest Royal Charter (2017–27) and in its public statement of *Mission, Values and Public Purposes* 'To provide impartial news and information to help people understand and engage with the world around them' and to 'offer a range and depth of analysis and content not widely available from other United Kingdom news providers' (BBC 2023). To this end, the BBC uses 'the highest calibre presenters and journalists' committed to 'championing freedom of expression' (BBC 2023). The BBC is a well-resourced and leading institution in the world of journalism and is positioned at the heart of the UK and wider international news ecology (Cottle 2012). Its news agenda can be regarded in broad terms as generally encompassing of that of most mainstream UK news broadcasters as well as some sections of the news press.

Table 10.1, based on a descriptive and inductive content analysis documenting the news reports' principal themes as presented, sets out the main patterns of the BBC's War in Ukraine news coverage.

As we can see, military-related events including threats of nuclear war and threats to nuclear plants, weapons provision and war crimes when combined with general political reactions to the war, together comprise almost two-thirds of all reporting. The reporting of refugees, aid and civil society responses as well as life on the home and war front constitute a further fifth of coverage. When these are combined with human-interest stories (reports about sports and cultural events and celebrities linked in some way to the war in Ukraine), together these account for the vast majority (87.1 per cent) of all the reporting. The remaining 12.9 per cent of the war coverage variously reports on the energy, cost of living and world food crises prompted by the Russian invasion as well as the costs of war including reconstruction. To what extent and how these reports have incorporated or distanced and dissimulated an ecological awareness of the war in Ukraine is now explored more analytically and deductively.

Ecological dissimulation: *Displacement*

In November 2021, the UK news media including BBC news devoted considerable resources and news time to its coverage of COP26 and the world's pledges to reduce carbon emissions and pursue mitigation and adaptation strategies. With the invasion of Ukraine, however, the latter soon dominated

Table 10.1: BBC News Online 'War in Ukraine'

	n.	per cent
Military events	201	23.4
Nuclear risks	60	7.0
Weapons/support	59	6.9
War crimes	42	4.8
Political reactions	153	17.8
Refugees	92	10.7
Charity/Aid	19	2.2
Civil society responses	43	5.0
Home front life	23	2.7
Energy/cost of living crises	60	7.0
Human Interest	57	6.6
Food crisis	32	3.7
Costs of war	9	2.2
Total	*860*	*100%*

news headlines often becoming the BBC's leading news story. The preceding agenda granted additional focus by the COP26 on climate change and the world necessity to transition away from fossil fuels now became displaced from its former position of news salience.

The latest release of the IPCC report, *Climate Change 2022: Impacts, Adaptation and Vulnerability*, for example, was released on 28 February 2022, four days after the invasion but this did not register in the BBC's online news reporting. The message of COP26 including the stark warning of the UN General Secretary that 'Our addiction to fossil fuels is pushing humanity to the brink' (UNFCCC 2022) quickly evaporated in BBC news reporting generally, as well as news now focusing on the war in Ukraine.

As the war in Ukraine proceeded, the BBC produced several detailed analyses concerning the growing world energy and cost of living crises prompted in part by Europe's dependency on Russian fossil fuels and President Vladimir Putin's weaponisation of the same. Here, occasionally, the preceding backdrop of COP26 and concerns over continuing use of fossil fuels and carbon emissions might find a brief mention, typically toward the end of the journalist's report. But for the most part these reports omitted any reference to either COP26 or growing calls to cut back on fossil fuels and the need to pursue green energies. All the following reports about energy and cost of living crises as well as their headlines below, for example, make no mention of these fundamental concerns and are typical of this crucial neglect.

> 'British Gas-owner reopens storage ahead of winter' (28.10.2022),
> 'Gas taps can still be turned on to EU – says Vladimir Putin' (12.10.2022)
> 'EU leaders consider how to cap gas prices' (6.10.2022)
> 'UK at significant risk of gas shortage this winter, warns energy regulator' (3.10.2022)
> 'Russia sanctions: How can the world cope without its oil and gas?' (29.9.2022)
> 'Germany nationalises gas giant amid energy crisis' (21.9.2022)
> 'EU clubs together on energy and invites UK' (8.9.2022)
> 'No going back to reliance on Russian gas' (3.9.2022)

These and other reports about energy and rising costs of living related to the war in Ukraine, define the 'energy crisis' as one of reduced energy supplies on world markets, and not as an enforced opportunity to break the dependency on fossil fuels and transition to green energies. Fuel price rises and their impact on costs of living invariably became focused in terms of economic consumers struggling to pay for fuel and other daily goods, rather than as a matter of ecological citizenship and political calls for action over climate and ecology (Lester and Cottle 2013). The following news report, for example, not only positions the energy crisis entirely as an economic rather than as an ecological crisis, but also normalises the expectancy of continuing tourism flights. Again, at no point in this report is the world backdrop of climate change, fossil fuel consumption and the carbon footprint of the aviation industry mentioned, much less the responsibility of all of us to reduce flights.

> Flights will be more expensive, says ex-BA chief.
> The price of airline tickets will go up 'without doubt' as fuel costs rise, an air industry boss has warned. Oil prices have jumped as economies recover from the Covid pandemic and due to the war in Ukraine. These costs will be passed on to

consumers, Willie Walsh, director general of the International Air Transport Association (IATA), said. (BBC News, 10.7.2022)

But the problem is more entrenched than the changing and temporary nature of news agendas, as we hear below.

Ecological dissimulation: *Disregarding*

BBC war reporting has not only displaced environmental concerns momentarily catapulted into the headlines by COP26, it has also disregarded the ecological consequences of war. Images of the terrible destruction of war on cities and urban infrastructure, often relayed by drone cameras, are plentiful across the military event reporting, but this reporting has not sought to situate such damage in respect of preceding ecological concerns of climate change, military carbon boot-prints or the wider ecological damage caused by weapons of war, including those offered by Western governments in support of Ukraine. A detailed report, 'Ukraine weapons: What military equipment is the world giving?' (9.9.2022), for example, explores the military expenditure and equipment provided by more than thirty countries to Ukraine, including Himar rocket launcher systems, M777 howitzers, S-300 air defence systems, Bayraktar TB2 drones and T-72M1 tanks, all contrasted with Russian weapons systems. But we hear nothing of their ecological costs and environmental consequences, whether measured in terms of carbon boot-print, ecological despoilation or ecological opportunity costs. In this report, better suited perhaps to a military enthusiast or potential buyer at an international arms fayre, we also hear nothing of these weapon systems' destructive power on human bodies.

Reports of war crimes have also confined their focus on documented and alleged human atrocities and torture, but they have yet to consider the wider environmental consequences of war, notwithstanding possible legal precedents to do so. The Rome Statute of 2002 states, for example, that it is a war crime to intentionally cause 'widespread, long-term, and severe damage to the natural environment which would be clearly excessive'. Though such a legal definition may prove underdeveloped in an international court of law, news media are not professionally or morally bound to ignore the ecological consequences and crimes of war.

Ukraine war reporting has reported extensively on the military danger posed to nuclear power plants, including decommissioned Chernobyl, and the largest nuclear power plant in Europe, Zaporizhzhia, housing six reactors, but less so on the risks of a nuclear exchange. These reports for the most part provide the latest update on military actions in or near these nuclear plants and the calls, for example, for independent safety inspections by the UN's International Atomic Energy Agency. Some reports go into greater depth concerning 'risks'. 'Ukraine nuclear plant: How risky is stand-off over Zaporizhzhia?' (BBC 21.11.2022) begins, for example, by noting how 'Rafael Grossi, the head of the International Atomic Energy Agency, has warned of a very real risk of nuclear disaster' and proceeds to ask: 'What, then, is the risk to this nuclear plant which houses six reactors – and is Europe facing a Fukushima-type meltdown?' Though the report provides expert commentary on the risks of shelling and power supply failure to nuclear plants and the robustness, in this instance, of the Zaporizhzhia plant, this and other reports have yet to set out in equal detail the possible devastating consequences of a nuclear reactor 'accident' and major radiation release. This would necessarily include consideration of its potential global scope, longevity and detrimental impacts on not only human bodies but all life forms and ecosystems into the future.

A similar reluctance to report on the apocalyptic outcome of a nuclear exchange between Russia and NATO is also evident in the reporting of President Putin's barely veiled threats to use nuclear weapons. For example, 'Putin not bluffing about nuclear weapons, EU says' (24.9.2022), provides analysis and expert commentary about the weapons involved, tactics of response and constraints involved in nuclear deployment – but does not envision the nuclear nightmare and ecological winter that would result. When the capabilities of nuclear weapons are described, as in 'Putin threats: How many nuclear weapons does Russia have?' (7.10.2022), this is stated in somewhat matter-of-fact terms, simply defining, for example, nuclear 'fireball', 'blast wave', 'radiation', 'electromagnetic pulses' and 'fallout'. Such oblique, matter-of-fact reporting produces a somewhat under-whelming sense of the possibility and consequences of a nuclear exchange, especially when described in factually abstract, geographically unspecified and ecologically understated ways.

A minority of news reports have begun to address the costs of war and processes of reconstruction, but these are generally estimated in economic and not ecological terms of environmental impacts and carbon footprints and focus on the human toll of war rather than opportunities to creatively redesign urban spaces and infrastructure systems for a sustainable future. The following are representative of this ecological disregarding. 'The cost of occupation in Kherson region. As Ukraine retakes territory, villagers tell the BBC about their precarious life under Russian rule' (23.10.2022), 'As UK counts pennies, we count casualties – Olena Zelenska' (3.9.2022), 'Death in Donbas – the toll on Ukraine's front line' (17.7.2022), and 'Kyiv residents hope to rebuild damaged flats' (20.7.2022).

Ecological dissimulation: *Diminishment*

In addition to Ukraine war reporting that disregards crucial concerns of ecology and displaces previously established ones, so important ecology stories can also be indirectly impacted and diminished by the prominence afforded to Ukraine war reporting. For example, the BBC news story, 'Amazon near environmental tipping point – researchers say', was relegated to the very last of the twelve pictured news items and positioned at the bottom of the BBC news homepage, with all eleven preceding stories focused exclusively on the war in Ukraine.

> The Amazon rainforest is moving towards a 'tipping point' where trees may die off en masse, say researchers. A study suggests the world's largest rainforest is losing its ability to bounce back from damage caused by droughts, fires and deforestation. Large swathes could become sparsely forested savannah, which is much less efficient than tropical forest at sucking carbon dioxide from the air. The giant forest traps carbon that would otherwise add to global warming. But previous studies have shown that parts of the Amazon are now emitting more carbon dioxide than can be absorbed. (BBC News, 8.3.2022

As the scientists quoted in the report stated, such a dieback would be devastating given the implications for climate change, biodiversity and the local community. Notwithstanding the world significance of this latest research finding concerning the impact of deforestation and climate change on the Amazon's capacity as 'the lungs of the world', this was relegated and diminished in prominence by the preceding eleven war reports all about the war in Ukraine.

Ecological dissimulation: *Duplicitousness*

Ukraine war coverage unsurprisingly, given what we know about propaganda war and the efforts to win over hearts and minds and demonise the enemy, can also involve ecological duplicitousness. That is, the attempt to deceive and exert pressure through claims and counterclaims about the use or intended use of chemical and biological weapons, so-called tactical 'dirty' bombs, and nuclear weapons. It also includes claims and counterclaims about the deliberate targeting of nuclear power plants such as Chernobyl and Zaporizhzhia and the bombing of the Nord Stream gas pipeline – all of which pose huge environmental consequences. The Russian invasion has given rise to numerous and continuing examples of such duplicitousness communicated via the news media, including so-called 'false flag' alarms of possible use of biochemical weapons or dirty bombs by the other side, and how these may then be used as a pretext for use of these same weapons by those supposedly raising the alarm. The following BBC report headlined 'Russian dirty bomb claims "feel like scare tactics"', is typical of these reports.

> Russia is standing by its claim that Ukraine is preparing to use a so-called dirty bomb – an explosive device laced with radioactive material. It made its case at the UN Security Council on Tuesday. But such allegations have been typical of Russia's conduct during the war. (BBC News, 25.10.2022)

While such reports help to raise awareness of the possible egregious use of barbaric weapons and how this underpins the scare tactic of thinly veiled or explicit threats, they detract nonetheless from the everyday and ongoing ecological consequences of warfare and how this is profoundly entwined in today's world-in-crisis.

Ecological dissimulation: *Dominating worldview*

The forms of ecological dissimulation evident in the reporting of the Ukraine war noted above, are based on a general review of BBC online news reporting. To what extent and how they obtain across the entirety of today's news landscape and in different countries requires more extensive exploration than possible here. With few exceptions, such as *the Guardian* newspaper with its pledge to report on the climate and ecological crisis, it seems probable that these forms of *disregarding*, *distancing*, *diminishment*, and *duplicitousness* are all widespread and at work within mainstream news reporting today. A further form of ecological dissimulation, *disparagement*, or the sceptical undermining and ridicule of accessed voices and ecologically committed viewpoints, may also be in play, particularly in populist TV news formats and partisan and tabloid press reporting (Cottle forthcoming). These analytically distinguishable forms of ecological dissimulation generally cohere under mainstream journalism's general subscription to the prevailing *dominating worldview*.

The current dominating worldview in late-modern capitalist societies is founded on the elective affinity with normative assumptions about constant economic growth, material progress and human exceptionalism or speciesism. It is this that filters and infuses news agendas and journalism's basic orientation to the world it reports on – including in times of war. I call this today's *dominating worldview* rather than, to borrow from an earlier lexicon, 'dominant worldview' or 'dominant ideology' or 'dominant discourse', to help signal the shared belief in the presumed exceptionalism of human beings and their hierarchical sense of active entitlement in the domination of not only each other (seen in times of war and peace), but also non-human species, nature, the planet – and, courtesy of space entrepreneurs like Elon Musk and Richard Branson, far beyond. This faith in humanity's capacity to successfully master and exploit nature rather than to see ourselves as deeply implicated within nature and the web of life, appears increasingly fatally hubristic.

This dominating worldview, antithetical to ecological consciousness, generally infuses news reporting and its daily disaggregation of the world into separate stories, news categories, news beats and specialist correspondence – as if the complex web of life can be so easily reduced and confined to separate categories. The dominating worldview also informs journalism's selective gaze and subsequent framing of news stories – and this is also enacted when reporting on war as we have heard. We see it in the ways in which the war in Ukraine is reported as a military and political contest, not an ecological devastation with planetary consequence, even when scorched earth policies are visualised through scenes of ruined human habitats or devastated infrastructure. We see it in the ways in which impacts of war beyond Ukraine are invariably focused through the business-as-usual prism of consumer price rises or the rapid return to find new sources of fossil fuels in times of economic recession. We see this dominating worldview in the disaggregation of the war in Ukraine from a preceding world-in-crisis and at the very moment that it exemplifies the compound economic and ecological interdependencies of a world now accelerating down existential tracks. Here presumptions of human species exceptionalism as well as normative ideas of perpetual economic growth, and human progress measured in materialist terms, all militate against an ecological consciousness of interconnectedness and symbiotic interdependency.

To conclude let's be clear ...

Journalism is neither historically static nor is it outside of the changing sensibilities, priorities and movements for change that help characterise civil societies. Most news media today, for reasons that are well known, remain behind the curve of change and have yet to fully recognise and report on the complex interdependencies and compounding nature of today's world-in-crisis (Cottle 2006; 2009a; 2023; forthcoming). This, as we have seen in the case of BBC reporting, is etched into the seemingly separate news issues and stories that they report on. This discussion has identified in preliminary terms several ways in which this happens in respect of the distancing and dissimulation of an ecological sensibility in the BBC's reporting on the war in Ukraine. But even the BBC with its institutionalised presence and expectations of journalist performance is not a reporting monolith and nor can it, as well as other news organisations, entirely ignore the encroaching entanglements of today's world-in-crisis.

The Russian war in Ukraine in all its brutality has illuminated the world's interdependencies in terms of energy, food shortages and consumer prices as well as military (in)security. These have all forced their way onto the news agenda. In a BBC report: 'Cost of living: what do COVID, war and drought have to do with my bills?' (3.9.2022), the journalist sets out to explain the impact of multiple global crises on price rises and everyday life and in so doing begins to communicate something of their mutually entangled and exacerbating nature. A similarly exceptional report, 'Ukraine grain ship with aid for Ethiopia docks in Djibouti' (14.11.2022) also explored the interconnections between the Russian invasion of Ukraine, world food prices, climate change, drought and famine. Though highly infrequent and together constituting a mere 0.2 per cent of all BBC war in Ukraine reports, they nonetheless illustrate how the BBC can, exceptionally, in a process of 'enforced enlightenment' (Beck 2009), begin to respond to the evident interplay and mutual reinforcement of multiple world crises.

An explicit concern with environmental despoilation in times of war is also not entirely absent from all BBC war in Ukraine reporting. A report entitled 'Wildlife abandons "Europe's Amazon" nature reserve' (9.10.2022), reflexively observed, 'The human and material cost of Russia's invasion of Ukraine is well documented. But rare species of animals and flowers that had flourished in the country's north have also been badly hit by the invaders' destructive use of weaponry and landmines, with fears they will take decades to recover.' It also noted how Russian artillery shells fired into northern Ukraine had ignited forest fires that 'burnt through more than 2,000 hectares (nearly 5,000 acres) of previously untouched forest, sending wildlife scattering, incinerating recently-discovered orchids and hundreds of other rare plants'. This rare report proved exceptional in the identified patterns of

BBC's reporting, given its explicit focus on the ecological consequences of war – even though such concerns are not situated in relation to the world's wider ecological crises both informing and, as here, exasperated by the war in Ukraine.

We began this discussion by situating the war in relation to COP26 that ended not long before the Russian invasion began and noting how Ukraine war reporting soon moved on from the pressing existential issues of climate change and ecological destruction. COP27, a year later, also afforded a renewed opportunity to finally raise and incorporate these existential concerns in the context of the war in Ukraine. A BBC report, 'COP27: War causing huge release of climate warming gas, claims Ukraine' (14.11.2022), outlined Ukrainian claims of the estimated 33 million tonnes of greenhouse gases caused by the war, the destruction of precious animal and plant life and referenced the Ukrainian government's compiling of evidence on environmental crimes. Ukraine's environmental protection minister was also quoted as saying, 'Russia has turned our natural reserves into a military base. Russia is doing everything to shorten our and your horizons. Because of the war, we will have to do even more to overcome the climate crisis.' This isolated report no doubt gives expression to Ukraine's efforts to seek enhanced political legitimacy and diplomatic advantage in international fora. But it also once again underlines the nature of today's world-in-crisis and how war, including 'environmental crimes' (see above), are deeply implicated in wider ecological crises and climate change, even though news media for the most part are institutionally and ecologically blind to them.

To conclude, I want to be clear, the vantage point of this article and its related argument is not suggesting that the reporting of war and its atrocious impacts on human beings, human society and human ways of life should be disregarded or diminished all in favour of ecological reporting. The human consequences of war must be witnessed by news media, and this rightly calls forth moral outrage as well as differing political responses. Concerns of ecology in planetary context, however, cannot be left to when the fighting stops. When the very biosphere of life on Earth is under existential threat, so the news media, as much as the rest of us, must seek to develop a deeper ecological awareness and consciousness of human life and its deep imbrication within the planetary web-of-life. It is only on this basis that a future society in symbiotic relationship with nature can be imagined and the deepening trajectories of ecological and societal collapse adequately recognised and responded to.

References

Allan, S., and Zelizer, B. (eds) (2004). *Reporting War*. London: Routledge.
Bast, E. (2008). 'A Climate of War: The War in Iraq and Global Warming', *Oil Change International*, https://priceofoil.org/2008/03/01/a-climate-of-war/, accessed 6 January 2023.
Beck, U. (2009). *World at Risk*. Cambridge: Polity.
Beck, U. (2016). *The Metamorphosis of the World*. Cambridge: Polity.
Bendell, J., and Read, R. (eds) (2021). *Deep Adaptation*. Cambridge: Polity.
Berners-Lee, M. (2021). *There Is No Planet B*. Cambridge: Cambridge University Press.
BBC. (2023). 'Mission, Values and Purposes', British Broadcasting Corporation, https://www.bbc.com/aboutthebbc/governance/mission, accessed January 2023.
Capra, F., and Luisi, P. L. (2014). *The Systems View of Life*. Cambridge: Cambridge University Press.
Clarke, N. (2014). 'Geo-Politics and the Disaster of the Anthropocene', *Sociological Review*, 62 (1), 19–37.
Cottle, S. (2006). *Mediatized Conflict*. Maidenhead: Open University Press.
Cottle, S. (2009a). *Global Crisis Reporting*. Maidenhead: Open University Press.
Cottle, S. (2009b). 'Global Crises in the News: Staging New Wars, Disasters, and Climate Change', *International Journal of Communication*, 3, 494–516.
Cottle, S. (2012). 'Global Crises and World News Ecology'. In S. Allan (ed.), *The Routledge Companion to News and Journalism Studies*, pp. 473–84. London: Routledge.
Cottle, S. (2022). 'On the Edge of the World: Peace and Conflict Reporting in a World-in-Crisis'. In K. Orgeret (ed.), *Insights on Peace and Conflict Reporting*, pp. 10–31. London: Routledge.
Cottle, S. (2023). 'Reporting Civilisational Collapse: Notes from a World-in-Crisis', *Global Media and Communication*, 19 (2), 269-288.
Cottle, S. (forthcoming). *Reporting Civilizational Collapse: A Wake-Up Call*. London: Routledge.
Cottrell, L., and Darbyshire, E. (2022). 'Explosive Weapons Use and the Environmental Consequences: Mapping Environmental Incidents in Ukraine', *The Journal of Conventional Weapon Destruction*, 26 (1), 44–50.
Cowie, R., Bouchet, P., and Fontaine, B. (2022). 'The Sixth Mass Extinction', *Biological Reviews*, 97 (2), 640–63.
EJF. (2022). 'Putin's War Fueled, Funded and Facilitated by Fossil Fuels', Environmental Justice Foundation, https://ejfoundation.org/resources/downloads/Putins-war-fuelled-funded-and-facilitated-by-fossil-fuels.pdf, accessed 6 January 2023.
FAS. (2022). 'Status of World Nuclear Forces', Federation of American Scientist, https://fas.org/issues/nuclear-weapons/status-world-nuclear-forces/, accessed 6 January 2023.
Ghosh, A. (2022). *The Nutmeg's Curse: Parables for a Planet in Crisis*. London: John Murray.
Goulson, D. (2021). *Silent Earth*. London: Jonathan Cape.
Hanh, T. (2021). *Zen and the Art of Saving the Planet*. London: Penguin.
Haque, U. (2021). 'The Age of the Great Dying', *Eudaimonia*, July 9, https://eand.co/the-age-of-the-great-dying-is-beginning-651b1a210432, accessed 6 January 2023.
Haraway, D. (2016). *Staying with the Trouble*. Durham, NC: Duke University Press.

IPCC. (2022). *IPCC Sixth Assessment Report: Impacts, Adaptation and Vulnerability*, https://www.ipcc.ch/report/ar6/wg2/, accessed 6 January 2023.

IRC. (2019). *Natural Environment: Neglected Victim of Armed Conflict*. International Red Cross, https://www.icrc.org/en/document/natural-environment-neglected-victim-armed-conflict, accessed 6 January 2023.

Kelly, S., and Macy, J. (2021). 'The Great Turning'. In J. Bendell, and R. Read (eds), *Deep Adaptation*, pp. 197–208. Cambridge: Polity.

Kimmerer, R. (2013). *Braiding Sweetgrass*. London: Penguin.

Kolbert. E. (2014). *The Sixth Extinction*. London: Bloomsbury.

Korton, D. (2021). *Ecological Civilization*, https://davidkorten.org/ecological-civilization-from-emergency-to-emergence/, accessed 6 January 2023.

Lawler, O., Allan, H., and Baxter, P. (2021). 'The Covid-19 Pandemic is Intricately Linked to Biodiversity Loss and Ecosystem Health', *The Lancet*, 5 (11), 840–50.

Lent, J. (2021). *The Web of Meaning*. London: Profile Books.

Lester, E., and Cottle, S. (2013). 'Visualizing Climate Change: Television News and Ecological Citizenship'. In A. Hansen (ed.), *Media and the Environment: Volume III, Covering the Environment*, pp. 920–36. London: Routledge.

Lewis. S., and Maslin, M. (2018). *The Human Planet: How We Created the Anthropocene*. London: Penguin Books.

Macy, J. (2021). *World as Lover, World as Self*. California: Parallax Press.

Matheson, D., and Allan, S. (2009). *Digital War Reporting*. Cambridge: Polity.

McGilchrist, I. (2022). *The Matter with Things*. London: Perspectiva Press.

Meadows, D. H., Meadows, D. L., Randers., J., and Behrens, W. (1972). *The Limits to Growth*. New York: Universe Books.

Millman, O. (2022). *The Insect Crisis*. New York: Atlantic Books

Moore, J. (2015). *Capitalism in the Web of Life*. London: Verso Books.

Naess, A. (2021). *There is No Point of Return*. London: Penguin.

OCHA. (2022). *Global Humanitarian Overview*. United Nations, https://gho.unocha.org/, accessed 6 January 2023.

Pantti, M. (ed.) (2016). *Media and the Ukraine Crisis: Hybrid Media Practices and Narratives of Conflict* New York: Peter Lang.

Parkinson, S. (2020). 'The Carbon Boot-Print of the Military', *Responsible Science Journal*, 2, 18–20.

Patel, R., and Moore, J. (2018). *A History of the World in Seven Cheap Things*. London: Verso.

Raworth, K. (2017). *Doughnut Economics*. London: Penguin.

Read, R., and Alexander, S. (2019). *This Civilization is Finished*. Melbourne: Simplicity Institute.

Sayre, R., and Löwy, M. (2022). *Romantic Anti-Capitalism and Nature*. London: Routledge.

Servigne, P., and Stevens, R. (2020). *How Everything Can Collapse*. Cambridge: Polity.

Steffen, W., Broadgate, W., Deutsch, L., Gaffney, O., and Ludwig, C. (2015). 'The Trajectory of the Anthropocene: The Great Acceleration', *The Anthropocene Review*, 2 (1), 81–98.

Timperley, J. (2018). 'Why Cement Emissions Matter for Climate Change', *CarbonBrief*, https://www.carbonbrief.org/qa-why-cement-emissions-matter-for-climate-change/, accessed 6 January 2023.

Toon, B. (2018). 'I've Studied Nuclear War for 35 Years – You Should Be Worried', TEDxMileHigh, https://www.youtube.com/watch?v=M7hOpT0lPGI, accessed 6 January 2023.

Tsing, A. (2015). *The Mushroom at the End of the World*. Princeton, NJ: Princeton University Press.

UNEP. (2015). 'UNEP Marks International Day for Preventing the Exploitation of the Environment in War and Armed Conflict', United Nations Environmental Programme, https://www.un.org/en/observances/environment-in-war-protection-day#:~:text=On%205%20November%202001%2C%20the,RES%2F56%2F4, accessed 6 January 2023.

UNFCCC. (2022). COP 26 Speeches and Statements, https://unfccc.int/cop-26/speeches-and-statements#Statements-given-at-official-opening-ceremony-of-t, accessed 6 January 2023.

Wallace-Wells, D. (2019). *The Uninhabitable Earth*. London: Penguin Books.

Weir, D., Neimark, B., and Belcher, O. (2021). 'How the World's Militaries Hide Their Huge Carbon Emission', *The Conversation*, https://theconversation.com/how-the-worlds-militaries-hide-their-huge-carbon-emissions-171466, accessed 6 January 2023.

Williams, R. (1985). *Marxism and Literature*. Oxford: Oxford University Press.

World Bank. (2022). 'Ukraine Recovery and Reconstruction Needs Estimated $349 Billion', Press Release, https://www.worldbank.org/en/news/press-release/2022/09/09/ukraine-recovery-and-reconstruction, accessed 6 January 2023.

WFP. (2023). *A Global Food Crisis*, World Food Programme, https://www.wfp.org/global-hunger-crisis, accessed 6 January 2023.

Yunkaporta, T. (2020). *Sand Talk*. New York: Harper Collins.

PARTICIPATIVE WAR: THE NEW PARADIGM OF WAR AND MEDIA

Andrew Hoskins

Walking through a minefield and along trenches in Donbas in 2016 and 2017, the then (2014–22) Russian war against Ukraine, seemed to me like something firmly located in the twentieth century. The 2022 war is also a traditional 'hot' war of trenches, artillery and tanks. As I write, the tens of thousands of casualties on both sides accumulate further in the eastern Ukrainian city of Bakhmut, in 'the bloodiest battle on European soil since World War II' (Washington Post 2023). Yet this is also the first state-on-state war in Europe to be entirely mediated by digital technology (Ford 2022). This includes Bakhmut, where the US technology company Palantir supplies software to Ukraine to crunch and fuse data quickly for the purposes of targeting and damaging assessment. Other US companies such as Starlink, Microsoft and Clearview AI, have all contributed support to Ukraine in the form of secure satellite-based communications, digital infrastructure and cloud data storage and facial recognition technology, respectively.

The dominance of US tech companies on the Ukrainian battlefield is the latest twist in President Eisenhower's (1961)[1] 'military industrial complex', which threatened US democracy. A 'military–social media complex' (Merrin and Hoskins 2020) is a different form of dominance, whereby a set of predominantly US-owned technologies, platforms and apps can be globally accessed and weaponised by states, but also by a digital multitude.

Newly empowered 'citizen militia' smartphone warriors take on and take down governments, militaries and media propaganda units. This is 'my war' (Boichak and Hoskins 2022). With the smartphone, individuals can communicate, coordinate, recruit and wage effective informational war from anywhere in the world. This wonderful volume clearly illuminates how emergent forms of digital participation mark a paradigm shift in the relationship between war and media.

A key tension in how we come to understand or misunderstand, adapt to or deny changes in technologies and media, is that ideas and concepts once established to explain perceptions, experiences and effects in an earlier era are difficult to shift. Astonishingly, but effectively, Merrin (2014) levels this charge against the discipline of Media Studies, showing how it cannot even register the revolution in digital media, as its view is too clouded by the 'broadcast era' lens it insists on looking through. This translates into adaptation to the new order being hampered through the clinging to the security that comes from the familiarity of long-established theories and practices.

Some journalists and news organisations think they can re-establish their profession – and trust – with fact-checking. Some militaries think they can prohibit smartphones from the battlefield. Some governments think that social media platforms can contain horrific content through moderation. All these approaches to rapid technological change stutter, as they require self-awareness of the demise of their (organisational and institutional) monopoly over information and experience. Instead, the unleashing of the productive and distributive capacities of individuals, empower them as commentators, critics, producers and sharers of their own material or messages (Merrin 2014).

Although the tipping point of participative war is firmly located in the smartphone era, its precursors are found in the 1990s development of the idea of 'network-centric warfare' (Cebrowski and Garstka 1998). This is the idea of a networked military form, a decentralised structure enabling connected individuals' greater agility in moving rapidly to unbalance the larger, less mobile, oppositional force. Thus, overlapping and continuously available networks are the organisational basis of a particular type of decentralised warfare, for instance, 'netwars' (Arquilla and Ronfeldt 1993; 2001; Hoskins and O'Loughlin 2010).

For Merrin (2018: 60) the establishment of ideas around the decentralisation of the organisation of war was not only a military transformation but 'more fundamentally *a global, societal and personal revolution* in information technology and information' (italics in original). This revolution is certainly defining the 2022 Russian war against Ukraine. There is an ongoing rapid exploitation of the smartphone and social media platforms and apps, and sensing, mapping and tracking technologies, built for war. Smart devices are both a way to represent war and a node in its practice (Ford and Hoskins 2022).

The new paradigm of participative war is evident on the Telegram messenger app (used by more than 70 per cent of Ukrainians and 25 per cent of Russians) enabling anyone to create a public newsfeed with videos, audios and texts. It is a unique platform in its openness to weaponisation by an array of actors including civilian society groups, NGOs, journalists, militaries and states. This includes the crowdsourcing for humanitarian assistance or military equipment (drones, advanced optics, uniforms and armour). However, it is on the Russian side that there is a greater civil society participation in this war via Telegram.

From 2022 into 2023, Russian civil society was increasingly mobilised on and through Telegram as the country fell considerably behind Ukraine in fighting the wider information war. On Telegram, you can sponsor a Russian sniper rifle, having your own message stencilled onto a gun that will shoot Ukrainians or inscribed on a 152 mm rocket shell.[2] But the civil-military nexus on Telegram is not just a one-directional flow of aid and crowdsourced donations. In return, images and videos on Telegram depict the damage caused by your personalised weapon, as well as an emergent genre of images and videos of gratitude, including a message of thanks for the donation from the sniper who fired it.[3]

These kinds of participation represent a new hyper-individualisation of war, where war is increasingly something in your personalised digital feed (Hoskins and Shchelin 2022), a media ecology of one. As this war has progressed, most of its actors have migrated onto, adapted and exploited Telegram, transforming the platform into the pivotal digital battlespace. War accelerates into media as media accelerates into war. Telegram renders the war in and against Ukraine up close and personal. Never has such media content been weaponised so quickly and on such a scale. Nor has the world seen blunt psychological warfare on the scale of millions of images and videos of human suffering and death so readily available, streaming from the battlefield. Or to be accurate, much of 'the world' still has not, as despite the astonishing availability of this digital battlespace, it is mostly overlooked by Western and Westernised mainstream media, incapable of showing what is shown there. Moreover, digital feeds that enable unprecedented personalisation of and participation in war enable unprecedented ignorance. Algorithms are not necessarily required for today's splintering of multiple realities of experience.

Overall, we might easily arrive at a conclusion of participation as the ultimate realisation of decentralised warfare. The original idea was that battlefield information and data dominance would feed downwards, allowing decentralised operations, rapid decision-making and the self-organising of an array of actors including those on the ground. Yet the same technologies, platforms and devices that enable participation, also produce information that can pour upwards. Every action of an individual is potentially locatable, trackable, traceable and recordable, so the future of war is not network-centric warfare. It will not be decentralised warfare.

The future is instead more likely the re-centralisation of war. The challenge with the most datafied and documented war in history is that its informational scale makes it resistant to ready human intelligibility. In real time, AI commanders have the greatest prospects of managing war. In future, whoever owns and can mine the new digital archives of participation, of citizen-militia messaging systems and social media platforms, will have most influence over legitimatising war, including in pursuing accountability and justice for its victims.

Notes

1 President Dwight D. Eisenhower's Farewell Address (1961), https://www.archives.gov/milestone-documents/president-dwight-d-eisenhowers-farewell-address.
2 Telegram, https://focus.ua/voennye-novosti/518432-za-donat-nadpis-na-snaryade-volontery-zapustili-neobychnyy-sposob-pomoshchi-armii-foto.
3 Telegram, https://t.me/lobaev_vlad/5544.

References

Arquilla, J., and Ronfeldt, D. (1993). 'Cyberwar is Coming!', *Comparative Strategy*, 12 (2), 141–55.
Arquilla, J., and Ronfeldt, D. (eds) (2001). *Networks and Netwars: The Future of Terror, Crime and Militancy*. Santa Monica, CA: RAND.
Boichak, O., and Hoskins, A. (2022). Editorial: 'My War: Participation in Warfare', *Digital War*, https://doi.org/10.1057/s42984-022-00060-7, accessed 8 April 2023.

Cebrowski, A. K., and Garstka, J. J. (1998). 'Network-Centric Warfare: Its Origin and Future', *Proceedings*, USS Naval Institute, pp. 28–35, http://www.kinection.com/ncoic/ncw_origin_future.pdf, accessed 8 April 2023.

Ford, M. (2022). 'The Smartphone as Weapon (Part 1)', https://www.academia.edu/75845985/The_Smartphone_as_Weapon_part_1_the_new_ecology_of_war_in_Ukraine, accessed 8 April 2023, accessed 14 April 2023.

Ford, M., and Hoskins, A. (2022). *Radical War: Data, Attention and Control in the Twenty-First Century*. New York: Oxford University Press.

Hoskins, A., and O'Loughlin, B. (2010). *War and Media: The Emergence of Diffused War*. Cambridge: Polity Press.

Hoskins, A., and Shchelin, P. (2022). 'The War Feed: Digital War in Plain Sight', *American Behavioral Scientist*, https://doi.org/10.1177/00027642221144848, accessed 8 April 2023, accessed 14 April 2023.

Merrin, W. (2014). *Media Studies 2.0*. London: Routledge.

Merrin, W. (2018). *Digital War: A Critical Introduction*. London: Routledge.

Merrin, W., and Hoskins, A. (2020). 'Tweet Fast and Kill Things: Digital War', *Digital War*, 1 (1), 184–93.

Washington Post. (2023). 'Opinion – Bakhmut's "Slaughter-Fest" Holds Lessons for the West', 3 April, https://www.washingtonpost.com/opinions/2023/04/03/bakhmut-battle-ukraine-resolve/, accessed 3 April 2023.

NOTES ON CONTRIBUTORS

GÖRAN BOLIN is Professor of Media and Communication Studies at Södertörn University. His research focuses on information management, branding, media generations, datafication and digital markets. He is the author and editor of *Value and the Media: Cultural Production and Consumption in Digital Markets* (Ashgate 2011), *Cultural Technologies: The Shaping of Culture in Media and Society* (Routledge 2012), *Media Generations: Experience, Identity and Mediatised Social Change* (Routledge 2016) and *Managing Meaning in Ukraine: Information, Communication and Narration since the Euromaidan Revolution* (with Per Ståhlberg, MIT Press 2023). He is a member of the Executive Board of ECREA and Chair of the section Film, Media and Visual Studies in Academia Europaea.

KATERYNA BOYKO is a PhD student in Media and Communication with the Institute for Russian and Eurasian Studies (IRES) at Uppsala University. Her doctoral research explores civic cultures of pirate online communities in Ukraine. She focuses on conjunctions and interplays between civic and peer-to-peer file-sharing practices: how and under what conditions file-sharing becomes embedded in the civic context. She has contributed to the anthology *Post-Soviet Women: New Challenges and Ways to Empowerment* (Palgrave

Macmillan), focusing on representations of Ukrainian women during the Russo–Ukrainian war.

SIMON COTTLE is Professor Emeritus of Media and Communication in the School of Journalism, Media and Culture (JOMEC) at Cardiff University, where he was Head of School (2013–15) and Deputy Head of School (2008–13). Before this, he was Inaugural Chair and Head of the Media and Communications Programme at the University of Melbourne and has held honorary professorships at various universities internationally. He is the author of 13 books and around 150 articles, chapters and reports on media, conflicts and global crises, and is Series Editor of the Global Crises and Media series for publisher Peter Lang. His books include *Global Crisis Reporting* (2009), *Transnational Protests and the Media* (ed. with Libby Lester 2011), *Disasters and the Media* (with Mervi Pantti and Karin Wahl-Jorgensen 2012), *Humanitarianism, Communication and Change* (ed. with Glenda Cooper 2015) and *Reporting Dangerously: Journalist Killings, Intimidation and Security* (with Richard Sambrook and Nick Mosdell 2016). He is writing and lecturing on ecological collapse and how journalism can perform better in communicating pathways to transition and processes of societal transformation. He is currently writing *Reporting Civilizational Collapse: A Wake-Up Call* (Routledge 2024) and editing *Communicating a World-in-Crisis* (Peter Lang 2024).

TOM DIVON is a PhD student in the Department of Communication and Journalism at the Hebrew University of Jerusalem, Israel. Divon focuses on digital culture, platform affordances, and user-generated content. Specifically, Divon explores TikTok's sociopolitical subcultures and their potential for education in three areas: (1) TikTok users' engagement with Holocaust commemoration and education, (2) TikTok users' performative combat against hate speech (he has published a co-authored book chapter on this topic in *TikTok Cultures in The United States by Routledge*), and (3) TikTok users' memetic participation in nationalism-driven conflicts, with a focus on Palestinian resistance (he has published a co-authored paper on this topic in *Social Media + Society*).

ROMAN HORBYK is a Senior Lecturer in Media and Communication Studies at Örebro University. His research is interdisciplinary, and his interests concern media and conflict, military communication, media practices, transmedia storytelling, propaganda and disinformation, journalist professional cultures, sociolinguistics, media history and history of ideas. His research has been published in journals such as *Digital War, Place Branding and Public Diplomacy, Baltic Worlds, Studi Slavistici* and *East/West: Journal of Ukrainian Studies*. He is also the author of *Mediated Europes: Discourse and Power in Ukraine, Russia and Poland during Euromaidan* (Stockholm 2017) and has frequently contributed to edited volumes, most recently to *Contemporary Challenges in Mediatisation Research* (Routledge 2023), where he wrote on mediatisation of war and the military. Before his career in academia, he worked as a journalist. He is also active as a playwright and screenwriter, with notable credits including *Strayed* (*Pryputni* 2017).

ANDREW HOSKINS is Professor of Global Security in the College of Social Sciences at the University of Glasgow. He has been writing on the relationship between media, war and memory for over 20 years. His current work exposes how the smartphone has remade self and society and what this means for the future of war, memory, privacy, identity and anonymity. He is the founding Co-Editor-in-Chief of *Memory, Mind & Media* and *Digital War*, founding Editor-in-Chief of *Memory Studies* and founding Co-Editor of the Palgrave Memory Studies Book Series. His books include *Radical War: Data, Attention & Control in the Twenty-First Century* (Oxford University Press 2022, with Matthew Ford); *Risk and Hyperconnectivity: Media and Memories of Neoliberalism* (Oxford University Press 2016, with John Tulloch) and *Digital Memory Studies: Media Pasts in Transition* (Routledge 2018, ed.).

INGA JASINSKAJA-LAHTI is Professor of Social Psychology at the Faculty of Social Sciences at the University of Helsinki. She has done extensive research on intergroup relations and immigrant integration, particularly in Finland. Currently, she is a co-leader of the Academy of Finland–funded research project PREVENT, which focuses on emotional prejudice in virtual reality, and a leader of a project funded by the Strategic Research Council on collective psychological and epistemic ownership of knowledge. She is an author of more than 100 international publications in the field of social psychology of intergroup relations.

JOHANA KOTIŠOVÁ is a Marie Skłodowska-Curie Postdoctoral Fellow at the University of Amsterdam, Media Studies Department. She has written on media professionals' emotional labour and crisis/conflict reporting for journals such as *Journalism, Journalism Studies, European Journal of Communication* and *International Journal of Press/Politics*. She authored the creative non-fiction book *Crisis Reporters, Emotions, and Technology: An Ethnography* (Palgrave Macmillan 2019).

MOA ERIKSSON KRUTRÖK holds a PhD in Sociology from Umeå University and is Associate Professor of Media and Communication Studies at Umeå University and affiliated researcher at the digital humanities lab (Humlab). She is also the editor of the *Journal of Digital Social Research* (JDSR). Her research interests concern discourses on societal crises and expressions of trauma, grief and resilience on social media, primarily Twitter and TikTok.

ZIXIU LIU is a Teaching Fellow in Communications and Media Studies in the School of International Communications at the University of Nottingham Ningbo China. Her research interests centre on the relationship between politics and media, with a particular focus on media, war/conflict and propaganda. She gained her PhD from the University of Liverpool in 2020. She has published journal articles on the war in Ukraine in *Media, War & Conflict* and *International Communication Gazette*.

MARJA LÖNNROTH-OLIN is a doctoral researcher in Social Psychology at the University of Helsinki's Doctoral Programme in Gender, Culture and Society. Her research interests concern intersectionality, gender and religion, and the discursive construction of the nation and its boundaries, particularly in times of conflict. She is currently working on her doctoral thesis focusing on these topics.

JAMIE MATTHEWS is Principal Academic in Communication and Media at Bournemouth University. His research covers international communication, journalism studies and risk perception, with a particular interest in disaster communication and the mediation of conflict. Some of his recent work has been published in journals including *Health Communication*, *The Journal of International Communication* and *International Communication Gazette*, as well as in several edited collections. He is the co-editor of *Media, Journalism and Disaster Communities* (Palgrave Macmillan 2020).

RUSTEN MENARD is a Senior Lecturer of Critical and Social Psychology in the Sociology Department at the University of Portsmouth. Using primarily critical discourse analytic and critical discursive psychological methodologies, his broad research interests include the production of values and identities from subjugated standpoints, hegemony and resistance, and social inequalities and power imbalances in the production of text and talk. His publications have focused on the production, reformulation and use of hegemonic equality discourses in Finland from various social positionings and standpoints. His current research deals with trans and gender non-conforming persons' experiences of gender-based and sexual harassment and violence.

NOTES ON CONTRIBUTORS

BORIS NOORDENBOS is Associate Professor of Literary & Cultural Analysis at the University of Amsterdam and is affiliated to the Amsterdam School for Cultural Analysis (ASCA). His publications focus on issues of conspiracy theory, nostalgia, trauma and cultural memory, with a special interest in the former Soviet Union. He is the author of *Post-Soviet Literature and the Search for a Russian Identity* (Palgrave Macmillan 2016) and the co-editor of the volume *Post-Soviet Nostalgia: Confronting the Empire's Legacies* (Routledge 2019). He is also the Principal Investigator in the ERC-funded research project Conspiratorial Memory: Cultures of Suspicion in Post-Socialist Europe (2021–6).

TEEMU PAUHA is a University Lecturer in Islamic Theology at the University of Helsinki and an Associate Professor (Docent) in the Study of Religion at the University of Turku. In his research, Pauha focuses on the social psychology of religious identity and interreligious relationships. He has published peer-reviewed studies in, for example, the *International Journal for the Psychology of Religion*, *Journal of Muslims in Europe*, *Journal of Religion in Europe*, *Approaching Religion*, and *Temenos: Nordic Journal of Comparative Religion*. Since 2014, Pauha has authored or co-authored the Finnish section in the *Yearbook of Muslims in Europe* (Brill).

MATTI POHJONEN is a Senior Researcher at the Helsinki Institute of Social Sciences and Humanities (HSSH), University of Helsinki. He previously worked as a researcher for the University of Oxford and the VOX-Pol Network of Excellence, and as a Lecturer in Global Digital Culture at the School of Oriental and African Studies (SOAS). He has published on topics related to global digital communication and online extreme speech for journals such as *International Journal of Communication*, *Popular Communication* and *Social Media + Society*.

PER STÅHLBERG is a media anthropologist and Associate Professor in Media and Communication Studies at Södertörn University. His research interests include cultural production, meaning management and professional cultures. He has conducted ethnographic fieldwork on journalism and book production in India and on information management in Ukraine. Currently he is studying digital platforms and vernacular fiction in India. Among his publications are *Writing Society Through Media: Ethnography of a Hindi Daily* (Rawat 2013) and *Managing Meaning in Ukraine: Information, Communication and Narration since the Euromaidan Revolution* (with Göran Bolin, MIT Press 2023).

MARC TUTERS is a Senior Lecturer in New Media and Digital Culture and a researcher affiliated with the Digital Methods Initiative and the Open Intelligence Lab, all housed at the University of Amsterdam, where his research aims to make sense of political subcultures at the bottom of the Web through combining computational methods with concepts from critical theory.

SATU VENÄLÄINEN is a University Lecturer in Social Psychology at the University of Eastern Finland and an Associate Professor (Docent) in Social Psychology at the University of Helsinki. Her research interests include gender, violence, intersectionality and the social constitution of identities and affects. She has published articles on these topics in journals such as *Social Problems, Men and Masculinities, European Journal of Cultural Studies, European Journal of Women's Studies, The Sociological Review, Feminist Media Studies, European Journal of Women's Studies* and *Feminism & Psychology*.

ANTAL WOZNIAK is a Lecturer in the Department of Communication and Media at the University of Liverpool. His research focuses on political and environmental communication with a particular emphasis on media representations of climate change, environmental politics and violent conflicts. He has published in journals such as *The International Journal of Press/Politics, Environmental Communication, Interest Groups & Advocacy, The International Journal of Communication, Journalism* and *Journalism Studies*. He has also contributed to the *Research Handbook on Communicating Climate Change* and the *Oxford Research Encyclopedia of Climate Science*.

EDITORS

METTE MORTENSEN is Professor and Deputy Head of Department at the Department of Communication, University of Copenhagen. She specialises in visual media studies and was the Principal Investigator of the collective research project 'Images of Conflict, Conflicting Images' (2017–22) funded by the Velux Foundation. She is the author or editor of ten books, including the monograph *Eyewitness Images and Journalism: Digital Media, Participation, and Conflict* (Routledge 2015) and the volumes *Social Media Materialities and Protest: Critical Reflections* co-edited with Christina Neumayer and Thomas Poell (Routledge 2019) and *Social Media Images and Conflicts* co-edited with Ally McCrow-Young (Routledge 2023). She has edited nine special issues, including on witnessing with Lilie Chouliaraki for *Journalism* (2022) and on the playful politics of memes with Christina Neumayer for *Information, Communication and Society* (2021).

MERVI PANTTI is Professor in Media and Communication Studies at the Faculty of Social Sciences, University of Helsinki. Her research is concerned with war and disaster journalism, emotion in media, humanitarian communication, media and immigration, digital platforms, disinformation and media accountability. She is co-author of *Disasters and the Media* (with Karin Wahl-Jorgensen and Simon Cottle, Peter Lang 2012) and editor of *Media and the Ukraine*

Crisis: Hybrid Media Practices and Narratives of Conflict (Peter Lang 2016). She has edited special journal issues with Karin Wahl-Jorgensen on journalism and emotion for *Journalism Studies* (2021) and *Journalism* (2021). Currently she is director of the research consortium The Democratic Epistemic Capacities in the Age of Algorithms (DECA) funded by the Strategic Research Council, and PI of the research project Media Platforms and Social Accountability: Dynamics, Practices and Discourses (MAPS) funded by the Academy of Finland.

INDEX

A

accountability 60–6, 69–71, 90, 218
The Act of Declaration of Independence 23
advertising and user profiling 25
AI tools 2
Airwars 81, 90
algorithm-driven platforms 5
Al-Qaeda 58
Amnesty International's Crisis Evidence Lab 82
Anthropocene 197
Attenborough, David 196
audience's consumption 53
Azv vs Zombies 47

B

BBC news 12, 196, 200–2, 206
Bellingcat 81
 and forensic architecture 7

blogs
  cybersecurity authorities 67–8
  guardians of democracy 68–70
  humanitarian actors 65–7
  narratives and credibility building 64–70
  social media 63–4
BRICS 175
broadcast media 40–1
Bucha massacre 8, 9, 89, 98, 101, 102, 105, 108
Buddhism 198
Business Insight 25–6

C

Capitalocene 197
catastrophes 57
censorship 2, 44, 51, 63, 178
centralised organisational institutions 22
Centre for Emerging Technology and Security (CETaS) 83

chatbots 46–47
civic engagement 46
civilian communication infrastructure 82
climate crisis 12, 195–210
collective grief 119
commercial business model 25
commodification of trauma 120
community organisation 27
Conflict Intelligence Team (CIT) 86
conflict reporting 157–8
  emotions 159–61
  fixers 159–61
content moderation 60, 62, 63, 70
Cook, Tim 60
COP26 210
COP27 210
corporate credibility 67
corporate social responsibility (CSR) 66
counter spectacles 122
COVID 209
credibility building 64–70
crowdsourced knowledge production 9, 98
cultural journalism 157–8
cultural translation 160
cultural trauma
  meme-based expressions of 119–32
  TikTok, memes 122–3
cyberattacks 70
cybersecurity authorities 67–68

D

Daily Mirror 84
Dattalion 84
decentralisation 52, 53
  strategic communication 51
deep ecology 198
diffusion 52, 53
digital ecology 5
digital platforms
  accountability demands 63
  blogs 63–64
  in global crises 57
  in information war 59–61

information warfare 58
digital sedatives 47
Digital Services Act (DSA) 2, 60
digital television package 48
digital war 38–9
disastrous events 57
disinformation channels 58
Disinformation Coordination Hub 4
dominant ideologies 178

E

ecological awareness 198
ecological dissimulation
  diminishment 206
  displacement 201–4
  disregarding 204–6
  dominating worldview 207–8
  duplicitousness 206–7
  in dying world 195–210
economic system 197
emotional labour
  affective proximity 170
  between international journalist and locally based media professionals 163–6
  detachment 158, 160, 162–6
  trauma and mental-health issues 165
emotions
  conflict reporting 159–61
  distance/proximity 158
  empathy 158
environmental despoilation 209
Espreso TV 48
EU blocked Russian media channels 5
Euromaidan Revolution 6, 22, 24, 32
European security order 2
Eurovision Song Contest (ESC) 30, 32
existential threats 196–7

F

Facebook 4, 24, 27, 50, 60, 61, 63, 70, 112
  research tool 105

Fedorov, Mykhailo 60
fixers
    conflict reporting 159–61
focusing events 57
forensic architecture 81–3
fossil fuel revenues 12
framing 3, 4, 11, 12, 67, 101, 106, 110, 176, 178–80, 182, 188, 208
Frank, Anne 121

G

gamification 46–47
Geneva Conventions 87
geopolitics
    alignment between platforms and governments 59, 70, 71
    of news coverage 10–13
    security 11, 12, 67, 71, 179
GEOSINT 109
global climate change 12, 13, 195–7, 199–200, 202–4, 206, 209, 210
global humanitarian hierarchies 11
Global Internet Forum for Counter-terrorism (GIFCT) 58
Google 7, 61, 64–6, 68, 69, 81
grandmotherhood in Ukrainian context 139–52
GriefTok community 125
The Guardian 83, 84–6
guardians of democracy 68–70

H

Human rights challenges 6
Human Rights Watch 82, 106
humanitarian actors 65–7
hybrid funding scheme 25
hyper-individualisation of war 13

I

iArmy 27
imitation publics 125
indexing hypothesis 176, 177, 187, 188
Indian press coverage
    blame/responsibility 182
    critical political economy perspective 176
    descriptors for conflict 186–7
    domestic political elites 177
    general-purpose models 177
    home country's geopolitical positioning 189
    human-interest topic 189
    international affairs 189
    media attention 182–4
    moral evaluation 182
    national interests in reporting about international conflicts 189
    open-ended public discourse 190
    research, violent conflicts 176
    resolutions 187–8
    responsibility 187
    of Russia's invasion of Ukraine 175–90
    sociopolitical and economic contexts 176–8
    sourcing 185–6
    treatment recommendation 182
India–Russia relationship 179–80
Information Forces of Ukraine 27
information management 44–5
Information Security 27
information war 2–4, 67, 68, 101–3, 110, 137, 195, 217
information warfare 5, 7, 58–61, 103
informational order
    management 24
    Russian war 21–33
Instagram 61, 70, 87, 123, 129
international news reporting 11
International Renaissance Foundation 26
investigative aesthetics 101

Invincibility Points 42
ISIS 58, 122

J

journalism
  emotional gap 167
  ethics 169
  exploitation 169
  'local' and 'foreign' distinction 168–9
  normative constructions 166
  outsourcing of empathy 167
  practice of 'shielding' local sources 166–9
  professionalism and objectivity in 166
  research 157–8
  retraumatisation of sources 168
Journalists Without Borders 11, 26

K

Konstantynovska, Valentyna 141

L

LETA 137
limited war 38
local journalism 157–8

M

Mail Online 84, 85
mass media coverage of foreign policy 190
maternal imagery 138
media infrastructures
  actors and their practices 42–43
  audiences and media practices 49–52
  communication blackout 42
  and geopolitics of Russia 179
  information management 43
  infrastructural transformations 41
  overcoming polarisation 49
  and shaping of connected war 4–7
Media Group Ukraine 47
media manipulation 49
media professionals 27, 38, 47–9, 157–66, 168, 169
mediascape 39
meme-based expressions, cultural trauma on social media 119–32
Meta 51, 60–5, 70
Microsoft 61, 215
military carbon boot-print 204
military communication 45–46
military conflicts
  age, womanhood and motherhood, intersections 144–50
  grand narrative 144
  masculinised agency, construction of 149–50
  maternal objects of protection 144–6
  older women, symbol of national heritage 146–9
military (in)security 209
Ministry of Culture and Information Policy 26
Ministry of Digital Transformation 30
Ministry of Economic Development and Trade 25
Ministry of Foreign Affairs of the Czech Republic 26
Ministry of Information Policy (MIP) 25, 26
Ministry's communication strategy 27
mobile media 9–10

N

narratives and credibility building 64–70
National Endowment for Democracy 26
National News Agency of Ukraine – Ukrinform 27
National University of Kyiv-Mohyla Academy 26
Neo-Nazis 2

networked information management
 degree of centralization and hierarchization 28
 global infrastructure 28
 and grammar of internet 28–33
 organised network 28
 persuasive language of advertising 28
 state 22
news coverage, geopolitics of 10–13
newsgathering practices and approaches 82

O

Odniklassniki 24
open-source intelligence (OSINT) 79–92
 civilian harm, disinformation and verifying incidents 85–89
 conflict and crisis journalism 83
 conventional military conflicts 83
 digital volunteers and investigations 79
 discrediting claims and disinformation 89
 human rights violations 90
 investigative journalism 82, 83, 85, 91, 92
 mining and processing data 82
 online data sources 79–80
 online verification 98
 participatory propaganda 101
 practices 80–83
 privacy protection and intellectual-property enforcement 83
 professional norms of objectivity and impartiality 91
 pro-Kremlin propaganda 97–113
 public online data sources 79
 quality news outlets 85
 reuse of online audio and video content 83
 social media geolocation 79–80
 war crimes 89, 90
 weaponizing 98–101
organisational networks 22
Orwellian 'Ministry of Truth,' 26

over-the-top (OTT) services 41

P

participative war 215–8
participatory propaganda 101–3
participatory reconnaissance 46
patterns, reporting in UK news media 200–1
plateau 40
Pro-Kremlin propaganda
 messaging on Telegram 103–5
 open-source intelligence (OSINT) 97–113
propaganda-spewing accounts 87
pro-Russian disinformation 58
Pryamy 48

R

Radical War 5
recommendation algorithms 5
Reform Watch 25
The Revolution of Dignity 24
Russia-EU relations 12
Russian aggression 3, 12
Russian illegal annexation of Crimea 162
Russian propaganda strategy 98
Russian war 1
 informational order 21–33
Russia Today (RT) 5–6, 26, 59–61, 70, 81, 98, 102, 105, 111
'Russian warship – Go fuck yourself!,' 31
Rybar 104, 109–12

S

social media
 blogs 63–64
 communication 28–9
 emergence of 9–10
 revolutions 58

social media platforms 1, 4–7, 9–10, 24, 41, 45, 57, 59–62, 65, 70, 71, 81, 97, 98, 102, 104, 111, 123, 124, 131, 140, 216–18
social media war 89
social systems 177
sourcing 81, 178, 182, 185–6
Sputnik 61
Starlink satellite internet terminals 42
  civic engagement 46
  direct official and military communication 45–6
  information management 44–5
  participatory reconnaissance 46
  and support networks 43–7
StopFake 26
swarm communication 37
  and hop-on/hop-off activism 53
Symbiocene 196, 198

T

Taoism 198
Telegram 4, 8, 37–8, 50–2, 97, 98, 102, 217
  pro-Kremlin propaganda 103–109
The Telegraph 84, 86
Things That Just Make Sense in a Bomb Shelter 121
TikTok 4, 5, 10, 31, 52, 60, 62, 64, 224
  affordances 132
  audio-meme challenges 125, 126
  bomb shelter 126–9
  critical societal conditions 132
  cultural trauma memes 122–3
  memetic text 126
  pro- and anti-Russian memes 131
  sociopolitical subcultures 222
  sound referencing corn 129–30
  storytelling 129
  structural elements 129
  technological features 119

trauma aesthetic 131
trauma on 123–6
user-generated videos 130
war influencers 120–1
war-related content 130
The Times 85–6
total mobilisation 39–40
total war 38, 39
transnational journalism, postcolonial understanding 158
Trauma on TikTok 123–6
  audiovisual grammar of memes redefines 125
  genres of communication 124
  stitch 124
  users' online grassroots coping mechanisms 123
Twitter 4, 21, 24, 29, 31, 37, 51, 61, 63–5, 87, 99, 104, 129, 137

U

UK news coverage 79–92
Ukraine Crisis Media Center (UCMC) 4, 24–25
Ukraine Now 29
Ukraine Today (UT) 25
Ukraine's Ministry of Defence 4
Ukraine's resilience to Russian information campaigns 4, 37–53
Ukrainian mediascape 37–53
Ukrainian Neptune anti-ship missiles 31
Ukrainian resistance, victories 37
Ukrainska Pravda 51
Ukrinform 24, 26, 27
UN Environment Programme 199
UN Independent Investigative Mechanism for Myanmar (IIMM) and 92
UN Security Council resolution 175
United News 41, 48–50
user-generated content 91, 222

V

VKontake, 24

W

war communication
   blackout 40
   and informational state 21–33
   periods of 39–40
   plateau 40
   total mobilisation 39–40
WarFakes 8–9, 97
   coverage on Bucha 105–10
   OSINT-style practices of reading 108, 110
warfare and ecology 198–200
war influencers 10, 120–1, 131
weaponizing open-source intelligence 98–101
Western democracies 58
Western journalism cultures 178
Western Romanticism 198
world civilizational community of fate 197
world-in-crisis 196–8

Y

Yanukovych, Viktor 23, 24
yeVoroh 46
YouTube 61, 63, 137–52
   babushkas, Russian war 140–3
   Battalion video 142, 143
   grandmotherhood in Ukrainian context 139–52
   interactional dynamics 140
   perception of morality and legitimacy of military action 152
   political opinions 151
   spatial and temporal contexts 151
   traditional gendered portrayals of women in war 150
   warrior societies 151
Yushchenko, Viktor 23

Z

Zelensky, Volodymyr 1

Simon Cottle, *General Editor*

From climate change to the war on terror, financial meltdowns to forced migrations, pandemics to world poverty, and humanitarian disasters to the denial of human rights, these and other crises represent the dark side of our globalized planet. They are endemic to the contemporary global world and so too are they highly dependent on the world's media.

Each of the specially commissioned books in the *Global Crises and the Media* series examines the media's role, representation, and responsibility in covering major global crises. They show how the media can enter into their constitution, enacting them on the public stage and thereby helping to shape their future trajectory around the world. Each book provides a sophisticated and empirically engaged understanding of the topic in order to invigorate the wider academic study and public debate about the most pressing and historically unprecedented global crises of our time.

For further information about the series and submitting manuscripts, please contact:

>Dr. Simon Cottle
>Cardiff School of Journalism, Media and Culture
>Two Central Square Central Square
>CARDIFF, Wales CF10 1FS
>United Kingdom
>*CottleS@cardiff.ac.uk*

To order other books in this series, please contact our Customer Service Department at:

>peterlang@presswarehouse.com (within the U.S.)
>order@peterlang.com (outside the U.S.)

Or browse online by series:

>www.peterlang.com

www.ingramcontent.com/pod-product-compliance
Lightning Source LLC
Chambersburg PA
CBHW061711300426
44115CB00014B/2640